THE POWER TO WIN

World Champion Keke Rosberg, shrugging off the effects of a virus infection, gave the performance of his career to date when he completely dominated the 1983 Monaco Grand Prix at the wheel of his Saudia Williams FW08C against formidable turbocharged opposition. His achievement marked the 154th victory in a World Championship qualifying race for the Ford Cosworth DFV engine, the success story of which had begun in 1967, when it powered Jim Clark's Lotus 49 to victory in the Dutch Grand Prix at Zandvoort, its inaugural race.

THE POWER TO WIN

The design, development and achievements of the FORD COSWORTH DFV, DFX, DFL and DFY V8 racing engines

JOHN BLUNSDEN

MRP

MOTOR RACING PUBLICATIONS LTD
28 Devonshire Road, Chiswick, London W4 2HD, England

ISBN 0 900549 77 7
First published 1983

Photosetting by Zee Creative Ltd., London SW16
Printed in Great Britain by Netherwood, Dalton & Co. Ltd.,
Bradley Mills, Huddersfield, West Yorkshire

Contents

Introduction		6
Acknowledgements		6
Chapter 1	The V8 solution Ford and Cosworth bridge an energy gap	9
Chapter 2	Back to the drawing-board DFV design and development	29
Chapter 3	The milestone years 1967-1972: Wings over wheels	73
	1973-1977: The 12-cylinder challenge	95
	1978-1982: The ground-effects era	113
	1983 and after: A short-stroke strategy	137
Chapter 4	Living with a DFV The cost of competitiveness	145
Chapter 5	Creating a new Indy legend DFX and the boost factor	165
Chapter 6	A matter of endurance DFL and the C100 saga	193
Chapter 7	A rewarding partnership Fruits of the Ford-Cosworth connection	207
Appendix A	Ford DFV World Championship race winners	223
Appendix B	Cosworth DFX CART/USAC race winners	227
Appendix C	Ford Cosworth V8 racing engine data	229
Appendix D	Engines manufactured by Cosworth Engineering	230
Appendix E	Useful addresses	232

Introduction

Towards the end of 1965, the Board of the Ford Motor Company in the United Kingdom sanctioned the design by Keith Duckworth and the manufacture by Cosworth Engineering of a Ford Formula 1 engine, initially for the exclusive use of Team Lotus, who at the time were desperately seeking a competitive power unit to use under the forthcoming 3-litre Grand Prix racing regulations.

The initial financial cost was to be £100,000, although Ford's commitment to the project's success would put the true value of the investment much higher than that. It was an audacious plan, primarily aimed at keeping Grand Prix racing's most competitive team at the front of the field, but the rewards were to be immeasurably greater than that. The Ford DFV engine would transform Grand Prix racing, just as a decade later its turbocharged derivative, the Cosworth DFX, would help to rejuvenate Indianapolis-style racing at one of its most critical periods.

The high level of professionalism seen today in both these racing categories owes much to the existence of these highly competitive and readily available V8 engines at the time when they were most urgently needed. They helped to bring new teams into the sport and they have facilitated greatly the difficult transition into the world of high technology as the lessons of the aerospace world have been applied to the race track.

Way back in 1970 it seemed sensible to write a book on the DFV's achievements before the engine ran out of steam. At the time David Phipps and I finished *Such Sweet Thunder* (MRP, but long since out of print) it had won 34 Grands Prix. People have been predicting its imminent demise on and off ever since, and when I began to work on *The Power To Win* early in 1982 the end really did look to be in sight. At that time the score of victories had risen to 144; as I write these words the total is 154 and soon, no doubt, the first success will be recorded by the DFV's successor, the short-stroke DFY. In North America, the DFX's score of victories has passed the 80 mark and is rising fast. So this great motor racing success story is far from over. Yet it seems an appropriate time to take stock, to look back over a period of 16 years of motor racing, and to the events which immediately preceded them, and to recall the turning points of the most significant period of change the sport has ever witnessed. The decision of a large multi-national corporation to back the entrepreneurial flair of a brilliant young designer and his talented team of engineers was to bring each of them considerable rewards. But the chief beneficiaries of their long-lasting association have been the ever increasing number of people for whom motor racing has been their livelihood and the countless thousands of spectators for whom the sight of battle between professionally run teams of well-matched cars and drivers continues to be of such absorbing interest. They should all be grateful for that day when Ford and Cosworth sat down together and decided to 'do an engine'.

Acknowledgements

There are some motor racing books which an author is able to produce entirely from first-hand knowledge, but this most certainly is not one of them. Nor would I have wished it to be so. Although this is a book about a series of racing engines, their impact upon the people who have been associated with them — drivers, team owners, racing managers, mechanics, as well as the people involved in their design, development and manufacture — is in a sense at least as important as their successes on the track.

Many people, therefore, have been approached — often at the most inconvenient of times — in the hope that they might add a further viewpoint to one of motor racing's longest-running success stories. Without exception they have responded most generously with their time and their interest, and I am most grateful to them all. I am only sorry that space considerations have precluded me from using all of their comments and recollections. I also apologize in advance should any errors of fact have slipped through, because if so the mistakes will have been mine, not theirs.

I could scarcely have chosen a less convenient year in which to worry Keith Duckworth, for in 1982, with Formula 1 still in a state of turmoil, the future of the 3-litre engine in some jeopardy, Group C providing a series of unexpected dramas and the American racing scene still recovering from the backlash of politics, his mind must have been on many more important things than merely recalling the past. Nevertheless, he came up trumps and I know that what follows is much the better for his major contribution to it.

His colleagues at Cosworth Engineering must also have tired of my interminable questions, and in particular I would like to thank Jack Field, for bearing the brunt of my frequent queries and requests; Mike Costin, for reminding me of that special blend of entrepreneurial flair and good humoured dedication which has motivated the Cosworth team from the beginning; Dick Scammell, for the hours of quizzing he endured so politely at various race tracks between tending to the needs of the Ford-powered teams; Malcolm Tyrrell, for explaining so lucidly many of the development milestones of the DFV over a period of more than 16 years; Paul Morgan, for his most helpful suggestions concerning the section devoted to the DFX; and Martin Waters, who similarly vetted the DFL part of the manuscript.

I was particularly fortunate that Walter Hayes, one of the chief architects of the Ford Cosworth partnership, who these days spends much of his time at Ford's Dearborn headquarters in the United States in his capacity of Vice President — Public Affairs, should be visiting London at a crucial stage in the preparation of my manuscript. I am more than grateful to him that despite a characteristically hectic schedule he gave me several hours of his valuable time during which the many ramifications of Ford's long and successful association with Keith Duckworth and his colleagues became so much clearer to me.

To John Waddell, who holds a similar position within Ford of Europe, I owe a particular debt of gratitude for his enthusiastic support of this project right from its inception; to Karl Ludvigsen, my thanks for explaining the rationale behind the C100 operation; to Stuart Turner, for his sagacity in confirming the strategic aims of Ford of Europe's competition involvement, which have recently become his responsibility; and to Harry Calton, who is forever a fund of information on any aspect of Ford's high-performance activities, and whose enthusiasm for motor sport knows no bounds.

Ford's photographic archive at South Ockendon was an obvious early port of call when the time came to begin selecting illustrations for the book, and my particular thanks go to Steve Clark, who manages this talented unit so efficiently and who shortlisted likely material for me so helpfully, and to Sheila Knapman, who processed my later requests most speedily despite the particularly heavy pressure of work from other sources at that time. Ford's individual photographers are not identified on the prints I selected, but I believe I can detect the particular skills of Ken Shipton, Jack Wright, Danny Fraser, Ken Denyer and Mike Wilkins amongst them. Beedle and Cooper were responsible for the photographs I chose from the Cosworth files and I am especially grateful to them for burning the midnight oil in order that I could include shots of the latest version of the DFY engine.

I have been happy to draw upon the work of many accomplished motor racing photographers, including Gerhart Brinkmann from South Africa, Diana Burnett, Geoffrey Goddard, Michael Hewett, Peter McFadyen, David Phipps, Nigel Snowdon, Gerry Stream, Colin Taylor, Peter Tempest and Paul Thompson, all of them from the United Kingdom, Mark Clifford, James Cutler, Jon Magge, Chris Mullen and Marc Sproule from the United States, and David Stone from Canada. The superb cutaway drawings of various engines are, of course, the work of Ford's Terry Collins and of Theo Page and Tony Matthews.

Inevitably the published work of many journalists has been of considerable reference value as a memory-jogger and I thank them all and the publishers of the magazines in which their work has appeared. But to Gordon Kirby, American Editor of the British weekly *Autosport,* I owe a particular debt of gratitude for the sheaves of background notes he prepared for me on the early days and subsequent history of the DFX. It was most important to have the American as well as the European viewpoint for this section of the book.

Amongst the appendices is an almost complete listing of the engine numbers involved in the first 154 Grand Prix victories with the DFV engine. These have come from a variety of sources, including the teams involved, who have often gone to immense lengths to find a missing number; my thanks to them all. Also to *Autosport* once more, who in years gone by used to record this information in their race reports, and to Peter Windsor, Sports Editor of *Autocar*, who carries on the good work today and whose industry has enabled me to fill all the more recent gaps.

Finally, to all those who have been so helpful in 'talking shop' to me over the past year — many, though not all of them, are quoted on the pages that follow — thank you all for spending the time and giving me the encouragement to complete what has inevitably been a long and complex story, but one which, I believe, deserved to be told.

Croydon
May 1983

JOHN BLUNSDEN

Cause for celebration. Keith Duckworth and approximately 200 of his fellow directors and colleagues of Cosworth Engineering who have contributed so much to the Ford Cosworth success story gather together behind a pair of DFV engines at their base in Northampton. In 1983, the year of Cosworth's 25th anniversary and the engine's 17th season, the tally of World Championship Grand Prix victories has passed the 154 mark, a new short-stroke DFY derivative has become available to Formula 1 teams, the turbocharged DFX continues to dominate CART/USAC racing in the United States and the long-stroke DFL continues to do battle in endurance racing. Few if any partnerships in motor racing have accomplished so much, over such a long period, for the benefit of so many people.

CHAPTER 1

The V8 solution

Ford and Cosworth bridge an energy gap

Early in 1964, as Jim Clark set about the defence of his recently won World Championship and the current Formula 1, for $1\frac{1}{2}$-litre single-seater racing cars, moved into its fourth season, there came some welcome news. From January 1, 1966, World Championship Grands Prix would be run under revised Formula 1 regulations which would permit the use of engines of up to 3 litres displacement if they were normally aspirated. The new rules would also admit cars fitted with supercharged engines of up to $1\frac{1}{2}$ litres, just in case anyone wanted to modify their existing power units.

The enthusiasm with which the British teams reacted to this decision by the *Commission Sportive Internationale (CSI),* the sporting wing of the world governing *Federation Internationale de l'Automobile (FIA),* was in marked contrast to their reaction, rather more than five years earlier, when the same body had announced that the then-current $2\frac{1}{2}$-litre Formula 1 would be changed to one with a $1\frac{1}{2}$-litre limit from 1961 onwards.

On that earlier occasion, reading the decision as a political move to undermine the British position just when the UK-based teams had finally achieved a position of dominance in Grand Prix circles after years of endeavour, there was a wave of indignation and rage from the British entrants, who threatened to boycott the new formula unless it was changed to something more acceptable.

However, they had underestimated the level of support which the $1\frac{1}{2}$-litre formula would attract from elsewhere, possibly overlooking the fact that a change of regulations which seemed likely to considerably reduce the speed of cars was not only acceptable, but for public relations reasons was actually desirable, in the aftermath of no fewer than three Grand Prix driver fatalities in the previous four months, and when the Le Mans holocaust of 1955 was still painfully vivid in the memory.

The British teams' reluctance to accept the inevitable and their late realization that their 'alternative solution', a proposed Intercontinental Formula with a capacity limit of 3 litres, would be so poorly supported from overseas as to render it little more than a temporary makeweight novelty, was to cost them dearly in 1961. That year, only Ferrari were fully prepared, with a team of purpose-built V6-engined cars, and their domination was inevitable against what, in the main, amounted to hastily converted Formula 2 cars with underpowered four-cylinder engines. Indeed, only the driving brilliance of Stirling Moss (in his last full season of Grand Prix racing before his near-fatal Goodwood accident halted his career) and Jim Clark (emerging as Stirling's natural successor) prevented a complete whitewash by the Italian team.

However, with BRM speeding the development of a new $1\frac{1}{2}$-litre V8 engine for their own team cars and Coventry Climax preparing a power unit of similar configuration for the Lotus, Cooper and Brabham teams, 1962 was to mark a turning point in British fortunes, and aided by Ferrari's failure to maintain their earlier form and Porsche's decision to pull out of the Formula 1 scene at the end of 1962 after only two seasons, the $1\frac{1}{2}$-litre formula was to prove a lot kinder to the British teams than they had had much right to expect.

By the end of 1965 they would have won no fewer than 36 of the 47 Grands Prix run under the $1\frac{1}{2}$-litre formula, the top scorer being Lotus with 22 victories, followed by BRM with 11, Brabham with two and Cooper with one. Ferrari had been able to add only four more wins to the five they scored in

It was only the mastery of Stirling Moss and Jim Clark in their relatively underpowered Lotuses which prevented the 1961 season — the first under $1\frac{1}{2}$-litre Formula 1 rules — from being a complete walkover for the Ferrari team. Here is Moss at the wheel of Rob Walker's Coventry Climax-powered Lotus 18 harrying Richie Ginther's Ferrari in the Dutch Grand Prix, a race in which every competing car was to run through non-stop.

The previous weekend Moss recorded probably the best drive of his racing career when he overcame the power deficiency of his four-cylinder engine to take on and beat the might of Ferrari in the Monaco Grand Prix. The body side panels have been removed to improve the air flow through the cockpit during an invariably exhausting race.

1961, Porsche had taken just one victory before their withdrawal, and Honda, a new arrival on the Grand Prix scene, was to be credited with winning the last of all the $1\frac{1}{2}$-litre World Championship races, the 1965 Mexican Grand Prix.

A significant ingredient of the British comeback had been the marked superiority in chassis design and technology shown by the UK-based teams, with Lotus proving the most innovative and encouraging the development of the monocoque structure as the logical successor to the traditional multi-tubular spaceframe. But engine power and efficiency had also played an important part in the success story, and there was considerable excitement and speculation, when details of the next formula were announced, concerning the configuration which BRM and Coventry Climax might adopt for their 3-litre engines.

BRM were the first to announce their intention. They had considered two solutions and had chosen the more complicated of them. They would be developing a 16-cylinder engine comprising a pair of horizontally-opposed 'eights', one on top of the other, in H-formation and geared together. It sounded both ingenious and frighteningly complex, and so it was to prove, and in due course the layout which had been thought about but discarded — a relatively simple V12 (effectively one-and-a-half of their existing 2-litre V8s which had been developed from their $1\frac{1}{2}$-litre engine for use in Tasman Championship events in Australasia) — was to replace the frustratingly unreliable H16.

Meanwhile, there had been only rumours as to Coventry Climax's intentions. One school of thought was that their first 3-litre racing engine would be a V8, an idea encouraged by the knowledge that a $2\frac{1}{2}$-litre V8 had been hiding under a dust sheet since 1960, when further development of this engine had been abandoned because of the forthcoming change of formula to

1½ litres. It would be a comparatively simple job, went the reasoning, to increase the displacement of this engine to a full 3 litres.

The more exciting rumour was that the 3-litre Coventry Climax engine would be a flat-16, a notion prompted by optimism rather than by evidence, but given some semblance of authenticity by the fact that the company had designed and built four engines to this configuration in 1½-litre form and would have loaned them to their contracted teams for the 1965 season had not their V8 in its latest 32-valve form proved more than adequate to win races.

Then, early in 1965, came some bad news and with it the realization that there would be neither a V8 nor a flat-16 from Coventry Climax for the 3-litre

By 1965 the position had changed dramatically. With a V8 Coventry Climax engine behind him, Jim Clark was about to repeat his World Championship success of 1963 and record his fourth consecutive victory in the Belgian Grand Prix on the Spa-Francorchamps circuit.

A victory wave from Clark at Silverstone after taking his Lotus 33 to the fourth of six Grand Prix wins he would score that year. But it was the last year of the 1½-litre formula and the future looked uncertain.

formula. There had been earlier threats that Coventry Climax Engines Limited was about to withdraw from motor racing, but each time the company had pulled back from the brink, largely through the dedication of Sir Leonard Lee, their chief executive and major shareholder. This time, however, there could be no turning back.

The company had recently been absorbed into the expanding Jaguar empire (which in turn was soon to become submerged in ever larger groupings within what ultimately would become British Leyland) and the time had come to measure the real cost of Coventry Climax's involvement in racing. In purely financial terms it was estimated to have been between £500,000 and £1,000,000, but this was only part of the story. Motor racing had put tremendous demands on key personnel and facilities and as a result various research and development projects concerned with the company's mainstream activities, notably the manufacture of industrial engines and forklift trucks, had been disrupted. The company's heavy and successful involvement in motor racing had done wonders in publicizing the Coventry Climax name, but at a cost which it could no longer be allowed to bear.

The motor racing world was saddened at the news that a company which had contributed so much to the sport and had enabled it to develop so healthily over a period of several years would no longer be part of the scene. But for teams like Lotus, Brabham and Cooper, sadness was laced with an element of desperation with the realization that, with less than 11 months to the start of the new formula — one which, ironically, had been billed enthusiastically as The Return of Power — their anticipated source of power had suddenly been switched off.

The next few weeks were a hectic and worrying time as the various team bosses searched for alternative power units. Cooper was to conclude a deal with Maserati for a supply of their heavyweight V12 engines, which had been developed for sports car use, and later they were to switch to the V12 BRM engine when this became available, but the change in formula was to mark a sad decline in the fortunes of a team which had been on top of the Grand Prix world as recently as 1960.

Jack Brabham, with characteristic depth of thought, decided that a simple, lightweight engine — even one with a relatively modest power output — would suffice, at least in the short term, and he encouraged the Australian Repco company to develop just such an engine, based on a General Motors V8 design. He was right, for it was to serve his team well, but only in the short term. . . .

Lotus chief Colin Chapman could also see the merit of simplicity and light weight but he was looking to a longer-term solution, and this, he reasoned, meant an engine with a target output of around 400 brake horsepower as a starting point. No such engine existed, of course, so he decided that someone must be persuaded to finance one.

For a short while, news of the Coventry Climax withdrawal had led to a rare level of unity in adversity amongst the rival teams who had been most immediately affected by it, but as is so often the case, lobbying in a common cause was to prove less effective than eyeball-to-eyeball discussions on an individual team basis. Clearly, each team had to look after its own destiny.

Chapman decided to approach the Society of Motor Manufacturers and Traders, reasoning that as the British motor industry had been a major

A Coventry Climax-powered Lotus 18 equipped with the infamous Lotus five-speed gearbox, the complexities and deficiencies of which were to prove so frustrating to Keith Duckworth after he had been charged with the job of making it work. His recommendation that it should be completely re-designed was declined and soon Duckworth had left Lotus to set up on his own. Cosworth Engineering was on the move.

beneficiary of the country's success in international motor racing through the publicity rub-off and the association with engineering achievement, it was appropriate that they should be invited to offer something in return — a desperately needed engine.

He stated his case most eloquently, yet he was probably not entirely surprised when it became apparent that the SMMT could offer little more than a sympathetic ear. The Society, in turn, agreed to make overtures to the Government, but all this achieved was to confirm that there was a formidable combination of ignorance and indifference within the corridors of Whitehall as to what British motor racing had achieved in international competition in the past, and a total lack of concern as to what it might or might not do in the future.

Yet, in a convoluted way, Chapman's approach to the SMMT was to bear fruit in an abundance which would transform Grand Prix racing and provide it with a measure of stability and growth never previously seen, although he was not to know this when he invited Walter Hayes to dinner at his home in Hadley Wood, Hertfordshire, shortly before he and his Lotus factory moved to Norfolk.

The two men had first met some years previously when Hayes was Editor of the *Sunday Dispatch* and had decided to employ Chapman as a freelance motoring correspondent. They got on very well together, but it is unlikely that they would have retained such close links had it not been for the close friendship of two other people. When Sir Patrick Hennessey, the dynamic Chairman of Ford of Britain, undertook a major reorganization of his company's management in 1961 and required someone to take the key post of Director of Public Affairs, he turned to his long-time friend Lord Beaverbrook for advice. The press baron, renowned as an unusually perceptive judge of people, immediately recommended Walter Hayes.

The former newspaper Editor soon found life at Ford to be full of surprises, one of which was the discovery that one man on his staff was required to combine the duties of Publications Manager and Competitions Manager. The logic of this eluded him, for it seemed to ensure that neither job would be handled with the necessary efficiency, and so he prevailed upon Sir Patrick Hennessey to relieve the Public Affairs department of responsibility for competitions activities. This was a particularly astute move, for Hayes had arrived on the scene as essentially an ideas man who at that stage was in no sense an expert on cars and whose knowledge of motor sport was even more slender — a situation which was destined not to last for long.

Sir Patrick agreed to Hayes' request, but was soon to regret his decision and early in 1963 he brought Competitions back under the Public Affairs umbrella, and with good reason. Under Hayes' guidance, the whole concept of Public Affairs at Ford had been transformed and its influence within the company had become stronger than ever before. Now it was essential that Ford's competitions policy should be administered with similar flair for Ford worldwide was embarking upon the projection of a Total Performance image as a major marketing tool, and the competitions activities of Ford of Britain would be required to play a significant role in this strategy.

The timing could scarcely have been better for the British company. Since 1959, not only had the little Anglia 105E saloon proved its worth as an effective rally and production racing car, but its overhead-valve engine had been race-tuned by specialists so successfully that it had become a mainstay of Formula Junior, the most prolific class of single-seater racing, and was also widely used for other racing categories.

1962 had seen the launch of the Cortina — destined to become the most successful European Ford car over the next two decades. It had appeared first with an engine similar to the Anglia unit, but increased in displacement from 997cc to 1,198cc. This had been followed by a 1,498cc derivative, incorporating a new cylinder block and a five-bearing crankshaft — two improvements which were to markedly enhance the engine's competition potential. A higher-performance version of this larger unit had since been

The graduation of Formula Junior from an Italian national formula to one of international status, coupled with the announcement of a new short-stroke 'Kent' engine with which to power the new Anglia saloon, was to provide Cosworth Engineering with a vital launching pad for their journey to recognition as competition engine builders of high quality. Here, two Lotuses with Cosworth-modified Ford engines start from the front of the grid at Mallory Park, Peter Arundell's in pole position. BMC, DKW and Fiat accounted for most of the opposition to Ford in the earlier days of FJ racing.

developed to power a Cortina GT saloon, which had proved a magnet for competitions enthusiasts, but even more exciting things were imminent. Within a few months the public would see a special Lotus-developed version of the Cortina, powered by a twin-overhead-camshaft 1,558cc derivative of the five-bearing engine, which had also been developed by Lotus, who were now to be entrusted with final assembly of the car as well as having responsibility for suspension and other high-performance-related modifications to the Cortina's specification. A Lotus-Ford link had already been forged in Formula Junior and the Cortina Lotus would be the next link in a chain which would soon spread as far as Indianapolis and ultimately embrace every Grand Prix circuit in the world.

Inevitably, Ford's rapidly growing influence in the European motor sporting scene, in which Lotus were so actively involved either on their own account or through their racing car customers, ensured that Chapman and Hayes saw a good deal of each other over the next two years, and it is fair to assume that each learnt a great deal from the other. There was certainly an abundance of mutual respect, and although in many respects they were very different people, they shared several elements of character which must have given substance and stimulation to their many discussions, including a healthy disregard for stodgy convention, a keen appetite for innovation and a facility for transforming complex problems into simple yet ingenious solutions.

Colin Chapman certainly found in his dinner guest that evening in Hadley Wood an interested and receptive listener as he expressed his concern about the situation caused by the Coventry Climax withdrawal. Naturally, he was worried that his own team, one which had been far and away the most successful under the $1\frac{1}{2}$-litre formula, would be going into the next formula in a few months' time without a competitive power unit — the best he could do would be to run his existing cars with engines enlarged to 2 litres on the tighter circuits, and gamble that the heavyweight H16 which he had arranged to buy from BRM would be reliable enough to serve him reasonably well in a purpose-built car on the faster tracks.

He had opted for the complex BRM engine because it seemed potentially to be the most effective of the 3-litre engines on offer, and at least it had the virtue of compactness. However, he did not disguise his opinion that complexity, and the weight penalty which went with it, was the wrong path to travel, whatever the power advantage on paper. The solution, he was convinced, was a compact and relatively simple engine — probably a V8. This would enable him to build a small, reasonably lightweight car of excellent aerodynamic form, which would be easier to work upon and would be much less tiring to drive than the heavyweights, thereby enabling his drivers to sustain their competitiveness throughout the duration of a hard race.

He also spoke with passion of his concern that all that had been achieved by British teams for their country's prestige, as well as for their own satisfaction and benefit, was in danger of being wiped out for the lack of a really effective power unit, and that the Grand Prix arena was likely to be handed back on a plate to Ferrari, whose consistent inability to match the performance of the British cars since 1961 had highlighted their design inferiority as well as an apparent lack of resolution. It would be a tragedy, Chapman argued, if a foreign team which had been taken on and beaten fair and square should now be let off the hook. It was not simply a matter of winning races, national pride

A young farmer called Jim Clark had been making headlines in his native Scotland for some time in a variety of production cars, but it was his series of outstanding drives as a member of the works Lotus Formula Junior team in 1960 which confirmed him as a racing driver of exceptional calibre.

Ford Cosworth engines were also to be found in road-going Lotus cars. Here is a conversion of the $1\frac{1}{2}$-litre Ford 116E five-main-bearing pushrod engine with twin dual-choke sidedraught Weber carburettors helping to enhance the performance of a Super Seven sports car.

was at stake, at a time when there was evidence of an increasing awareness by foreign governments of the value of international motor racing success in terms of a nation's prestige, and more than a hint that financial support might be available on a national basis. (Soon after, President De Gaulle was to offer the equivalent of £500,000 to anyone who would develop a race-winning French Formula 1 engine.)

By the time Walter Hayes left Hadley Wood that evening he was convinced about what needed to be done. There must be a Ford engine — another link in

A 1961 Ford Cosworth-powered Lotus Formula Junior chassis showing that in the days of tubular construction both chassis designer and engine builder had to accept considerable compromises in order to fulfil the needs of each other.

A wider version of the same structure provided the framework for the Lotus 23 sports-racing car. The first examples were fitted with the $1\frac{1}{2}$-litre Ford Cosworth pushrod engine, but during 1962, when a works car was fitted with one of the Twin-cam engines developed for the Cortina Lotus, Jim Clark staggered the racing world by leading all the 'heavy metal' in the Nurburgring 1000-kilometres race until he became affected by exhaust fumes and slid off the track.

Formula Junior's swansong at Brands Hatch in 1963 with Peter Arundell in his Lotus 27 already inching ahead of Denny Hulme and Frank Gardner in their Brabhams and Mike Spence in the other works Lotus. The following year FJ racing was to be replaced by both Formula 3 and Formula 2, each with a 1-litre displacement limit, and Cosworth Engineering were to give top priority to the latter category for which they produced the SCA engine.

the Lotus-Ford chain of collaboration — around which Colin Chapman could design his compact, slippery-shaped, lightweight, comfortable-to-drive and easy-to-maintain Grand Prix car with which Jim Clark, in particular, could continue to dominate the Formula 1 scene.

At first, the idea might have seemed far-fetched, yet it had a certain compelling logic. After all, Ford were firmly committed to the Total Performance image, Ford engines had become dominant in many racing classes and Ford mainstream products, like the Cortina in its various guises, were already benefiting greatly in the marketplace through their association with competition success. Grand Prix racing represented the pinnacle of the sport, so why should there not be a Ford involvement at this level, too, especially if there could be seen to be a tangible link between the engineering of a Formula 1 engine and that of Ford's high-performance production power units?

Hayes had not been aware of the approach to the SMMT until a few days later, when he was summoned to Sir Patrick Hennessey's office. In addition to his Ford responsibilities, Sir Patrick at that time was President of the SMMT, and he asked his Director of Public Affairs for his opinion of the concept of a motor industry-sponsored Grand Prix engine. Hayes' response must have surprised him, for he left no doubt in his Chairman's mind that in his opinion the idea was a complete non-starter. Having done so, he continued to prepare the groundwork for his own alternative solution.

When Harley Copp had arrived from the United States to take over the position of Vice-President in charge of Engineering with Ford of Britain, Walter Hayes had been quick to discover in his new colleague a considerable passion for motor racing, a trait which he did all he could to encourage. It was clear that if Hayes' intended proposal to the Board — that Ford should finance a Formula 1 engine — was to have any chance of success it had to have Copp's support, and so he arranged for him to have a long discussion with Colin Chapman and hear at first hand the Lotus boss' concept of an engine of the utmost compactness and efficiency. Copp was duly impressed, the more so when he discovered that an intermediate stage in the development of such a power unit could be the construction of a four-cylinder Formula 2 engine based on the Cortina cylinder block.

There was never any real doubt, assuming that the proposal got off the ground, as to who should be entrusted with the design of the proposed Formula 1 engine, or that such a power unit would be anything other than a V8, despite all the subsequent talk in racing circles about forthcoming or proposed Ford 12-cylinder and 16-cylinder engines. Keith Duckworth, who had already earned an enviable reputation as the most knowledgeable and successful producer of competition versions of Ford production engines, was the obvious choice.

Duckworth, a graduate in mechanical engineering from London University, had been initially a customer of Lotus Cars (having bought and assembled a Lotus 6 sports car from a kit of parts), then a part-time employee (having been enticed to lend a hand during one of his frequent visits to their modest premises in the north of London) and ultimately a full-time gearbox development engineer (having proved himself unusually adept at Austin A30 gearbox assembly during the absence at a race meeting of the company's transmission specialist, one Graham Hill).

It was during his time with Lotus that he met and formed a close working relationship with Mike Costin, who had previously worked for the De Havilland aircraft company but had been lured away by Chapman during the formative years of Lotus and was by now a senior member of the staff. Duckworth's strength in engineering theory and Costin's ability to apply practical solutions to engineering problems complemented each other extremely well, but in due course Duckworth's frustration with having to spend so much time attempting to cure the ills of a troublesome Lotus five-speed gearbox, which he believed needed a fundamental redesign, persuaded him to resign, with the intention of starting his own engineering business.

Duckworth and Costin had been discussing for some time the possibility of joining forces and exploiting their combined talents in the motor racing field, and Duckworth's departure from Lotus provided further impetus after the formation, in 1958, of Cosworth Engineering Limited, a title which, of course, combines part of their two surnames. The original intention was that whereas Duckworth would devote all his time to the company, in which he would be the major shareholder, Costin's contribution would be confined to evening and weekend work, but this idea was soon to be knocked on the head by Colin Chapman, who offered Costin the post of Technical Director of Lotus, with a three-year contract, one clause of which expressly excluded any outside activities of a similar nature. It was not until 1962, therefore, that Costin was to be free to join his new partner.

Sir John Whitmore with the works Cortina Lotus which he co-drove to victory in the 1964 six-hours touring car race at Brands Hatch with Peter Procter. Immediately the Lotus Twin-cam engine was available Cosworth Engineering set about its further development for racing.

In the meantime, Cosworth Engineering progressed quickly from a company operating out of someone else's workshop to one with premises in North London with its own dynamometer, a growing reputation for the race-preparation of Coventry Climax engines and an ever-lengthening list of satisfied customers. One of these had been Howard Panton, for whom Duckworth had agreed to design and construct a Cosworth Formula Junior single-seater, the Italian-born racing formula having been granted full International status for the 1959 season. However, Duckworth was experiencing difficulty in extracting what he considered to be sufficient power from the Fiat 1100 engine which he intended would drive it, whereupon Panton, who worked for Ford of Britain, revealed that a new short-stroke Ford engine was on the way to power the forthcoming 105E Anglia saloon, due to be unveiled that autumn.

Motor racing spectators first caught sight of the new car at Brands Hatch, on October 4, the day on which the British Racing and Sports Car Club staged the first race in Britain specifically for Formula Junior cars. Ford had provided one of their brand new Anglias for use as a course car, and commentator Anthony Marsh, in drawing attention to the new saloon, suggested perceptively that it would not be long before someone got down to race-developing its short-stroke engine into a Formula Junior power unit and that the Italian engines which had predominated so far would soon have a formidable rival. How right he was!

Duckworth obtained an early example of the 105E and all work on the Cosworth FJ car was forgotten as the staff carried through a frantic development programme on the new engine in time for the first Cosworth Ford racing power unit to make its debut in the traditional Boxing Day meeting at Brands Hatch. It was the beginning of a remarkable success story, both for the engine and for Cosworth, for its superiority over all rival engines was soon firmly established, and Mike Costin was able to convince Colin Chapman that the best way of ensuring sales of the newly designed Lotus Formula Junior car was to offer it with an engine developed by his former employee. The Lotus contract — which was to be worth 126 engines in the first year — provided that element of commercial stability which is so essential for a new company during its formative period.

Cosworth Engineering was now in need of some sound business administration, and this was to be provided by Bill Brown, with whom Duckworth had shared a twin-bedded room in their London University days and who had become an unofficial part-time Cosworth employee whilst completing his National Service in the Royal Air Force. Brown was to remain in charge of the company's business affairs until well into the 1970s, when he decided to move on to further develop his interests in other fields, including powerboat racing.

The fourth key member of the team in the company's early years was Benny Rood, who ran a machine shop in the Walthamstow area of East London and was one of the team present at Brands Hatch for that inaugural appearance of the Cosworth Ford FJ engine. Rood carried out sub-contract work for Cosworth and eventually this became such a dominant part of his business that his company was put under the Cosworth wing and he accepted a position on the Board. He has remained in charge of the company's manufacturing facilities throughout its dramatic growth from a modest engineering enterprise to the multi-million pound publicly owned Group it is today.

The widespread appeal of Formula Junior had provided the foundation for

Jack Brabham, searching for an engine to use in 1966 under the new 3-litre rules, decided that simplicity and lightness, even coupled with modest power, was preferable to mechanical complexity and excessive weight. He found his solution in Australia, where Repco Engineering had successfully race-modified a General Motors V8 engine. The Brabham-Repco combination had a highly successful first season, and here Brabham is heading for victory in the French Grand Prix at Reims, which made him the first driver to win a Grand Prix in his own make of car. With three more victories in succeeding races Brabham was well on the way to his third World Championship.

A day for the heavyweights at Watkins Glen in 1966. Jim Clark, a lap clear of the field in his BRM H16-powered Lotus 43, is being followed by Jo Siffert and John Surtees in their Cooper-Maseratis, and Bruce McLaren in his own Ford DOHC-engined car.

After a relatively troublefree run Clark scored the only Grand Prix success for the compact but complex H16 engine which, like the Ford DFV on the way, bolted directly to the back of the chassis monocoque.

the Cosworth success, and its demise at the end of 1963 was to mark another important milestone along the road towards the design and construction of a Formula 1 engine. Formula Junior had grown from a 1,000cc to a 1,100cc engine displacement limit early in its career, but the two categories which replaced it — Formula 3 and Formula 2 — each had a 1,000cc limit, the fundamental difference being that whereas Formula 3 called for engines which were production power units with only limited modifications, Formula 2 offered the freedom of replacement rather than mere modification of key components, including the cylinder head, although the production cylinder block had to be retained.

For Duckworth, the opportunity to produce his first complete cylinder head was a stimulating challenge, and the result was his Cosworth Ford SCA engine, based on the Cortina 116E cylinder block, but with a gear-driven single overhead camshaft; it was to prove as effective in Formula 2 racing over the next two years as his FJ power units had been over the previous four. Duckworth's next success came with his MAE engine, based on the Ford 105E, which similarly became a leading contender in Formula 3 during the

A surprise in store at Kyalami. The Brabham-Repcos of Jack Brabham and Denny Hulme leave the front of the grid, with Jim Clark's tyre-smoking Lotus-BRM behind them and John Love barely on the move in the foreground with his four-cylinder Cooper-Coventry Climax. But the winner of the 1967 South African Grand Prix was to be Pedro Rodriguez, whose Cooper-Maserati is alongside Clark's car at the start.

same period.

Although single-seater racing provided the mainstream of Cosworth Engineering's activities during this period, the company was also active in other racing categories, one of their more interesting projects being the further development of the Twin-Cam version of the Cortina engine which Lotus were assembling and fitting to the Cortina Lotus high-performance saloon. However, it was another 1.6-litre racing engine which was to provide the final stepping-stone along the path towards the Grand Prix scene. Formula 2, like Formula 1, was about to undergo a fundamental change, with a substantial increase in the engine capacity limit, in this instance from 1 litre to 1.6 litres. The new Formula 2, however, was not to be introduced until the beginning of 1967, one year after the 3-litre Formula 1 was due to come into operation.

The new regulations allowed considerably more scope for design ingenuity than had been provided by the previous Formula 2, and Duckworth applied his fertile mind to the creation of a pure racing engine with a power output in excess of 200bhp,based around the Cortina 116E cylinder block. However, it was at this point that confirmation of the withdrawal of Coventry Climax from the Formula 1 scene raised far more fundamental questions, and suddenly Duckworth found himself faced with a challenge which, for all his understandable faith in his own ability — after all, his batting record had been a remarkably successful one — was sobering in its magnitude.

He had never designed a racing engine completely from scratch — all his efforts to date had been built around someone else's cylinder block — yet it was soon clear from the discussions in which he became involved, first with Colin Chapman and then with Walter Hayes and Harley Copp, that if these gentlemen were to get their way, his design expertise would soon have to be tested in the showplace of international motor racing. His first effort at producing a pure racing engine, starting with a blank sheet of paper, would inevitably attract tremendous publicity, so much so that failure to get the job done could not only dent the fortunes of the Lotus team and hinder the career of its star driver Jim Clark, but it could also put the credibility of Cosworth Engineering into jeopardy.

Fortunately, the simultaneous requirement of the new Formula 2 engine, though adding to the work load (on the assumption that the Formula 1 engine project would be given the go-ahead by the Ford Policy Committee), would provide Duckworth with one more design exercise pointing towards a Formula 1 power unit. It also fitted in very neatly with Ford's requirements, because not only was it important that the company's association with success in Formula 2 be continued under the revised regulations, but any Formula 1 engine with the Ford name on it would have to be a V8, and not only because such a cylinder configuration could best satisfy Colin Chapman's needs for a lightweight and compact engine. Although there was no longer a V8 in Ford's European car catalogue, the parent company was still essentially a producer of cars with V8 engines, many of which were to be found in other parts of the world, some as imports and others the products of local assembly plants. The association with a V8 racing engine which would be seen in the United States, Mexico and South Africa, as well as throughout Europe and possibly in Australasia as well, was not to be underestimated as a potential marketing tool.

From Duckworth's point of view, a two-stage project in which the successful production of a 1.6-litre four-cylinder Formula 2 engine could be followed by a 'doubled-up' V8 power unit, with suitable modifications to the cylinder dimensions in order to bring its displacement within the 3-litre limit, made good sense. Most important of all, it would mean that the cylinder head — in Duckworth's opinion the key component of any of his competition engines — could first be tested and proven on the four-cylinder block before it was committed to a V8. Such an arrangement also had a special attraction for Walter Hayes in so far as his Public Affairs people would justifiably be able to point to a link between the proposed Grand Prix engine and the best-selling Cortina, with the Formula 2 engine, incorporating twin overhead camshafts and four valves per cylinder over a Cortina block, representing the halfway stage.

The all-important meeting of the Ford Policy Committee, comprising some dozen or so of the company's top executives who meet at regular intervals to take the major decisions concerned with the operation of the company, took place only six days after Stanley Gillen had arrived in England from the United States as Ford of Britain's new Managing Director. He had been looking forward to the new challenge which his appointment offered him, but he must have been rather surprised when, after running smoothly through the fixed agenda of his first meeting of the Policy Committee, he turned to Any Other Business and heard Walter Hayes say, 'Yes, Harley and I would like to do a Grand Prix engine'.

Hayes then expanded on the proposal, outlining the content of the various discussions which had been going on with Chapman, Duckworth and Copp, who in the ensuing discussion confirmed his own support of the proposal, which was to commit the company to a minimum expenditure of £100,000. Although this represented just about one-tenth of the cost of putting synchromesh on the Cortina's bottom gear, it was nevertheless a considerable amount of money in terms of contemporary motor racing costs, and especially for an activity in which Ford at that time had had virtually no first-hand experience. However, the proposal, when put to the vote, was passed without any apparent misgivings; it was another example of Ford's corporate policy of relying upon the judgment of its own senior specialists. Walter Hayes and Harley Copp had been given the support of their colleagues for which they had asked, now it was up to them to see that the support — and the expenditure — would be fully justified.

Hayes asked Ford's legal department to draw up a draft contract in the form of a tripartite agreement involving the Ford Motor Company, Cosworth Engineering and Keith Duckworth, and including the following clauses:

1. In consideration of the payment by Ford to Cosworth of the sum of £100,000 . . . Cosworth and Duckworth agree to design and develop for Ford Formula 2 and Formula 1 engines to be known as 'Ford' engines . . . suitable for racing in international competitive events.
2. That the engines to which this Agreement refers are (a) a 1,600cc four-cylinder inline engine designed for the 1967 International Formula 2 category designated the FVA using the Ford 120E cylinder block and a light alloy four-valve-per-cylinder head, and (b) a 90-degree V8 3,000cc engine using cylinder heads basically the same as/or developed from the above FVA suitable to race in international Formula 1 races under the regulations which started in 1966.
3. Cosworth and Duckworth will develop the FVA engine during 1966 and produce at least five engines for racing during 1967.
4. Cosworth and Duckworth will design and build and develop the Formula 1 engine and have engines ready for use by May 1967. They will build at least five engines by January 1, 1968 and maintain such engines until December 31, 1968. Cosworth will supply to Ford a total of five engines suitable for Formula 1 by January 1, 1968 for the purpose of equipping one Formula 1 team. The choice of team will be at Ford's discretion, Cosworth being available in an advisory capacity if required.

The agreement was to become effective on March 1, 1966, although it was not until June 23 that year that Keith Duckworth put pen to paper, his reluctance to do so earlier stemming from a desire to see how things progressed on the design side before being committed to a contract, even one which offered a break clause in so far as his undertaking to proceed with the Formula 1 engine was dependent upon the successful completion of the Formula 2 part of the project.

Meanwhile, Colin Chapman had also been reluctant to sign an associated engine supply contract, but this was due to his desire to see contained in it a longer-term supply commitment than Ford felt able to make at that time. Consequently, he received from Walter Hayes a letter of intent in lieu of the formal contract in which was outlined the basic terms of the agreement which Ford's legal department had drafted.

Whilst the sum of £100,000 was a conveniently round figure, Hayes felt that Duckworth had reached this figure on the basis of some rather arbitrary costings, and that it was probably little more than an inspired guess on his part,

The last Grand Prix under the 3-litre rules to take place without a Ford DFV-engined car in the entry list was the 1967 race at Monaco, which marked Denny Hulme's first Grand Prix success in the year he was to win the World Championship. Here he applies a touch of corrective lock as he accelerates his Brabham-Repco BT20 out of the Station Hairpin.

rather than an accurate assessment of the value of the time, services, materials and equipment needed to complete the job. Accordingly, he told Duckworth that, provided the FVA engine proved to be successful, if he found that he had spent more than the anticipated £100,000 prior to the completion of the Formula 1 part of the contract, the Ford Motor Company would be prepared to reimburse him for any reasonable additional expenses incurred in finishing off the job. In the event, that original contract figure, however it had been arrived at, was to prove remarkably accurate, and although Ford were subsequently committed to further expense, this was largely as a result of their on-going involvement in Grand Prix racing and their separate agreement to finance the supply and maintenance of a certain number of engines for specific teams or organizations.

Ford at this time were heavily involved in motorsports activities on both sides of the Atlantic, but the European-based programme, which the company liked to contain within an annual budget of approximately one million dollars, had little in common with the considerably more substantial operation being mounted in the United States. Indeed, the only time when the two programmes came together was at Le Mans, for the famous confrontations with Ferrari during the mid-1960s. Nevertheless, it was valuable for each of the Ford companies to know what the other was doing and — even more important — planning to do on the motorsports front, and so once a year there would be a meeting in Detroit where all would be revealed.

It was just a few weeks after Ford of Britain's Policy Committee had given his Formula 1 engine project the go-ahead that Walter Hayes crossed the Atlantic to report on the European programme to the main Board. There, he explained that the main thrust of the company's activity would continue to be the further technical development of its production cars, but that it was about to engage in a new venture with a Grand Prix engine. The Board members listened intently as he outlined the Lotus position, explained Duckworth's involvement and so on, and eventually Mr Ford asked him what he thought the proposed engine would achieve? Walter Hayes recalls the conversion clearly: 'I said, well, I thought that it would win several Grands Prix, and I also thought that it could win a World Championship, in fact I said that I thought that this was fairly likely to happen. I had already told them what it would cost us, and of course they laughed, because it didn't sound like a very expensive programme, and then, after a pause, Mr Ford said, "Well, I think all we can say is Good Luck . . . and we'd like to know how it all comes out." But you know, people talk about luck, but I think you've got to create the circumstances in which luck has a chance. It wasn't just a question of money, it was a question of getting the right people together, and giving them the opportunity to do a job better than anyone else had been able to do it. Looking back from a distance of more than 15 years it may not look like a particularly bold act, but at the time it was a fair old gesture of confidence on my part. I hadn't been with the company all that amount of time, and I sort of hung my career on the line with that engine. In fact, I stuck my neck out a million miles. . . .

'I must say, though, that frankly it never occurred to me that Keith's engine would be anything other than a tremendous success. It was one of those things I always felt so right about. He'd had such a good record all along, and we knew where he'd been. Our 'Kent' engine, which we introduced for the Anglia, then used for the Cortina, Escort and the others, must be one of the great engines of all time, and no-one knew more about the 'Kent' and its potential than Keith, so nobody was in a better position to do the FVA for us (and later the BDA) and then move on to a V8 in the form of a 'double-FVA'. Also, he has always been a deep and clear thinker, and it was a great comfort to know that he had the whole of that engine designed in his mind, even before he started to put pencil to paper . . . he knew exactly what he was doing.'

CHAPTER 2

Back to the drawing-board

DFV design and development

It is one thing to have the layout of an engine and all its ancillary equipment visualized in one's mind, but quite another to get it all down on paper in such a way that everything fits, nothing gets in the way of anything else, and the total package is fully functional and contained within acceptable overall dimensions.

Keith Duckworth was breaking new ground with the DFV because for the first time he had no base unit — someone else's cylinder block — around which to build his engine. There were no predetermined dimensions, or fixed spacing of cylinder centres, or positioning of cylinder head bolts, or distance between front and rear main bearings, or any of the other fundamental measurements to influence his actions. This time he had total freedom, but with freedom came awesome responsibility.

At first it was not simply a question of drawing a complete engine, but rather of producing schemes for the major components, such as the crankshaft, cylinder block and cylinder heads, whilst retaining flexibility in design to enable such dimensional changes to be made to any of them as might subsequently prove necessary. For example, although it was always the intention to produce the shortest possible engine, this did not simply mean designing a crankshaft within target dimensions; Duckworth had to convince himself that at the length to which he had drawn it the crankshaft looked sufficiently strong. Similarly with the cylinder block. With the dimensions envisaged, had he provided adequate liner arrangements? Was the head joint sealing satisfactory? No longer was he inhibited by things like head bolts in the wrong places — if they were he could move them — but this complete freedom tended to delay rather than accelerate the production of definitive drawings. 'When you start with a clean sheet of paper you quickly find that you play around with an awful lot of schemes and sketches, while simultaneously you keep a lot of knowledge in your head, as well as make continuous reference back to the various schemes and half-schemes you've produced for all the individual pieces. It means that you do a colossal amount of work before everything can be fixed.'

There was a period of two to three months before Duckworth felt he had a fair grasp as to where everything would be on his engine, although there was

Keith Duckworth at his drawing-board in a room of his home, a few miles from the Cosworth Engineering factory in Northampton. Duckworth's long hours spent on FVA and DFV drawings during 1966 were relieved by regular weekly trips to St James' Mill Road in order to discuss progress with his colleagues — and to give his eyes a rest.

one exception, which was the cause of the first definitive DFV drawing being produced a considerable time in advance of all the others. He decided at an early stage that he would not be able to accommodate the starter alongside the engine, and it seemed sensible to integrate it into the gearbox casing, where there would be plenty of room. He was also forced to make a quick decision as to where the bolts would go between the gearbox and the bellhousing face of the engine, so that ZF, who were to supply the transaxles for the Lotus 49, could make a start on this work. Accordingly, Duckworth's first DFV drawing contained his scheme for the mounting of the starter, the detail of the rear face of the engine, plus a sketch of the general layout of the DFV as he envisaged it.

Another priority was to fix the layout and location of the various drives and to package the ancillaries in such a way that the fundamental requirement of a compact overall assembly could be achieved in a satisfactory manner. This meant that Duckworth himself had to do a certain amount of drawing of components at an early stage, especially the metering unit, the alternator housing and the distributor, to make sure that they could all be accommodated in the Vee between the cylinder heads, but the detailing of the majority of the ancillaries, including the various pumps, the metering unit and the alternator assembly, became the responsibility of Mike Hall. Duckworth detailed the major engine components, including the block, the heads, the valve gear and the gear and belt drives, plus the crank, rods and pistons, often with dimensions pencilled in quickly so that someone else could subsequently make fair copies as final working drawings. Whereas Duckworth worked at home, Hall was based at the factory, but the two would meet about once a week with Mike Costin to check on progress throughout the design period, which lasted approximately nine months.

Although the design of a V8 cylinder block from scratch was a formidable undertaking, Duckworth was able to draw on his considerable experience of modifying other people's blocks. 'We were used to working on standard blocks and seeing where they were weak, and I'd obviously got a fair idea of the way loads moved around in the block and the forces between the cylinder head and the main bearings.' The calculation of loads involved in engines is so complex, due to the effect of random vibrations, torsionals and other things creeping in, that Duckworth is convinced that to stress from calculated loads can be open to great errors and that past experience, plus an eye for avoiding stress concentrations, is much more likely to provide a satisfactory result.

The overall design of the DFV was governed by the decision to make it a 90-degree V8, and because it is difficult to construct an efficient chassis around such an engine, due to the considerable plan area of the cylinder heads, it seemed logical to end the chassis structure immediately behind the cockpit, attach the engine directly to it as a stressed member, and then use the engine-transaxle package, in conjunction with a small subframe, for carrying the rear suspension and wheels. Such a layout, of course, called for the provision of suitable pickup points on the engine, which had to be stressed to cope with the usual chassis loads.

'Obviously, I liaised with Colin Chapman over this, and once we had agreed what we wanted to do I went away, sketched my engine, looked at the situation, and eventually came up with the fact that we could use plates from the top of the cam carriers, plus bolts from the bottom corners of the sump, to give us a suitable configuration of pickups for the back bulkhead of a monocoque. Chapman's monocoque had a very narrow base, the two side sponsons being just 9in apart at the back (the original dimensions had been chosen to fit Jim Clark's bottom!), so it made sense for us to locate the two lower bolts with 9in centres. Fortunately, the position of my cam carriers when I had drawn them was such that the back face of a monocoque of appropriate size could be defined by the required positions of the mounting points.'

Although Duckworth was anxious to contain the overall length of his engine as much as possible, he had to accept that the insertion of wet liners in his light-alloy cylinder block meant that the spacing of the bores would have to be considerably greater than would have been the case with a linerless block. It would have been possible to reduce the length a little by adopting a smaller bore than the 3.373in dimension used on the Formula 2 FVA engine, but finally the decision was made to stick to the same bore and bring the displacement within the 3-litre limit by reducing the stroke to 2.55in, the conrod length being increased so as to avoid an unacceptable increase in piston acceleration.

In an effort to keep mechanical losses to a minimum, Duckworth decided that the aerodynamics of the crankcase should be as favourable as possible,

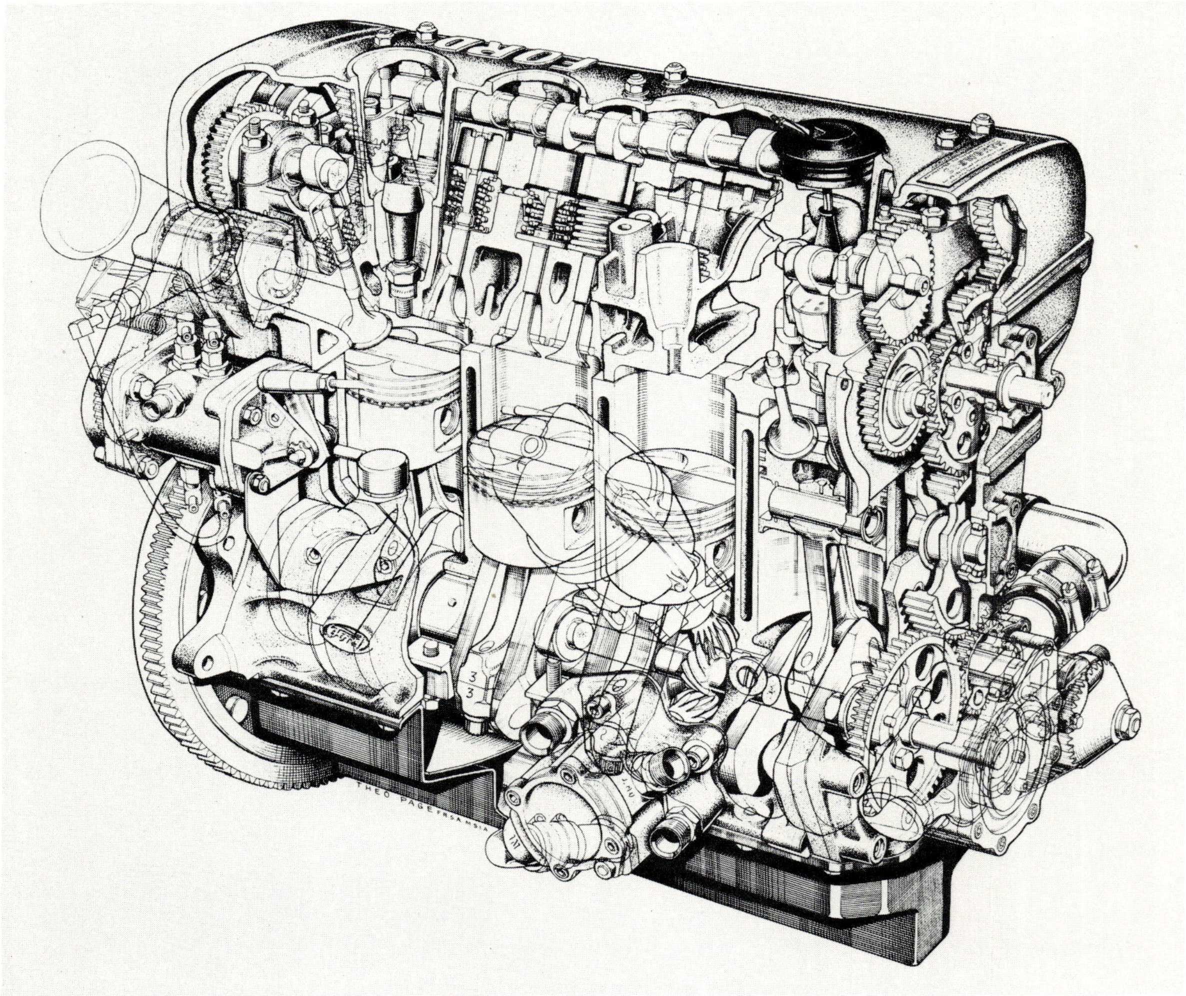

The Ford Cosworth FVA engine for Formula 2, which provided a useful halfway stage towards the design and initial development of the Formula 1 DFV. One quarter of the £100,000 fee negotiated with Ford was allocated to the FVA part of the dual project.

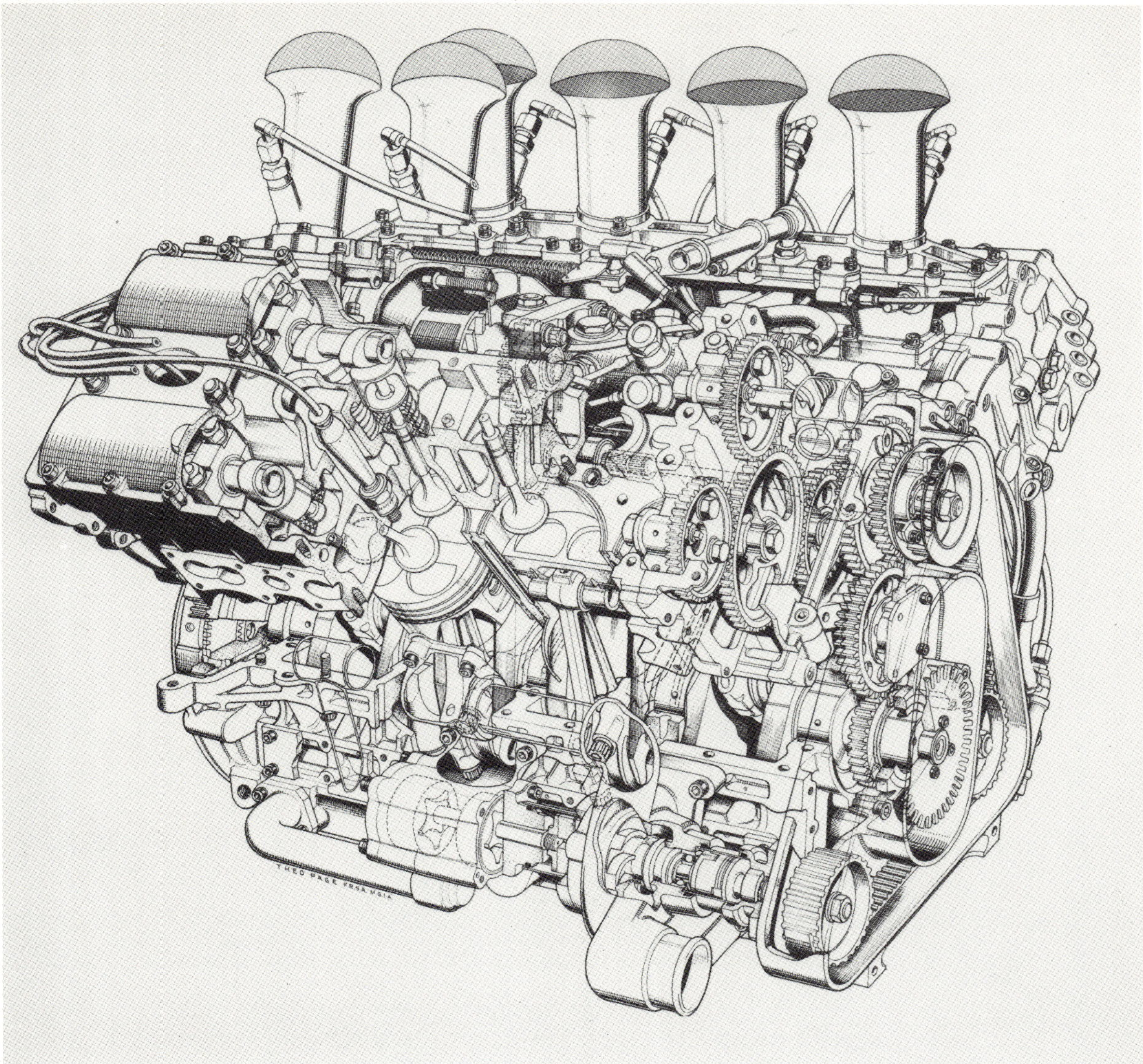

The DFV engine exposed. It was possible to transfer much of the work done on the cylinder head of the FVA to the Formula 1 engine, although the valve angle was reduced and in order to bring the V8 engine within the 3-litre limit a reduction in piston stroke from 2.72in to 2.55in was applied.

and to this end he made sure that the internal surfaces would be made smooth to minimize the interference to the air passing over them. He was also keen to get the centre of gravity of the engine as low as possible, and consequently he chose to use a small flywheel and to design the sump in such a way that the crankshaft would be mounted as close as possible to ground level. This called for a fairly complicated bottom half of the engine, and initially all the main bearing caps were built integrally with the sump, with holes through the intermediate diaphragms to look after the inter-cylinder breathing. It was also important that the structure should be strong enough to allow chassis loads to be passed through the bottom of the sump.

Duckworth's facility for cylinder head design had been a cornerstone of his success to date as a racing engine designer, and he was to draw heavily on his experience with smaller-displacement engines in scheming the heads for the Formula 2 and Formula 1 power units. His first complete cylinder head, as distinct from a modified version of someone else's component, had been for

Keith Duckworth explaining to Harley Copp the detail design of the valve gear of the FVA engine. Although Duckworth had had the opportunity to design his first cylinder head from scratch for his earlier SCA engine, the revised Formula 2 regulations provided him with considerably more design freedom in drawing the FVA.

his SCA (Single Camshaft — A) engine, based on the Ford 116E cylinder block, but built for the 1-litre Formula 2 which began in 1964. Duckworth had been used to working with bath-tub combustion chambers, and he reasoned that to achieve the appropriate compression ratio for the SCA engine he could obtain his required combustion chamber from the valve recesses in the piston crown. 'By putting the clearance slots in the piston — rather than recessing the valves into the head — I avoided masking the valves, because the piston was out of the way for most of the stroke.'

At the time he schemed the SCA the merits of four valves per cylinder were not fully apparent. The basic concept was sound, but the advantages of the greater valve area provided could only be exploited if all the detail work was to the highest standard, and it was not until Honda arrived on the Formula 2 scene with their four-valve engine producing more than 150bhp per litre that the limitations of the two-valve SCA became serious. 'We tried very hard for three years to get that engine to burn. The volumetric efficiency was very high, but judging from the 49-degree spark advance we needed we had a combustion problem and we never achieved very high bmep's. We had attempted to control the combustion by squish, but I felt that this was only

Mike Costin's considerable prowess as a racing driver was put to good effect when the time came to track test and race develop the FVA. Cosworth Engineering ran a Brabham chassis for this purpose, in which Costin is seen here warming up the FVA and checking the dials with Duckworth before venturing out on to the circuit for some early trials.

really useful for tidying up the remote parts of the chamber; in general it occurred too late to be a major combustion control.' In the end, Duckworth and his colleagues managed to get 143bhp per litre out of the SCA, compared with approximately 100bhp per litre which they had been obtaining from their pushrod-valve Formula 3 engine, but it had been quite a struggle, and there was no longer any doubt that twin overhead camshafts and four valves per cylinder would be needed for the next-generation Formula 2 engine, hence FVA (Four Valves — A) and its Formula 1 V8 derivative, the DFV (Double Four Valves).

With such a layout, Duckworth felt that it would be entirely feasible to aim for 200bhp from the 1.6-litre engine as an initial target. It had been his intention at first to use a pent-roof chamber with diametrically opposed inlet and exhaust valves — a layout subsequently adopted by BMW — but he abandoned the idea, partly because it would have called for three spark plugs per cylinder, and partly because it would have been very difficult to arrange the inlet and exhaust systems on the V8 version. Instead, the Formula 2 engine was given a simple valve layout, with inlets on one side and exhausts on the other, the two sets being angled at a relatively narrow 40 degrees. The two

One of the first Ford DFV engines to be assembled about to be given its first run-up in the Cosworth test house at Northampton. Although there were some early breathing problems internally, once these had been overcome the target of 400bhp was exceeded without further drama.

A Ford photographer finds an unconventional use for a DFV cam cover in order to record the tightly packaged distributor and metering unit assembly between the engine's two cylinder banks.

camshafts were gear-driven from the front of the crankshaft, and the original Ford camshaft was retained to drive the distributor.

For the Formula 1 engine, of course, each cylinder had to be reduced in capacity by some 25cc (from just under 400cc to just short of 375cc) to meet the regulations, and as the limitation on the amount to which the Ford cylinder block could be bored out had resulted in a relatively long stroke for the FVA engine, it was only sensible to apply a stroke reduction from 2.72in to 2.55in for the DFV. 'This necessitated keeping the pistons flat (apart from small valve cutouts) and decreasing the valve angle to 32 degrees, which I did with some trepidation as at this stage the Formula 2 engine was giving very good bmep's. However, there was an additional advantage in that this made the cylinder head slightly more compact, which was a consideration because at that time the engine looked in danger of growing very wide.'

The cam carriers were designed as particularly rigid castings so that chassis loads taken in through the plates attached to the cam covers could pass through them and into the heads and block without any risk of tappet seizure, and all the major castings were designed for direct metal-to-metal contact. The cast-iron cylinder liners were to be secured and sealed by two 'O' rings at their bottom end and by Cooper mechanical joints at the top, while the block was designed for a conventional V8 configuration, with the left-hand bank forward of the right-hand bank, to avoid the use of forked conrods, which Duckworth regarded as 'extraordinarily complicated and not worthwhile'. The diameter of the big-end bearings was to be the same as for the Formula 2 engine, but the main bearing diameter was increased to provide more overlap between the pins and the mains and to improve crankshaft stiffness.

The decision to produce a flat-fronted engine inevitably complicated the task of accommodating all the engine's accessories and their drives, but Duckworth's solution represented a particularly neat example of packaging,

The four prime movers of Cosworth Engineering from its early days, Bill Brown, Keith Duckworth, Mike Costin and Benny Rood, assembled in the test house at Northampton prior to a DFV being run on the bed. Brown was to move on during the 1970s, but has remained in touch with the other members of the Cosworth quartet.

with the oil pressure and scavenge pumps and the water pumps tucked along the side of the engine, and the metering unit, distributor and alternator assembly, as already recorded, nestling in the Vee between the cylinder banks. However, although the space between the inlet manifolds was just sufficient to house an integrated unit comprising a small-capacity alternator, a fuel injection pump and a metering unit, there was not quite enough space for the Lucas distributor as supplied and so the cap and base were assembled with a drive shaft of Cosworth's own design. The ignition chosen initially was the Opus system, which Cosworth had used in four-cylinder form on the SCA engine, and which Lucas were now making in an eight-cylinder version for the Rover $3\frac{1}{2}$-litre production car. Lucas fuel injection equipment was also chosen after satisfactory experience with it on the Formula 2 engine, and in designing his fuel system Duckworth arranged for excess fuel to be pumped through the inlet manifolds, where it could be cooled by the incoming air on its return to the tank, thereby helping to prevent vaporization problems in extreme conditions.

In choosing to use a single-plane crankshaft, Duckworth had certain misgivings because of the resulting out of balance, but as it seemed likely that the maximum transverse shake would be no more than plus or minus .003in he reasoned that this would be a tolerable price to pay for the significant advantage of being able to use an exhaust system which was both simple and compact, and about which he had already gained a lot of experience with his four-cylinder engines. Vibrations, in fact, were to be the cause of some of the most protracted development projects over the ensuing years, and although a great deal was done to minimize their harmful effects the DFV and its derivatives, and in particular the long-stroke DFL, were to earn the not entirely affectionate reputation for being 'a bit of a shaker' by the teams who operated them!

However, vibrations were not the most immediately obvious problem when the first engine was assembled and given its initial run-up on the testbed at Northampton. Duckworth recalls that the engine didn't sound at all bad, but that they had an immediate problem with oil drainage. 'We were breathing oil out of the breather and the heads tended to fill up with oil, then wouldn't drain properly down into the sump where the oil could be collected out by the pumps. We therefore had to do a collection of lashups to improve the breather system, which involved boxes and big pipes on the side — when it first ran in the Lotus 49 it had some tin boxes cobbled on the cam cover with big tubes coming up the side to feed it. Mike Costin and I spent several weekends as well as time during the week on testbeds trying various systems, but as soon as we had it breathing properly from top to bottom it gave 408bhp, which meant that we had met our target of at least 400bhp straight away.'

The first signs of a timing gear problem came before the engine had been installed in the Lotus. During one of the testbed runs a tooth had snapped off

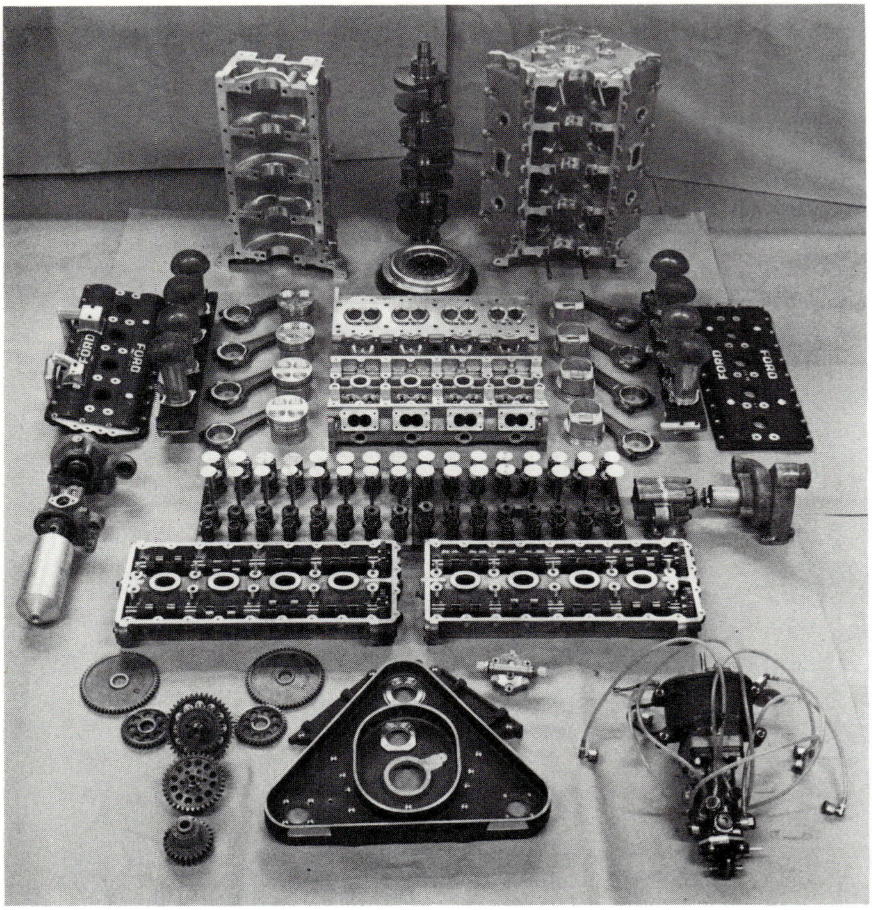

The major components of a Ford DFV engine displayed in an arrangement which emphasizes the precision as well as the compactness of Duckworth's design.

The cylinder block and front cover of the DFV. Although castings were bought out in the engine's earlier days the later establishment of Cosworth's Foundry Division in Worcester has helped to improve both material properties and quality control.

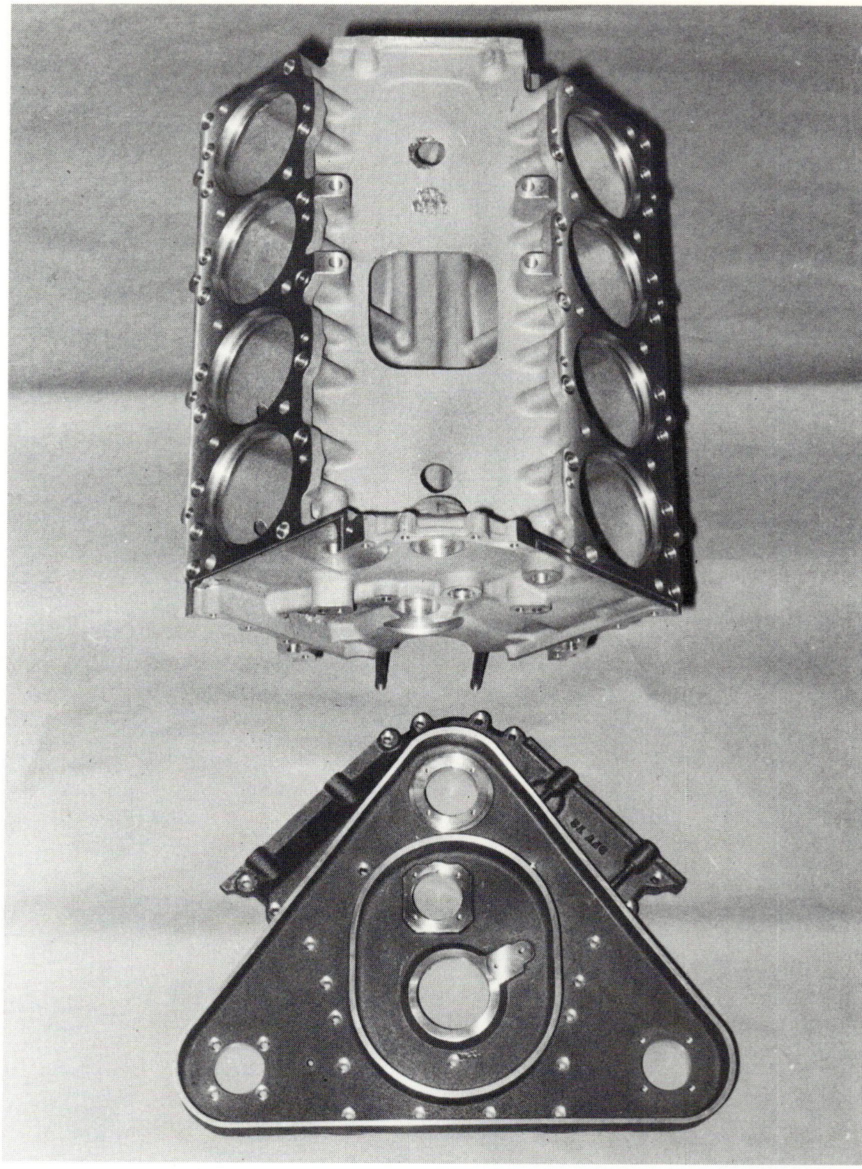

one of the gears — excessive backlash was suspected — and there were also some problems with the bearings supporting the gears. 'The whole of the 14-gear train was very heavily loaded by some torsional, some strange phenomenon that was to stay with us for a long time. However, we had done quite a lot of running before we lost that tooth, so it seemed to us that it wasn't a very short-life problem, and therefore it need not delay the engine's debut.'

Although Graham Hill was to be entrusted with most of the early development driving of the Lotus-Ford, the initial testing was carried out by Mike Costin, who ran the car up and down the Lotus track at Hethel, then later carried out some circuit testing at Snetterton before Hill took over the test programme. The initial track testing went off virtually according to plan, even down to the expected first failure. Duckworth and Costin were fairly convinced that the clutch as originally fitted would not be up to the job, and

The DFV gear train, which in the early life of the engine was to suffer considerably from the effects of the vibrations inherent in a flat-plane V8 engine. Duckworth's ingenious solution was to mount the critical second compound gears on tiny quill shafts.

sure enough it failed after the first start! Afterwards, they changed to the configuration of clutch plate which had been produced for the Formula 2 FVA engine, and this did the job satisfactorily.

With the relatively brief test programme completed and the second car built for Jim Clark, Team Lotus headed for Zandvoort for their first race with DFV power, and for that memorable first victory. For Cosworth Engineering this marked the end of the beginning, but only the very beginning of an on-going programme of detail improvement which would involve virtually every single component in the engine and would ensure that the Ford DFV remained on or very close to the front of the starting grid for the next 15 years. Some of the changes were brought about by the quest for improved reliability from a specific component, others were made in the search for more power, some were made necessary by subtle changes in Formula 1 regulations, which often

The DFV cylinder head, with inlet and exhaust valves directly opposed at an angle of 32 degrees. Duckworth had considered a layout incorporating pent-roof chambers and diametrically opposed valves for his Formula 2 FVA, but he abandoned the idea because of the complexities which would have arisen when applying it to the V8 engine.

An early crankshaft, cylinder liner and piston-and-rod assembly. All were to be the subject of considerable development attention, the move to a low-pressure crank proving particularly beneficial, while the eventual change to aluminium liners did wonders for oil consumption performance.

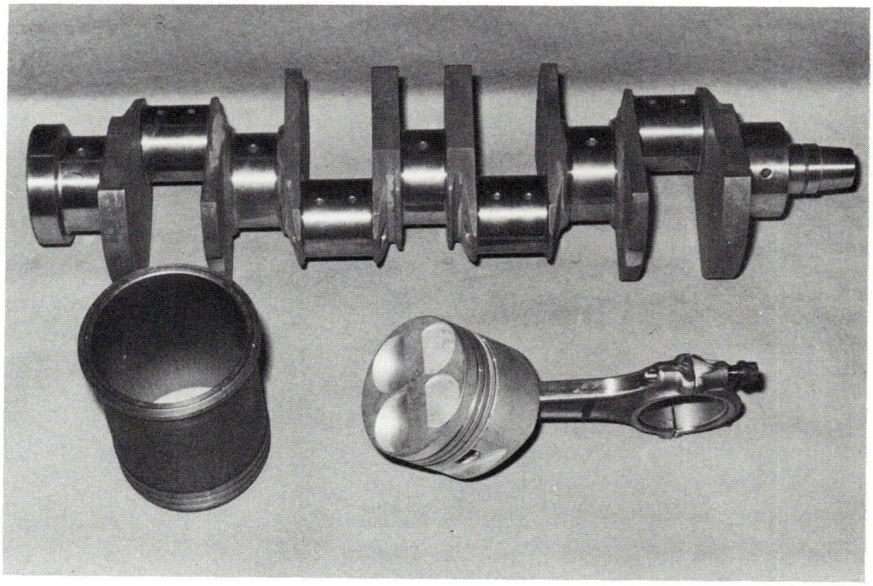

A DFV cam carrier with the cams installed. After a spate of early vibrations-induced breakages a modified cam profile was adopted, aimed at reducing the stab torque loadings on the highly stressed gear train. The modified cams have been run throughout much of the life of the DFV.

The packaging of the DFV's auxiliaries was made the more complicated by the decision to mount the engine directly to the rear of the chassis monocoque, thereby calling for a flat front face. However, Duckworth found space below the cylinder banks, one of the water pumps and the oil scavenge pump finding a home along the right side of the engine.

The second water pump, together with the oil pressure pump and a large filter canister helped to fill the space along the left side of the engine. A decade later, the introduction of ground effects to Formula 1 brought a call for even neater and more compact ancillaries, and the result was Cosworth's slimline auxiliaries.

had a dramatic influence on relative car performance, and others were dictated by the spectacular advances in chassis technology which have occurred during the DFV's long career. On the remaining pages of this chapter are recalled some of the most significant changes in specification which have been brought about by this development programme as well as a typical cross-section of the more minor modifications which have been made during the same period, some of which, though seemingly fairly insignificant, have brought major benefits in terms of engine reliability and component life.

Timing gear troubles

The loss of a timing gear tooth on the testbed prior to the engine's first race was followed by a similar failure which stopped Graham Hill's car while it was leading the 1967 Dutch Grand Prix, and when a post-race examination revealed that Jim Clark's engine had also lost a gear tooth it was clear that the shock loading to which the gear train was being subjected had been underestimated and that some urgent development work was called for.

It would have been very convenient if the problem could have been overcome by doing away with the gears altogether and using a cogged belt instead, but such a solution was out of the question because it would have meant that the concept of mounting the engine directly to the monocoque and taking the loads through the rocker covers would have had to be abandoned. It was necessary, therefore, to work on the gear train itself.

A comprehensive programme of detail improvements was initiated, which involved changing the specification of the bearings and the gear supports, improving the geometry of the gear teeth and re-examining their root diameter, as well as modifications to the grinding of the gears and an overall removal of backlash. But although the quality of the gears became progressively better, there were still breakages and some of the needle bearings in the idlers either failed or became pitted and consequently needed replacing between every race.

Duckworth and his colleagues were preoccupied with this problem for a considerable length of time. 'We did a lot of testing and discovered that there were very high and very short period loads in the gear trains driving the cams, and when we analyzed the cams and their interaction from one bank to the other we found that there was a very quick reversal in torque on that gear set-up. We concluded that this was the problem and we then designed new cams, which were specifically aimed at reducing the maximum torque needed to actually turn the cam against the valve springs, or to accelerate the valve gear. The modified cam is still being run, although when we introduced it its primary objective was purely to reduce the stab torques on the gear train.'

This alone, however, was insufficient to overcome the fundamental problem. 'We hawked around with all kinds of schemes, believing that if we

Keith Duckworth, Graham Hill, Colin Chapman and Harley Copp get together for the unveiling of the DFV to the press at the former Ford premises in Regent Street, in London's West End. Talking in the backgrond is national paper motoring correspondent Keith Challen.

A display version of the DFV engine, seen at the time of the press unveiling and revealing clearly the plumbing arrangements along the left side of the engine. As can be seen, the mechanical fuel pump, water pump, oil pressure pump and filter canister filled the lower space completely. Latterly, the mechanical fuel pump has disappeared, to be replaced by a combined pump, usually mounted on the fuel tank, while the remaining auxiliaries have been so compacted that there is room for an air starter behind them.

The other side of the same engine. Once again a water pump dominates the lower area, with the oil scavenge pump and drive coupling behind it. Subsequent removal of the right-hand water pump meant that the scavenge pump could be mounted further forward, with an air/oil separator immediately ahead of it, to leave the rearward part of the engine uncongested.

Maurice Phillippe, who led Colin Chapman's design team at the time of the Lotus 49, seems to be saying to Graham Hill: 'That's my job done, now it's up to you', as Hill sees the Lotus-Ford package for the first time.

Shortly afterwards, Hill donned overalls and helmet to give the new car and engine a few exploratory laps prior to beginning a serious test programme. Jim Clark's temporary exile abroad meant that Hill was solely responsible for chassis tests prior to the team cars being taken to the 1967 Dutch Grand Prix.

could get a bit of sponge into the gear train — if we could get a bit of give into it in place of the dead rigidity we were faced with at that time — we might get over the problem. So I talked to various people to see whether they thought that rubber would do the amount of work we were talking about, but with the instantaneous loads that were occurring in the gear train nobody seemed very happy about using bits of rubber. We had been recording instantaneous torques of over 300lb/ft, even with our modified camshafts, which had reduced the theoretical maximum from 36 to 26lb/ft.

'All our development work in strengthening, supporting and generally improving the gears had really only transferred the problem from one component to another, so it was vital that we provided some form of cushioning. In the end I decided that this could best be provided by mounting the second compound gears on a hub incorporating 12 tiny quill shafts, the reasoning being that with the twisting of this multiple quill we could store a certain amount of energy and that if the loads were as low as I hoped they would be, then it would survive. So it was an act of faith to make it, and after a short development period we managed to get it to work, and it has worked ever since. We have had failures when you use more savage cams with it, and if you try to run a DFX without a crankshaft damper (because the quill takes out torsionals from the crank as well as torsionals coming down from the camshafts), so this goes to prove that it has to work fairly hard, but fundamentally it has done the job, although it called for some very careful packaging and it presented us with quite a complicated lubrication problem.

'The cushioned compound gear was first fitted to the DFV in 1971, since when, apart from the odd failure on the gears below it due to crankshaft torsionals, all the bearings have been lasting more or less indefinitely and the gears in general are surviving on a permanent life basis, too. Mind you, we continue to make the gears with all the improvements which we introduced at

Boxes on the top of the exhaust cam cover of the DFV engine were a temporary expedient to overcome the oil drainage problems which had been encountered when the engine was first run at Northampton. In due course they would give way to a redesigned lubrication system incorporating Roots-type scavenge pumps of much larger capacity and air/oil separators and allowing the engine to be run at a considerable depression.

the time of our earlier failures, such as using very high specification vacuum remelted material, beautifully ground with minimal backlash, because we have never really found out whether it was required or not.'

Even during the height of the timing gear problems it was possible for a driver to obtain a level of reliability far beyond the norm, and perhaps the most remarkable example involved Jochen Rindt who, at the time when just about every other engine was suffering regular timing gear failures and ruining bearings in virtually every race, went through five races with the same set of gears and bearings installed. Obviously, the scatter between different engines was very high, but unfortunately, Duckworth recalls that they were never able to find out why certain engines 'would' and certain ones 'wouldn't'!

Transmitting the power

One of the earliest problems encountered with the Lotus 49 was concerned not so much with the power unit as with what was happening immediately behind it; the ZF gearbox was simply not up to the job of transmitting the DFV's power.

Although the box had been built specifically for the car, Keith Duckworth and Mike Costin were convinced when they first saw it that it had been underdesigned. 'When we examined the gearbox for the first time, looked at the stiffness between the pinion mounting and the crownwheel mounting and visualized the loads, we could forsee problems', Duckworth recalls. 'You must remember that I had had a little experience of crownwheels and pinions during my 10 months with Lotus in 1957.'

Colin Chapman had been attracted to the idea of a purpose-built box because it offered the possibility of some useful weight-saving, but any thoughts that it could perform the job required of it were effectively removed at the 1967 French Grand Prix, when the race took place (for the only time) on the very tight Bugatti circuit at Le Mans, where the preponderance of low-speed corners was guaranteed to expose any transmission weaknesses. The race was to be over 80 laps, but Hill's car lasted for only 14 and Clark's for just 23 before they were both retired with transmission failure.

The above-normal use of first and second gears had exposed the inadequacies of the pinion-to-crownwheel location, and after the race Duckworth gathered up all the bits of evidence and flew through a violent thunderstorm to Germany to set in train a whole series of modifications. 'My experience at Lotus had given me a vague idea of the sort of loads that were kicking around between crownwheels and pinions, and on reflection I think it was fairly remarkable that the box had performed as well as it had up to that point. But at Le Mans, of course, it had failed in no time at all.'

Substantial stiffening of the casing and a whole series of internal modifications were to do much to overcome the immediate problem, but this still did not alter a fundamental shortcoming of the ZF transmission in that it was not possible to change individual gearbox ratios to suit specific circuit requirements. Instead, Lotus had to arrive for races with a supply of complete boxes, which had been built up with different final-drive ratios, and if a car proved to be incorrectly geared the complete box had to be changed, and even then it was likely that it would not be ideally geared for every corner.

The Hewland gearbox which rival teams were using was certainly heavier than the ZF as originally designed, although this weight advantage of the German unit was markedly reduced after the necessary modifications had been made. The principal advantage of the Hewland, however, was that it allowed individual ratios to be changed, and when an improved Lotus 49B appeared early in 1968, with revised rear suspension, it was equipped with a Hewland transaxle, to the considerable relief of the Lotus mechanics, not to mention the team's drivers.

Throttle control

The DFV came into Formula 1 at a time when tyres were relatively narrow and adhesion was at something of a premium. It was somewhat disconcerting, therefore, for drivers to find that at around 6,000 to 6,500rpm the engine just about doubled its horsepower; in the dry the sudden increase in power was reasonably controllable, but it was making life in the cockpit rather difficult in the wet!

At the time, the solution seemed to be to devise a fully progressive throttle and a scheme was designed whereby a cam control enabled the throttle to be moved very slowly through the first half of the opening then very quickly through the last part. However, tyres started to grow quite early in the DFV's life and then came the move into wings, two developments which combined to offer drivers a significant increase in adhesion, so suddenly the throttle linkage requirement was reduced considerably and consequently the fully progressive throttle was never adopted.

One of the problems with designing an appropriate throttle system for a racing engine is that if you put on ordinary tension springs that are strong enough to ensure that the throttle closes properly — always difficult on slide throttles because the slide becomes sticky when the depression comes on top for the last bit of travel — they are too heavy for the driver to use over the rest of the range. Duckworth's solution was to introduce special closing springs on the throttle slides, which effectively go over-centre. These springs are provided on the trailing ends of the throttle slides and have a very high closing force, but the load goes down as the slides are opened.

Valve spring developments

It is probably fair to say that valve springs and their associated mechanisms have constituted the most persistent cause of mechanical malfunction of the DFV engine and its most frequent cause of failure. It is not surprising that this should be so because in a four-stroke piston engine the valve spring is probably the most highly stressed component of all. It is also fairly difficult to manufacture accurately and consistently.

Valve spring troubles tend to be a combination of the standard of manufacture of the spring, the damping of the spring and the characteristics of the camshaft. If you are aiming for maximum power you need to have high accelerations on your camshaft, which incites much more surge in valve springs than will a quieter cam. This means that you have to cope with the

Keith Duckworth taking a look at one of a batch of DFV blocks which have arrived at the machine shop in St James' Mill Road. During 1977 a limited number of engines were produced with experimental magnesium castings, but although they offered a useful reduction in weight, various problems ensued and it was decided to shelve the idea until such time as magnesium casting technology matched that of aluminium.

contrasting requirements of savage cams for performance and softer cams for valve spring life.

'As we seem to be performance-orientated we go for fairly hard cams, and it is difficult to say whether our compromise in that direction is in fact the right one', says Duckworth. 'Obviously, there can be a problem from batch to batch due to manufacture, which means that you tend to have certain problems, followed by a period with no problems, and it certainly strikes us as very dangerous to change your cam profile because it might be a long time before the inevitable failures manifest themselves. For example, when we ran a different camshaft in 1977 everyone thought that it brought a great improvement in the performance of the engine. Yet ultimately not only did it break more valve springs, it actually dropped a lot of valves, due to reasons which have tended to elude us as all our rig testing failed to reproduce the failure.'

A fundamental requirement is to minimize valve surge, and one of the ways of doing this is to run interference springs in which the inner spring is a push-fit inside the outside spring, causing the coils to rub together. The trouble is that this can lead to scuffing of the spring material, which in turn can cause a weakness in the spring and ultimately a breakage at that point. It is vital, therefore, to try to reduce surge at source, and this brings many factors into play, including the weight of the valve and valve gear, which will also influence the design of your spring in the first place.

'We have tried various solutions to the surge problem', explains Duckworth, 'including the use of non-interference springs with deep retainers at the bottom that cause some damping by interfering on the outside of the spring. You have to remember that although valve springs fail through surge, surge is an inevitable function of the spring and it is exacerbated by your cam. Your task is to find adequate ways of damping the natural surge of the spring which allows you to run at high speeds with fairly vicious cams.

'We changed the type of mounting of the spring and the fitted length of the spring, examined how far from coil-bound it is, and experimented with various types of damping, then we moved on to the interference-fitted springs. One of the problems is that it is very difficult to manufacture your springs sufficiently accurately so that you can guarantee that all pairs have in fact the same interference between coils in about the middle of the spring. As a result, the variability of the damping of contact springs, as they are called, can be very great between pairs, and therefore I would suspect that optimum interference springs don't break, whereas those which happen to have a bit less interference do break.'

A relatively recent development by Cosworth's spring suppliers, which at the time of writing is being evaluated, is the application of a special coating designed to prevent scuffing of the springs through interference. Simultaneously, Cosworth have been running a research rig with pressure transducers underneath the spring platforms and experimenting with a whole series of damping systems as well as evaluating the differences between cam profiles on the rig before they are fitted to engines.

'What this rig has shown', Duckworth reveals, 'is that the amplitudes of surge and the speeds over which it occurs are very much greater than I ever envisaged, and frankly I'm not surprised that springs break! We also have a problem of our age in that today you can collect a lot of data with modern instrumentation, high-speed recorders, electronic transducers, high-speed oscilloscopes, tape recorders and so on, but the complexity of most of what is happening is so great that to actually analyze the data you have gathered is a major undertaking. You then require somebody to sit down and think, and judge whether 'A' is in fact a satisfactory level when it looks awful.....but it's slightly less awful than 'B'. But judging what is likely to survive and what isn't requires a lot of experience of having collected data and tied that into your results in order to build a new picture as to what is acceptable and what is not. We are in an age when everybody collects data, but we are not training people with the thought processes to actually analyze it and say what is the solution. It is the invention of the solutions to the problems which the data has confirmed exist that is, in fact, the problem. That can only be done by creative thinking, and in my view we haven't trained anyone in creative thinking for the last 30 years!'

Nevertheless, despite Duckworth's concern in this respect, it seems reasonable to expect that major progress will have been made towards solving the engine's elusive spring-surge problems by the time this book has been published.

Desmodromic valve gear

One of the most interesting development exercises to be applied to the DFV was the investigation into the use of desmodromic valve gear. The programe, which was initiated in 1979 by Duckworth, was prompted by the difficulties in trying to solve the valve spring surge problem, which at that time looked so intractable that a study of desmodromics, whereby the valves are moved without the assistance of springs, looked to be a head-on approach that was likely to be more successful.

However, the task was to prove far more difficult than had been envisaged, and after a number of failures on the desmodromic test rig due, says Duckworth, to certain inadequacies in the design details of the rig, it struck him that what he had hoped would have been a fairly quick solution would, in fact, take an inordinately long time to get right. Therefore, it did not look to be a satisfactory solution to the surge problem after all. Duckworth also had some growing doubts about exactly how much could be gained by such a system because, in practice, the limitations on cam profiles and valve motions with desmodromic actuation were such that they did not seem to represent that big an advance on those which were possible with springs.

'We do not always know the importance of small amounts of cam changes — it is very difficult to evaluate them, and we've made loads and loads of cams, very few of which see the light of day — and we get very confused as to what really matters when cams open and when they shut, how high they go, and the manner in which they go from, say, half-lift to full-lift. It is the general area under the diagram which is very difficult to evaluate, and bearing in mind that you possibly have to tune your intake and exhaust for every cam change, to go through the whole thing is very time-consuming. Also, the required accuracy of your results, bearing in mind you are probably looking for an improvement of just one to two percentage points — which can make quite a good engine out of a very ordinary one — makes the whole subject one of great difficulty.'

After encountering the initial difficulties on the test rig, Duckworth decided that he ought to redesign the thing, but unfortunately he was unable to find the time to do this. 'I should have let the people who were working on it soldier on, and after a couple of years of steady endeavour something might have come out. But I find it very difficult to accept things being done by trial and error — I suppose you could say it is a colossal failing on my part — when more thought at the beginning should give it half a chance of success. The majority of the people involved think that I should never have stopped work on the desmodromic because, although it might have taken a long time and cost a lot of money, eventually we might have arrived at something. The trouble was, I thought it was going to take forever, which perhaps was being difficult and unreasonable.'

Although it would be possible to re-activate the programme, the case for doing so now is less pressing with the accent in racing generally getting away from power per litre and more towards fuel economy. In producing and running engines which will be designed to achieve the most efficient use of fuel it is unlikely that engine speeds will be high enough to give desmodromic any significant advantage over conventional valve gear. The other deterrent is the extraordinarily difficult manufacturing problems involved.

'The accuracy with which you have to make and set up your desmodromic parts is colossal, and this work is inherently exceedingly expensive as well as time-consuming on the part of the fitters. Therefore, because of the difficulty in producing enough good parts, and then ensuring that they are sufficiently skilfully assembled to make the engine a goer, the strain on manpower would be such that only a small number of desmodromic engines could be produced and maintained properly. If we were back to producing, say, just half a dozen engines for one team, more or less regardless of cost, maybe it would be a different matter.'

I sense that Duckworth has some regrets, however, that he did not allow his people to soldier on, even though he reckons that to continue the programme could have cost two or three man-years of work, possibly with no result at the end of it. 'I don't think that an appreciation of the manufacturing difficulties had dawned, or had been appreciated by people. If you are trying to design

Development engine tester Paul Squires reporting to Duckworth on a dynamometer run in one of Cosworth's test cells. The cone-shaped air intake trumpets have become a regular fitment after many experiments over the years with intakes of various lengths and shapes.

very difficult and precise mechanisms you must have a very precise approach to the situation and the mental capability to grasp precisely what is the problem. Without this you immediately get into a triumph of development over design, which costs a fortune.

'There's no doubt that my major fault is that when I see things that are going to take 11 more months and 10 more days to get anywhere I tend to say, "stop". And I shouldn't -- it's as simple as that. Or should I? It all depends upon how unlimited your rescources are to throw at something. The process of getting to the moon was by having enough thousands of people occupied on enough design solutions for a long enough time to achieve it. The development of the majority of cars and production engines happens in much the same way, with enough people grinding away at it so that what eventually emerges is reliable. But we are trying to do something which is far more exotic — and it doesn't matter quite so much if occasionally it breaks — and far more complicated, and we are trying to do it all with a relatively small budget. Under those circumstances I think you have to get things right first time, by good design, and concentrate your rescources on making the things you know you can make efficiently.'

Although the desmodromic programme was cut short, it was certainly not without value. It gave those involved in it a valuable insight into new and complex engineering and manufacturing problems and it also provided additional impetus to solving the valve spring surge problem by other means. Whether there will ever be a Ford Cosworth racing engine with desmodromic valve gear is another matter altogether.

Cylinder head plug tubes

One of the most important detail changes made to the DFV's cylinder heads concerns a modification of the casting and the insertion of separate spark plug tubes. As originally designed the plug tube formed part of the casting and water being used to cool the exhaust valve had to find its way past the tube on each side. However, there was a considerable restriction to flow, and when a damaged head was cut and examined it was discovered that in places the water passage was completely blocked, thereby causing local overheating.

The solution was to bore out the top section of the casting and insert a thin-wall sleeve, which not only provided more clearance for water than a cast piece could offer, but also enabled the casting to be examined much more thoroughly to ensure that all the holes were where they should be, and for the casting to be simplified considerably. That the structure of the head does not seem to have suffered unduly by the removal of this piece is, perhaps, indicative of Duckworth's facility for design with generous provision for the unexpected.

One of the enviable features of the DFV, which has been a major contribution to its enviable reliability record, has been its ability to keep temperatures within bounds in the area of the cylinder head, and Duckworth believes that the engine's heat-to-oil and heat-to-water readings are probably a lot lower than with many other engines, the very short exhaust passages in the head being particularly beneficial in this respect.

Cylinder liner changes

With replenishment of oil being forbidden under Formula 1 regulations, the control of oil consumption has been a high priority throughout the life of the DFV engine, yet it has been a difficult problem to overcome, with considerable variations of oil usage persisting from one engine to another. Because some teams' oil systems have from time to time been less than ideal, leading to excessive oil loss through poor plumbing and tankage arrangements, the need for the engine itself to consume oil at a modest rate has been given added emphasis.

The condition of piston rings is a widely recognized influence on oil consumption, but another factor can be the choice of cylinder liner material, and this has been the subject of considerable experimentation at Northampton. Initially, the DFV was fitted with steel liners, but the wear rate proved unacceptable, whereupon a lengthy development programme was initiated into the use of Tufftrided steel, but again the results proved unsatisfactory. Things might well have been different had not the airbox arrived on the Grand Prix scene, one effect of which seemed to be that a

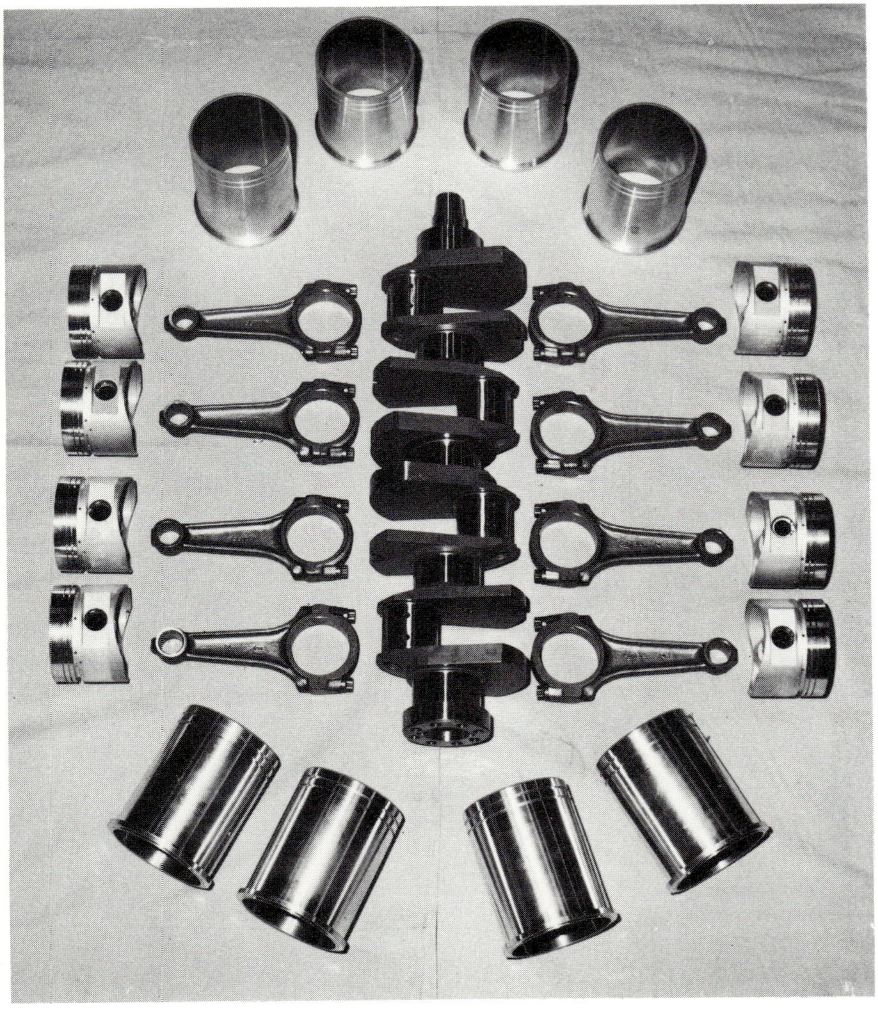

A display of DFV engine components, including steel cylinder liners and a set of moving parts which can only be described as works of art. Note in particular the meticulous detail work on the rods and the extremely narrow recesses for the compression rings, which are a feature of Cosworth's DFV pistons.

considerable quantity of dirt was drawn down the rearmost cylinders; once this had caused an initial amount of wear on the liners, further deterioration followed very quickly.

Another line of development involved the use of molybdenum-sprayed spheroidal graphite iron liners, but these were found to cost power, and so with some reluctance it was decided that the DFV's aluminium cylinder block should revert to the conventional cast iron liners which had replaced the original steel components. Duckworth had been keen to avoid using cast iron in the first place because he wanted a liner which, in the event of a piston or rod failure, would not shatter and lead to the destruction of the engine. Certainly with cast iron liners in use the spread of engine damage arising from a local failure such as a dropped valve has tended to be considerably greater than would have been the case if steel liners had been made to function satisfactorily and been fitted.

However, there has recently been a major breakthrough with the successful manufacture of lightweight liners in aluminium using the Mahle-Nikasil process, which have not only saved a valuable 8lb in the overall weight of the engine, but also appear to have cured the DFV's erratic oil consumption problem at a stroke! Inevitably, these are expensive components to produce compared with cast iron liners, but against this has to be set the reduction in the number of engine rebuilds which have been necessary and the amount of staff time which previously had to be devoted to such things as 'lapping rings, fooling about with surface finishes and sorting out all kinds of piston problems', which can now be devoted to other more pressing activities.

Cosworth forged pistons

It has been Cosworth Engineering's policy for many years to manufacture as large a percentage of engine components as is practicable in-house in order to maintain adequate standards of quality and supply. Initially, this facility was provided to satisfy the company's own requirements for pieces, but from it has grown an important additional arm of the business, concerned with the design and manufacture of components for outside customers. Forged pistons, of which Cosworth are the biggest supplier in the United Kingdom, are the best known example of this work.

In view of the performance levels involved, ordinary cast pistons could not be considered for racing, hence the move at an early stage in Cosworth's development into forged pistons. However, there were relatively few forging companies in England, and most of these were either involved in the aerospace business or else were very busy in other spheres and could not guarantee supplies. For some time Hepworth and Grandage were able to provide an excellent service, but the considerable decline in the number of forged pistons being used in motorcycle engines in England made it uneconomic for H & G to continue to operate their forging plant, whereupon Cosworth, concerned that their major source of supply would be cut off, bought the plant and moved it into a purpose-built building at Northampton, where it has operated ever since.

In the early life of the DFV there were a few piston reliability problems which led to a number of detail changes, including an alteration of the land clearance, but over the years Cosworth's development of forging techniques and their control of processes has been such that the strength and reliability of their pistons is now probably unequalled. Rings are still bought out, however, and Hepworth and Grandage, who originally did a fantastic job for Cosworth by specially developing a very thin type of compression ring, remain one of the company's suppliers of rings.

Inevitably, persistent oil control problems with the DFV has caused Cosworth to maintain a very close watch on ring performance and from time to time to question the consistency of manufacture, as Keith Duckworth explained. 'In this area we have to be concerned with particularly precise geometry. For example, you have rings which are supposed to have very slight tapers on the outside as compared with the flat face, and it's obviously an extraordinarily difficult manufacturing process, and I think that the consistency of some of these small tapers is sometimes leaving something to be desired. Much of the problem is due to our short running-in period. We don't want to run in engines for hours, as for normal road cars, and so new engines don't even get bedded-in. We could do with a higher rate of wear in the first few hours in order to correct the ring geometry, but our engine life is such that they're never run in. This means that the geometry needs to be perfect right from the word go, and that is a very difficult requirement. Actually, the reason that we are not in ring trouble with the Nikasil liners is probably that the abrasiveness of the liner from new is such that it rapidly corrects any ring geometry imperfections!'

Low-pressure crankshaft

The specification of the DFV's crankshaft has changed considerably over the years, and this important component has been the subject of a lot of development attention, the cause of considerable heartache on one occasion in 1970 and, more recently, the beneficiary of one of the most important changes concerning the engine's moving parts.

There were a number of failures early on for fairly complex reasons. The first shafts were made out of bar material, and then they were forged. The next stage was to forge them in better material, and a close inspection was made of the cleanliness of the steel. There was also a failure resulting from the way in which the core plugs had been inserted to block the crank drillings, and this led to a change in the way in which the core drillings were blocked.

The spate of failures in 1970, however, was due to a manufacturing error, when someone ground through the Nitriding layer in the corner of a radius. 'That was an epic way of making a good crank hopeless', recalls Duckworth. 'The whole batch of cranks had been given the same treatment, so they all either broke or they cracked while on the testbed. That batch, which should have lasted us the whole year, had to be written off, and of course it took three or four months to make a new set, so we had to spend most of that year running old engines and retrieving old cranks wherever we could. Inevitably there was a great shortage of engines, and big panics all round.'

It was the construction of the batch of experimental magnesium engines in 1977 which led to the big breakthrough in the design of the DFV's crankshaft. 'There was a considerable expansion of the magnesium main bearing housings, and we were anxious to keep down the oil flow through the engine, otherwise it would have been more difficult to get the oil out of the sump — you get churning losses. So we decided to redrill the crankshaft in such a way that it could run with a much lower main bearing pressure and thus give a lower rate of flow, even though the clearances were greater.'

With the earlier high-pressure crankshaft a minimum pressure of approximately 85psi had been necessary to get the oil out of the main bearing anulus into the crankshaft, from where it could be flung out to the big-ends, but with the revised drillings the oil has to travel a considerably shorter distance, and consequently requires less pressure, in order to reach the main gallery. The latest cranks operate at a pressure of 52psi, plus or minus a tolerance of 5psi.

Keith Duckworth maintains that the accurate measurement of big-end and main bearing pressures is more difficult than some people realize. 'A lot of people say that the crank acts as a pump to supply the big-ends and that the big-end pressure is very high. But this is not the case if you have problems with air getting into the middle of crankshaft drillings — and as to an extent cranks tend to act as centrifugal separators I would say that it's pretty well guaranteed that you will have air in the middle of your cross drillings. Therefore, nobody really knows precisely what their big-end oil pressures are, but by changing your style of drillings it is possible to make this more predictable. So now we say that theoretically we can run with lower oil pressure, and we've been proved right because we've shown that we can run them as low as 45psi; furthermore, the incidence of failures has gone down dramatically.'

Apart from occasions when teams have suffered a bit of 'finger trouble', such as failing to fill up their oil tanks to the correct level, or making a basic plumbing error, or perhaps suffering a detached union, big-end bearing failures have virtually disappeared with the arrival of the low-pressure crank, which is now standard equipment and to which the vast majority of earlier engines have been converted.

Oil system modifications

The external oil pipes and boxes on the cam cover were a temporary expedient to overcome the oil drainage problems encountered when the DFV first ran on the testbed, and efforts to find a tidier and more permanent solution began towards the end of 1967. One of the first steps was the introduction of an air pump to transfer air and blow-by from the bottom half of the engine to the cylinder heads, but unfortunately this caused a lot of oil to be pumped up with the air.

It was then decided to use the air pump as an additional oil pump, and instead of transferring air from the bottom to the top of the engine the total output of the scavenge pumps and the air pump was sent back to the tank, causing the whole engine to run at a depression and allow air to enter the engine through what had previously been a breather. However, this also brought problems for users, who discovered that so much oil and air was finding its way back to the tank via the coolers that their separation systems were inadequate; a number of bearing failures were caused when cars blew all their engine oil out through their tank breathers.

At this point, Duckworth decided to introduce a separation system on the engine and this led to the design of Roots-type scavenge pumps of much larger capacity, together with air-oil separators, so that very large volumes of air could be taken in through the cylinder head and used to assist the oil to drain into the sump. The oil and air were then separated, the air being taken directly back into the top of the tank to breathe out into atmosphere while the oil was sent through the coolers.

Over the life of the DFV there have been a considerable number of changes to the scavenging and separation systems as regards the design and capacity of pumps and their method of operation, many of them brought about by ever increasing demands resulting from the higher cornering speeds made possible through the use of wings, then ground effects. The need to use the underside of cars for airflow management in the ground effects era was also to lead to some major repackaging of auxiliaries, as is described later.

A series of scavenge pumps of increasing capacity led eventually to the DFV being fitted with the pump originally developed for the DFX engine, in which the amount of blow-by was greater. With the Cosworth system the scavenge pumps are required to pump the oil, the blow-by air, plus the extra air which is sucked in through the heads and allows the engine to be kept reasonably free from oil, despite the very high sideways cornering forces. With the aid of wings and ground effects these have been of such a magnitude that one would normally expect the oil to accumulate up on one side of the engine, but by having such a large depression in the sump, and therefore very large volumes of air being drawn down the drains from the head, as soon as any oil gets near one of them it can be gathered into the sump very quickly.

The actual method of separating the oil from the air has also been the subject of design improvements. The separation is achieved by means of a centrifuge assembly into which the oil and air are drawn, the oil then being thrown towards the outside while the air remains in the centre of the separator. As originally designed, the unit acted rather like an egg-beater, with the oil being flung outwards against a stationary wall, from which it was inclined to splash back and froth, as though from a hose being played against a garden wall. To overcome this difficulty the assembly was redesigned so that the outer canister of the centrifuge rotated, with the result that the oil thrown against it no longer hit a stationary surface, but instead made contact with something travelling at more or less the same speed, and consequently it tended to cling to it more effectively. The redesigned centrifuge is also lighter and more compact.

Ignition system developments

The ignition system has been the subject of as much change as any other item of equipment used with the DFV. Initially, engines were produced with a substantially modified version of the Opus contact-breaker ignition which Lucas had developed for production cars. In applying this equipment Cosworth found that its satisfactory operation was highly sensitive to the precise location of the pickup, and in the end they produced their own version of the Lucas distributor incorporating the original cap and base with a series of strengthening modifications. One of the problems had been a tendency for the pickup to wander around and there was a considerable amount of distortion due to heat to be overcome.

The next development was to replace the Opus pickup with a magnetic trigger, but this was less than satisfactory as the pickup was located in a hot area and the loss of strength of the magnet under the influence of heat proved crucial, and as a result relatively few engines were fitted with this equipment. Another problem during the early life of the DFV was that the engine required a speed limiter to protect it from over-revving beyond its fairly conservative 9,000rpm limit, and this was provided by partly electrical and partly mechanical means; unfortunately, the mechanical parts were amongst those which suffered from the engine's inherent vibration and the functioning of the limiter became erratic.

A major change followed the availability of capacitor ignition, Walter Scherag of Germany being the first on the scene with their Contactless system, which was first tried by the Tyrrell team. This enabled surface discharge plugs to be used, with their wider heat ranges, and with a lot more energy in the shorter-duration spark drivers could detect better pickup out of corners, even though it was difficult to discover any difference on the testbed. It was in places like Monaco that the drivers claimed to gain the maximum benefit from capacitor discharge ignition, especially when using part throttle out of tight corners, when the mixture tended to be ignited better during the first few bangs. Another advantage of these plugs was that they virtually eliminated any oiling problems.

Soon, this form of ignition was in heavy demand, and Marelli — anxious to get a foothold in the DFV camp — produced a system suitable for the V8 engine, and in due course Lucas also developed a capacitor discharge system, even though to do so went against their traditional policy of only providing the racing world with adaptations of equipment produced commercially for passenger cars. In this case, purpose-built racing equipment had to be provided, with its own built-in speed limiter, which has proved to be totally reliable. This equipment is also being widely used on the DFL and DFX engines, applications which seem likely to call for the development of some advance-and-retard management in the near future in place of the more or less fixed ignition which has been a feature of Formula 1 ignition systems hitherto.

Fuel system improvements

One of the early problems with the DFV during its first racing season was loss of fuel pressure caused by dirt entering the fuel system and blocking the filters. It was suspected that the trouble was caused in the main by material from the inside of tanks, and larger filters were used in an effort to overcome the problem, although the fuel pump was to remain very sensitive to dirt and consequently had to be assembled with great care. Subsequently, a modification was made to the 'O' ring on the in-line filter when it was discovered that it was not seating satisfactorily in its housing and as a result was allowing dirt to pass through it.

Fuel systems tend to be trouble areas in motor racing because different teams have their own ideas as to how to integrate their own pet systems to supply their engines. On reflection, Duckworth considers that the system used originally on the Lotus 49, with the fuel coming out of the bottom of the tank and the electric fuel pump put in a circuit around it, also mounted low and in a cool area, was probably one of the best systems to have been applied to the DFV, and that high-mounted pumps with longer pipes are not necessarily a good thing.

Nevertheless, the replacement of the original electric high-pressure pump (with which to start the engine) and the mechanical pump (to run it on full power) with a combined electro-mechanical pump has constituted the most important change so far to the DFV's fuel system. The combined unit incorporates a small electric motor and a one-way clutch assembly which ensures that for as long as the engine is running at low rpm, slower than the electric motor, the latter is driving the pump. This is sufficient for starting the engine and for low-speed running in the pit road. Then, as the revs rise, the drive speed increases, the one-way clutch comes into operation and from then on the armature in the pump is driven mechanically by the cable drive. Apart from the weight-saving, it is a much tidier arrangement and it has also meant that one filter element has been discarded.

The revised layout has also overcome a number of valve and associated problems which persisted with the former system. However, one problem of mounting the combined pump on the top of the fuel tank is that there is then a depression at the entry to the pump, which is not as good as if it were fed from the bottom. Duckworth has also produced an alternative scheme in which the fuel pump is located in the bottom of the tank and connected by a long drive from the tank top-mounted motor drive unit, which is also used as an electric generator. As is so often the case with new ideas, it was not easy at first to sell the arrangement to teams, who inevitably tend to be reluctant to change something which has been working well for them and enabling them to finish a lot of races for something else which may have theoretical advantages, but has yet to be tested in the heat of battle. However, once the Williams team took the plunge and tried the new system, with satisfactory results, other teams started to show more interest.

A less fundamental change to the fuel system, but nevertheless one which was widely welcomed because it removed a cause of metering unit failure, was to provide an effective front support for the unit, which was hung from a flange at the rear. Because of the inherent side-to-side shake of a flat-plane 90-degree V8 engine, with everything tending to move in that plane, the unsupported unit tended to crack the flanges of its end plate. The first, temporary solution, often referred to at Cosworth as the Frankenstein mod, comprised a pair of threaded stays with their ends ground to a point, which would be unwound until their tips bore on to the aluminium cylinder head. It was not terribly scientific, but it worked until a better engineered solution was evolved which incorporated the original Lucas sandwich plate with additional straps which were properly bolted up to it. The metering unit is now securely mounted, adjacent to the alternator and distributor, in what has become a fairly tightly packed Vee between the cylinder banks.

Slimline auxiliaries

These days it is not sufficient for a Formula 1 engine designer to produce a power unit which develops race-winning power, torque and reliability; it also has to be so packaged that it conforms to the latest and seemingly ever-changing requirements of the chassis designer. It was a series of requests from that direction which were to cause Duckworth to re-examine the whole question of the placement of the externally mounted engine components of the DFV and to produce a series of what became known as slimline auxiliaries which, since their introduction in 1980, have been used as standard equipment on new engines and have been adopted increasingly as conversions of existing power units.

Prior to their introduction there had been various layouts of auxiliaries along the sides of the engine beneath the cam carriers until the specification was settled with a pair of water pumps, one mounted each side, and on the right side of the engine, the oil scavenge pump, with the oil-air separator immediately behind it, plus the clutch drive to the scavenge pump; this was a safety device which, in the event of any debris getting into the pump or the back pressure increasing, would slip and prevent the internals of the pump being damaged. All this equipment extended the full length of the engine on the right side, which made it a pretty cluttered area.

On the left side, in addition to and ahead of the water pump, there was the mechanical fuel pump, and behind the water pump there was the oil pressure pump with a very long filter canister attached to the back of it, all of which meant that the left side of the engine was as cluttered as the right side. For the chassis designers, who wanted to provide underbody venturis to control airflow along each side of the engine, these auxiliaries represented a major obstacle, and the plea went out for them to be relocated.

Duckworth responded with several schemes, including one which would have involved mounting the pumps up the front of the engine and another which would have integrated them into the bellhousing, but after a close examination of all the requirements and a study of the size of ducts which were feasible because of other considerations it became clear that with some judicious redesigning and slimming down of components it would still be possible to accommodate them along the flanks of the engine.

The important thing was to move everything as far forward as possible into space which would be shadowed by the cars' fuel tanks and which therefore would interfere as little as possible with the path of underbody air. To a considerable extent this would be influenced by the space between the inside edge of the rear wheels and the outer edges of the rearward part of the engine, so it was vitally important that this space should be kept as free from pumps and other appendages as possible.

The solution provided represents a masterpiece of packaging. On the right side of the engine the water pump has gone altogether, while the redesigned scavenge pump has been moved well forward and it now has its separator mounted ahead of it, rather than behind, because the diameter of the separator is greater than that of the pump itself. On the left side of the engine the single redesigned water pump produces the same flow as the previous pair and is tucked well in with its inlet angled up high instead of being located low, in the path of the venturi. Behind it, the oil pressure pump now has a much smaller filter canister containing two tiny filters, and the high-pressure outlet from the filters is dog-legged upwards then back through 90 degrees, which leaves space behind for the air starter, which teams now like to mount inboard instead of hanging it on the back of the gearbox, as used to be the case.

The final clean-up operation on the flanks of the engine was to remove the mechanical fuel pump; as already mentioned, it was to be replaced, along with the original electrical fuel pump, by a combined pump mounted on top of the fuel tank and driven through a cable from a bevel drive off the back of the left-hand inlet camshaft, a modification which also had the virtue of saving a considerable amount of weight.

Matching performance with reliability

Prior to the arrival of the DFV engine on the Grand Prix scene the yardstick of performance was provided by the Repco engine which the Brabham team were using to such good effect, and as this was reputed to be giving 350 or 360bhp a target initial power output of 400bhp for the Ford engine seemed sensible. Consequently, the engine's valve and port sizes, the camshaft design and the shape and length of the intake trumpets were chosen with this in mind. Maximum power was achieved at a little over 9,000rpm, and a rev limit of 9,500rpm was established for the first season.

Only when a requirement for more power arrived, following evidence of Ferrari's growing competitiveness in 1970, was any serious development work applied to the DFV for this purpose. At this stage ports became larger and trumpets a little shorter, the peak power figure went up, but so did the revs, and of course the more the revs the more exacting became the task of ensuring that the engine would survive. It becomes something of a balancing act to provide on the one hand sufficient power and revs to achieve a potentially race-winning performance, and on the other the vitally important reliability to ensure that the performance could be maintained to the chequered flag. For Duckworth and his team at Northampton this has been a virtually non-stop programme, occasionally involving major changes of specification — such as the experiments with magnesium castings in 1977 — but more often than not being concerned with refinement in the manufacture and finishing of individual components in order to eliminate a potential local weakness or to enhance the efficiency of one system or another. Frequently, highly beneficial results were to be achieved by changes which might have seemed almost inconsequential, such are the complexities of racing engine design and development.

Inevitably, detail improvements to pistons and connecting rods were an important part of this work and one of the major landmarks in the development of the DFV was a machining change on the conrod caps around the bolt seat area, which took a lot of stress out at that point and resulted in a dramatic improvement in component life. Although a standard DFV conrod looks fairly conventional it is, in fact, something of a work of art, and what started out as being an ordinary forged steel item has become a vacuum remelted fat forging which is virtually the equivalent to having been machined from solid.

Another development coincident with the requirement for higher revs was an examination of big-end bolts and the introduction of modified thread forms, allowing the loads to be spread over more threads. 'I think a lot of people have been very surprised that we could run at the speeds we have with the size of bolts we have been fitting, especially when we are not using the strongest bolts that are available', says Duckworth. 'But the stronger the bolt the more brittle it tends to be, and it is my contention that it is very difficult to keep the geometry of your bolt — your mounting face and your thread squareness — sufficiently good to justify the use of materials which, though they have much higher strength, are very sensitive to out-of-squareness of the under-head. It comes down to the bolts themselves, because manufacturers seemingly are not able to make bolts truly square to the thread. I'm cynical enough to say that once you've proved you can make things decently in quite normal materials it might be worthwhile making them in better materials; unless you can keep your manufacturing standards very high the use of exotic materials in general brings more trouble than it's worth.'

As the DFV's power output and rev limit continued to rise so the need came to examine every component in order to relieve stress concentrations as far as possible and improve both life expectancy and operating efficiency. 'There are countless examples of very small changes having improved the life of things', recalls Duckworth. 'Even slight differences in the depth of hole drillings have stopped things breaking. I can remember a mistake we made, I think, on the second compound shaft when a tapped hole went too deep, so that the end happened to coincide with the shoulder on the shaft, and it just broke in no time flat. You've got to watch for this sort of thing, in fact you've got to watch just about everything.'

Human error is always a problem, and as the example of the 1970 crankshafts demonstrated so dramatically, a seemingly minor fault at the manufacturing stage can have disastrous consequences in such a highly stressed mechanism as a racing engine. 'Occasionally you will find people who, when drawings specify radii in undercuts, allow a sharp tool to go in and do a bit of damage, so it is dramatically easy to cause a failure through a minor manufacturing error. Constant quality control is not always easy to achieve, but it is vital nevertheless.

'There is another on-going problem, which is to do with the constantly increasing number of engines and components you're manufacturing. You find there is an increasing drag on the time of engineers in the place simply to sort out the problems which are due to making more of the same things. These people, capable of designing and building the things in the first place, can find themselves fully occupied instead in trying to ensure that manufacturing standards are being maintained in the production of more of the same components; the more you make, the more the chances of something not being 100 per cent up to standard.' This, perhaps, is one of the penalties of success, and Keith Duckworth can be forgiven if occasionally he looks with a trace of envy towards, say, Ferrari, with their need merely to service their own team's engine requirements.

So far, so good. The Ford DFV-powered Lotus 49s of Jim Clark and Graham Hill accelerate clear of the field at the start of the 1967 British Grand Prix at Silverstone, the first occasion on which the combination had performed in front of a home crowd. Following Clark's historic victory at Zandvoort six weeks earlier niggling troubles in Belgium and France had prevented a repeat performance, and back in England the Lotus mechanics had spent some sleepless nights rebuilding Hill's car following a practice accident caused by a suspension failure. So dominant were the team in the race, however, that Clark and Hill were able to play to the crowd by exchanging places up front until Hill was forced to the pits with further suspension trouble, leaving Clark out in front to win his fifth British Grand Prix in six years.

Nothing left to chance. Designer Keith Duckworth casts a careful eye over one of his first DFV engines nestling in the back of a Lotus 49. Although its neat packaging was the envy of rival teams, a considerable tidying-up of ancillary equipment and plumbing was to follow during the months ahead.

The 25th Grand Prix victory by a Ford DFV-powered car was also Jochen Rindt's first. It had been a long wait for the talented Austrian, but a rewarding one with first prize in the 1969 United States Grand Prix at Watkins Glen a record $50,000. Here, Rindt's Lotus 49B leads Jackie Stewart's Matra-Ford before it retired with a severe oil leak. Stewart was already 1969 World Champion, a title first won with DFV power the previous year by Graham Hill, who ended this race severely injured following a tyre deflation and a high-speed accident. Jochen Rindt's ambition to win the world title would be fulfilled in 1970, but alas, only posthumously.

Batting for a half-century! Jackie Stewart has just lapped Howden Ganley's Marlboro BRM P160C on his way to the DFV engine's 50th Grand Prix success. Driving his Elf Tyrrell 005, he led the 1972 Canadian Grand Prix for all but the first three laps on a misty Mosport Park circuit to finish well clear of the McLaren-Fords of Peter Revson and Denny Hulme.

Carlos Reutemann was at his formidable best for the 1974 Austrian Grand Prix on the Osterreichring, out-accelerating Niki Lauda's Ferrari 312B from the front row of the grid and leading from start to finish in his Brabham-Ford BT44. It was the 75th victory in a World Championship race for the DFV engine, and one of the most comfortable, with a winning margin of almost 43 seconds over Denny Hulme's similarly powered McLaren M23.

For 1977 Canadian tycoon Walter Wolf built a Grand Prix team around Jody Scheckter, who responded with a first-time victory in Argentina and, here at Monaco, recorded the Ford DFV engine's 100th success in a World Championship race. Cosworth Engineering had loaned some experimental magnesium-cast engines to certain teams, but Scheckter only needed a standard production DFV in his Wolf WR1 to score a narrow victory over Niki Lauda's Ferrari 312T.

Frank Williams parted from Walter Wolf in 1977 to reform his own team and begin the most spectacular comeback yet seen by a Formula 1 entrant. Alan Jones' victory in Canada in his Saudia Williams FW07, after a thrilling battle with Gilles Villeneuve's Ferrari 312T-4, was his fourth in five races during 1979 and marked the DFV's 125th Grand Prix success.

The start of the 1982 Austrian Grand Prix. Nelson Piquet's Brabham-BMW heads the field from pole position as teammate Riccardo Patrese is challenged by the Renaults of Alain Prost and Rene Arnoux to his left and Patrick Tambay's Ferrari from behind, while Keke Rosberg's Saudia Williams makes the best getaway amongst the Ford-powered cars. But what had looked to be a turbo benefit turned out very differently.... After Piquet and Arnoux had retired at the pits, Patrese had spun off and Prost had abandoned at the trackside, all as a result of engine problems, and Tambay had been delayed by a puncture, Elio De Angelis found himself out in front with his JPS Lotus 91. He resisted Rosberg's last-lap challenge to claim the first Lotus victory for four years and the 150th for the Ford DFV engine.

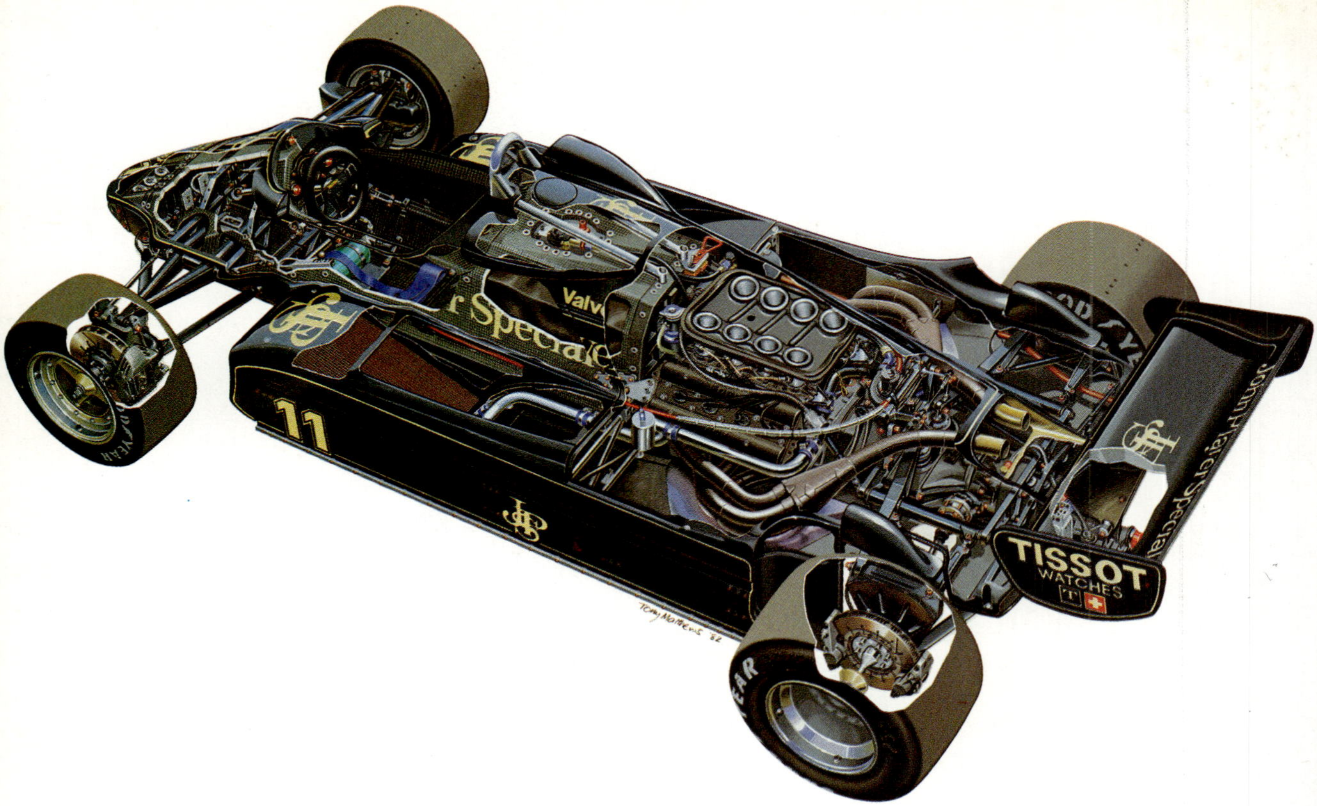

Variations on a Ford Cosworth single-seater theme. The upper cutaway drawing illustrates both the inherent complexity and the compact packaging of components in a Formula 1 car at the height of the ground-effects era. This is the JPS Lotus 91 which in Elio De Angelis' hands was to score the milestone 150th DFV Grand Prix victory. The lower drawing of the DFX-powered Penske PC10 which Rick Mears drove to the 1982 Indy Car Championship provides a reminder of the extent to which Formula 1-developed chassis technology has been applied to this type of racing.

Familiar scene. Like everyone else in the Indianapolis 500, Rick Mears and the Penske team had to pose for the official photograph before the race. Mears had qualified for pole position at 207.004mph, but he was to be beaten to the finish line by Gordon Johncock's DFX-powered Wildcat by the proverbial gnat's whisker.

One of the team's Cosworth DFX engines receiving some careful attention in the clinically spotless Penske workshop. The ultra professionalism of this team is aspired to by many of its rivals, but only rarely achieved.

The French Rondeau team used a mixture of Ford DFL and DFV engines for their five M382s at Le Mans in 1982. The car above, shared by Gordon Spice, Francois Migault and Xavier Lapeyre, retired with electrical failure after running third, but had won the Monza 1,000-kilometres race earlier in the year. The Ford C100, right, was driven to victory at Hockenheim by Klaus Ludwig, one of two 1982 German Championship successes for the Zakspeed-prepared car. The endurance racing season ended at Brands Hatch in a downpour with the C100s of Marc Surer and Manfred Winkelhock at the head of the field until they collided with each other.

CHAPTER 3

The milestone years

1967-1972: Wings over wheels

One of the few common denominators shared by the 1967 Dutch Grand Prix at Zandvoort and the 1982 Austrian Grand Prix at Zeltweg was that in each race the winning car was powered by a Ford DFV engine. During that interval of more than 15 years the Grand Prix scene had undergone a complete transformation, one which would not have been possible had there not been available, for all who chose to use it, a compact and competitive power unit, around which so many Formula 1 cars could been constructed and so many racing teams developed.

Even the DFV engine, for all its outward appearance of fundamental similarity, had undergone change in almost every detail during the intervening years, and whereas those first examples supplied to Lotus in 1967 could manage only a little more than 400bhp and were confined to a rev limit of 9,000rpm, the 1982 version was producing at least 100bhp more and could be revved to over 11,000rpm. The price had gone up rather more steeply, from an initial £7,500 when the engine was first put on general sale in 1968, to almost £27,000, which, after taking into account the effect of inflation and the more sophisticated specification, was still considered to be something of a bargain, particularly in view of the engine's impressive record of reliability.

The remarkable thing was that an engine which when it was conceived was expected to have a potential competitive life of perhaps three years should still be winning races after 15. Several times in its career its days were thought to have been numbered as, one after another, rival engines would appear, only to fail to live up to their promise or expectations, and it needed nothing less fundamental than the emergence of turbocharged 1½-litre engines, with the excessive power increases which this form of induction makes possible, to dislodge the DFV from its position of pre-eminence amongst Grand Prix power units. By that time it had served the sport not for its anticipated three seasons, but for five times as long, and had provided that essential element of stability on the technological front which had enabled so many other changes to take place over the same period. Indeed, to look back over the milestone victories as the tally of World Championship Grand Prix successes by DFV-powered cars rose to a remarkable 150 at an average rate of 10 per season is to recall the period of the most dramatic changes in the entire history

Settling down for some history-making. Jim Clark defending third place in the 1967 Dutch Grand Prix from Denny Hulme's Brabham-Repco a few minutes after the start. Graham Hill was leading at that point in the other Lotus 49, but he was soon to drop out, whereupon Clark immediately speeded up, took the lead from Jack Brabham a few laps later and went on to a score a clear-cut victory on the debut of the DFV.

of international motor racing.

For example, the nearest thing to a sponsor's decal visible on the Formula 1 cars which were assembled at Zandvoort for the 1967 Dutch Grand Prix was a team badge, usually worn on the nose of the car. The Lotus 49s, like the majority of cars present, were painted in the national colour of their team, the British green in this instance being relieved by a yellow band from nose to cockpit. The name 'Team Lotus' was carried along the sides of the body and the word 'Ford' was cast into the cam carriers of the DFV engine. In those days, the bodywork either ended at the rear cockpit bulkhead, as in the case of the Lotus, or else it flanked only the lower portion of the engine bay, thereby leaving the entire top end of the power unit exposed.

With the Lotus-Ford about to make its dramatic race debut, the new 3-litre Formula 1 was well into its second season, and already Jack Brabham's decision to aim for light weight and mechanical simplicity had paid him a handsome dividend. Not only had he won the 1966 World Championship in his Brabham-Repco V8, having been victorious in four of the nine qualifying races, but his team driver Denny Hulme had now won the second Grand Prix of the 1967 season, at Monaco, and was destined to become the next World Champion.

The very first race under the new rules — the 1966 Monaco Grand Prix — had been won by Jackie Stewart in a 2-litre V8 BRM, but the new 3-litre V12 Ferrari driven there by John Surtees had posed a considerable threat, and when Surtees took a comfortable victory in the Belgian Grand Prix three weeks later it looked as though the Italian team might prove to be as dominant during the first year of the new formula as they had in the first season under the $1\frac{1}{2}$-litre rules. But just a few days after his Belgian success, Surtees had had a major disagreement with Ferrari and had left the team; later he was to return to Grand Prix racing at the wheel of a Cooper-Maserati, with which he would win the final race of the year in Mexico. Although Ludovico Scarfiotti was to score a popular home victory that year at Monza, Ferrari never appeared as threatening after Surtees' departure, and now they had suffered a major tragedy with the death of Lorenzo Bandini following a fiery accident during the 1967 Monaco Grand Prix.

After Stewart's initial success, BRM had had little to celebrate, and as had been feared their H16-engined cars had proved to be excessively unreliable when pressed hard; it had been left to Jim Clark to record the only success for BRM's complicated engine, nestling in the back of his Lotus 43 at Watkins Glen for the 1966 United States Grand Prix.

Dan Gurney had demonstrated the considerable potential of his Eagle chassis when fitted with a four-cylinder Coventry Climax 2.7-litre engine, but the replacement 3-litre V12 Weslake engine, which had made its debut towards the end of 1966, had so far proved worryingly unreliable (although it was destined soon to win its one and only Grand Prix, in Belgium), a lack of interchangeability of certain components between the team's small number of power units being an added complication.

Surtees' success in Mexico apart, the Cooper team had found the weight penalty of their Maserati V12 engines to be a formidable burden during 1966, and although a programme of lightening was underway, the prospects for this formerly so dominant racing team did not look bright under the new formula, despite Pedro Rodriguez's rather fortunate victory in South Africa at the turn of the year. Surtees, meanwhile, had been merely biding his time with a Cooper, pending Honda's return to the Grand Prix scene, and although both Richie Ginther and Ronnie Bucknum had driven the Japanese cars towards the end of 1966, Surtees had been nominated as the new team leader for the 1967 season. There was little doubt that the V12 engine was delivering a lot of power, although the car's performance was handicapped considerably by its excessive weight, a problem which in due course was to be partly resolved by a Lola-designed chassis; this would appear just in time to give Surtees the

Returning to the pit area after his victory lap, Clark appears to have been indulging in a spot of grass-cutting along the way. The 90-lap race had ended just in time; a post-race examination of his engine revealed that a tooth had snapped off one of his timing gears — the fault which had sidelined Hill.

narrowest of victories at Monza the following September.

The change of formula had given Bruce McLaren the encouragement to follow Jack Brabham's lead and create his own Grand Prix team, but the lack of a suitable power unit had hampered him considerably. His initial ploy had been to use a specially developed short-stroke 3-litre version of the 4.2-litre Ford V8 engine used at Indianapolis and elsewhere on the USAC scene, but the conversion was less than a success, while the alternative solution of a 3-litre V8 Serenissima engine from Italy was soon to prove equally troublesome. McLaren was now obliged to run a converted Formula 2 chassis equipped with a 2-litre BRM V8 engine, pending delivery of one of BRM's

Potentially one of the biggest threats to the DFV engine under the 3-litre Formula 1 rules seemed to be coming from the V12 Weslake power unit which Dan Gurney had chosen for his Eagles. But the Californian's only Grand Prix success in his own car was to be here at Spa-Francorchamps in the 1967 Belgian Grand Prix.

Jim Clark at speed in pursuit of Gurney. He had won four of the previous five Belgian Grands Prix, but this time a long pit stop to replace a broken spark plug had dropped him far behind and he was to do well to finish sixth.

forthcoming 3-litre V12s, although the New Zealander was destined to drive an Eagle for Dan Gurney for three Grands Prix before he could give his McLaren-BRM its debut in 3-litre form.

It was into this somewhat confused technological scene, therefore, that the Ford DFV engine was to make its public debut in the back of the Lotus 49s of Jim Clark and Graham Hill. There was no lack of variety amongst the opposition, and ample evidence of considerable sums of money having been spent in various directions. Nevertheless, the measure of Jack Brabham's achievement so far with relatively underpowered engines augured well for the longer-term prospects for the Lotus-Ford combination. However, as the team set out from England, only the most rashly optimistic of its members were contemplating much more than a good practice performance at Zandvoort. To finish in the points first time out.... well, that really would be asking rather a lot.

1967 Dutch Grand Prix

It had been left to Graham Hill to carry out all the serious initial testing of the Lotus 49 in England because of Jim Clark's temporary overseas residency in order to minimize his tax liability, and even for Hill the test schedule had been complicated because of his involvement in the Indianapolis 500 race and the qualification runs which had preceded it during the month of May.

But at least he was able to start practice at Zandvoort knowing that his car fitted him and that it was in a reasonable state of balance, whereas Jim Clark was meeting his car, which had only been completed a couple of days earlier, for the very first time. Initially came the task of tailoring the controls to the driver, then Clark had to familiarize himself with the DFV's characteristic of a sudden power surge as the revs rose beyond 6,500rpm — a feature which called for great care in gearing the car to a circuit (both cars needed gearbox changes during the first day of practice).

To finish the day in sixth and seventh places in the combined list of practice times was a reasonable beginning, especially as Clark was within half a second of Hulme's fastest time of 1 minute 26.8 seconds with his Brabham-Repco, but the Lotus had yet to reveal its potential. On the second day Hill lowered his time to 1 minute 25.6 seconds and then, in the final session, he shaved a further second from this time to claim pole position on the grid, half a second clear of the next fastest car, Gurney's Eagle-Weslake. Clark, meanwhile, had been seriously delayed by a suspension problem, eventually traced to a faulty ball-joint, and his best time of 1 minute 26.8 seconds was only good enough for a place on the outside of the third row.

Although traction was not a strong card of the Lotus 49 during the early period of its development, Hill made an excellent start and led the field into the first corner, then increased his advantage over Brabham to more than a second by the end of the lap. Clark was in sixth position at this stage and about to mount a strong challenge against Chris Amon's Ferrari, although it was to take him three more laps to find a way past. The sudden slowing of Gurney's Eagle on the seventh lap elevated Clark to fourth place, and at the end of 10 laps the Lotus team looked to be in a strong position with Hill holding Brabham at bay by more than a second and Clark inching his way towards Jochen Rindt's third-placed Cooper-Maserati.

But the next time round Brabham was leading the field and after a long wait Hill appeared pushing his car back towards his pit and into retirement with a broken engine; a timing gear had failed. A similar problem had been encountered during earlier tests, so there was understandable anxiety about the health of Clark's engine. The only consolation was that it had covered a significantly lower mileage than Hill's, which had been used for a considerable amount of test driving. Seeing that Hill's race was run, Clark immediately applied the pressure, passing Rindt's Cooper on lap 15 and pulling out from Brabham's slipstream to take the lead just before the end of the 16th lap.

Once ahead he worked hard to break clear of Brabham, but the Australian proved hard to dislodge from his wake and it was not until lap 32 of the 90-lap contest that more than five seconds separated the two cars. After that it was a long and agonizing waiting game for everyone in the Lotus pit and for the considerable contingent of Ford and Cosworth personnel, including Walter Hayes, Harley Copp and, of course, Keith Duckworth himself, who were standing close by and doing their best to disguise the tension they felt.

By half-distance Clark had extended his lead to 12 seconds and by lap 60 it was up to 18 seconds. Another 10 laps and the gap had grown to 27 seconds and as they completed the 80th lap there were a comfortable 31 seconds separating the two cars. The remaining 10 laps seemed to take an eternity to the ever-growing crowd of people who had eased themselves into the vicinity of the Lotus pit, intent on associating themselves as closely as possible with what looked to be a piece of motor racing history in the making.

There was a heart-stopping moment as Clark began his 84th lap and his engine note faltered momentarily as he passed the pits. Surely nothing would rob him of victory at this late stage of the race? Or would it? Keen eyes and ears followed the car's progress past the back of the paddock and up the hill leading out of the banked Hunzerug corner. The exhaust note was crisp again and on the next lap Clark went through on schedule. He had merely eased off on the previous lap, content at this stage to cruise at a second or two per lap below his previous pace having seen off all opposition in the most convincing style.

After almost two-and-a-quarter hours of racing the chequered flag was unfurled and Clark passed by with an arm raised in acknowledgement of the tremendous cheers from the grandstands and the frantic arm waving from much of the pit road; it was 23.6 seconds before Brabham was to complete his race in second place. After the initial euphoria, the atmosphere amongst the Lotus, Ford and Cosworth personnel settled down to one of delight intermingled with intense relief. One engine, which had been subjected to a lot of work beforehand, had wilted under the strain, but the other had behaved itself throughout a long race — although the post-race strip-down would reveal that it, too, had lost a tooth from one of its timing gears and would not have run much further. The Lotus 49 had proven itself as a car with great potential, even though at this early stage in its career there were elements of its performance which could — and no doubt would — be improved. Perhaps most important of all, the faith of people like Walter Hayes, who had been prepared to put his reputation — and possibly his career — on the line in order to extend the boundaries of Keith Duckworth's talents and experience, had been examined in a blaze of publicity and found to be entirely justified. He and Harley Copp had flown back to England in the Ford executive jet — having toasted each other with a couple of cans of beer along the way — long before the jubilation had subsided that evening in the Zandvoort paddock.

Following Jim Clark's tragic death at Hockenheim in 1968 Graham Hill did his best to restore Lotus team morale by scoring a fine victory in the Spanish Grand Prix at Jarama a week later. He then followed up with his fourth of five wins here at Monaco, where his Lotus 49B raced with nose fins and a wedge-shaped engine cover.

The Zandvoort circuit on which Jim Clark scored the engine's first success was also the place where Jackie Stewart was to record his own first victory with the DFV, one year later. Held in soaking conditions, the 1968 Dutch Grand Prix became a Matra benefit, with Stewart comfortably beating Jean-Pierre Beltoise in the V12-engined works car.

Although the Lotus-Ford combination was to win only one of the next three Grands Prix, there was little doubt that the original plan, which was to service the engine needs of just one team, would have to be revised if Grand Prix racing was not to be put into jeopardy.

Other team owners, struggling with power units which clearly were about to be outclassed, could foresee a bleak future for their own operations unless they, too, could obtain a supply of the Ford engines and design new chassis to carry them. The Lotus 49 had only been prevented from winning the next two races, in Belgium and France, by petty problems and then it had won comfortably at Silverstone, despite handling problems which, when overcome, would make the car even more difficult to challenge.

Walter Hayes recalls that it was at the German Grand Prix that he decided to raise the delicate subject with Colin Chapman. 'I said to Colin, "You know, if we don't make this engine available to everyone else we'll kill the whole thing because there's no reason why anyone else will ever win". I've always said that I think it was a sign of extraordinary maturity by Chapman that he didn't even argue about it. He said something like, "Oh well, what a pity", and we agreed. It was as simple as that.'

By the time of the United States Grand Prix that year the Lotus team were so dominant that Hayes, anxious that nothing should occur to prevent an overwhelming victory on Ford's corporate doorstep, was able to insist that Clark and Hill should not race each other in anger, but that instead they should toss a coin on the eve of the race to decide their finishing order (there was never any doubt in his mind that they would be first and second!). He was right, but there were a few heart-stopping moments before the two Lotuses finished the race a lap ahead of the field. Hill had won the toss, but a gear-selection problem in the middle of the race had delayed him, leaving Clark well out in front until four laps from the end, when suddenly his right rear wheel sagged inwards following the failure of a retaining bolt in the suspension. He reduced speed and found the car to be still controllable — just — so he eased his way through the final laps to take the flag just six seconds ahead of Hill.

That two cars could finish a Grand Prix more than a lap ahead of any other survivor, after each had suffered a mechanical mishap along the way which had greatly reduced their speed for several laps, was the clearest possible evidence of their overwhelming superiority, and testimony to the good sense of that decision, taken two months earlier at the Nurburgring, to make the Ford engine available to other teams in 1968. This step, which was to have such a profound effect on the wellbeing of Grand Prix racing, also marked a turning point for Cosworth Engineering, for the manufacture and subsequent overhaul, rebuilding and testing of DFV engines on a regular basis was to commit the company to a major expansion of its facilities and rescourses and assure it of a lucrative new market.

The DFV was to end its first season with only four Grand Prix victories to its credit out of nine attempts, but from then until Jochen Rindt scored his own first and the DFV's 25th win at Watkins Glen, in 1969, on the second anniversary of that famous Clark-Hill one-two, only one World Championship race would fail to be won by a car powered by one of Duckworth's engines. The DFV common denominator by that time had become firmly established, yet it was a very different Grand Prix world in which Rindt was to score his first Formula 1 victory from that in which the DFV had made its debut.

The death of Jim Clark in a Formula 2 race at Hockenheim in 1968 had stunned the motor racing world into disbelief, for he had seemed so impregnable, but the sport was to lose three more drivers during the course of the next few weeks of that black season. Mike Spence died while testing a Lotus turbine car at Indianapolis, just when BRM were beginning to reap the benefit of his talent in their Formula 1 team, then Ludovico Scarfiotti, who had joined the Cooper team, lost his life while driving a Porsche in a hill-climb at Rossfeld, and finally Jo Schlesser was called upon to drive an experimental Honda with an air-cooled V8 engine in the French Grand Prix at Rouen and was killed when it crashed and was burnt out.

Clark's last Grand Prix victory, in South Africa, had also marked the last appearance of the Lotus Formula 1 team in their traditional green-and-yellow colour scheme. When the Lotus 49 appeared shortly afterwards in Australia and New Zealand for the Tasman Championship races, fitted with a short-stroke $2\frac{1}{2}$-litre version of the DFV engine designated the DFW (all such engines later reverted to 3-litre DFV specification), it carried the red-white-and-gold colours of the Gold Leaf cigarette brand in deference to John Player, the team's newly signed sponsor.

This marked the beginning of the era of commercial sponsorship of Formula 1 racing teams and the start of a trend, soon to be accelerated by the

A confusing collection of high-mounted wings forming almost an umbrella over the Brands Hatch starting grid dates this as the 1969 Race of Champions. Stewart had made the best getaway in his Matra, with Hill's Lotus on his right and Rindt's right behind him. To Stewart's left is Siffert in Rob Walker's Lotus, with Brabham behind him and Jackie Oliver and his BRM on the far left of the circuit. Wing breakages were soon to involve Hill and Rindt in frightening accidents in Spain.

relaxation of rules governing the display of advertising decals on racing cars, which would lead ultimately to the use of car bodywork as mobile billboards for the promotion not just of the products and services used on the car in question, but of anything from tobacco to perfumery, dairy products, airlines or anything which a sponsor might choose to expose through the medium of motor racing.

But it was not just the colour schemes of cars which changed so dramatically during this two-year interval; this was the period when Formula 1 cars sprouted wings. At first they were little more than tabs on the sides of the nose cone and an extended engine cover to give cars a wedge-shaped profile — an aerodynamic development which Lotus had already chosen to exploit for their Indianapolis cars. But this was merely an interim stage before teams explored largely uncharted territory with rear-mounted wings suspended high over the engine bay and attached at first to the structure of the car and later to the rear suspension. With frightening speed these aerodynamic devices grew both in size and number and before the end of 1968 cars were appearing with high-mounted wings over the front as well as the rear wheels.

There had already been warning signs, such as when Jackie Oliver's Lotus 49 had suddenly swerved out of control in practice at Rouen when it was caught by the turbulence behind a high-winged car immediately ahead of it. Then John Surtees' Honda lost its wing at Brands Hatch, where it flew into the path of Bruce McLaren's car, running close behind it. But the most dramatic evidence of the potential danger of these devices was reserved for the 1969 Spanish Grand Prix at Barcelona, where the two Lotuses of Graham Hill and Jochen Rindt, carrying larger rear wings than ever before, suffered virtually identical accidents following the collapse of their wings at the same point on the circuit. Hill's car remained upright and he was able to clamber out unscathed just in time to help in the rescue of Rindt, who was trapped beneath his totally wrecked car; the Austrian was most fortunate to escape with relatively minor injuries.

An emergency meeting at Monaco — the next race on the calendar — led to

The size and mounting of wings was strictly controlled following the accidents in Spain, but for the 1969 Italian Grand Prix at Monza both Stewart and Rindt decided to race without them, and to very good effect, Stewart just pipping Rindt to the line in a four-car photo-finish. Here they lead the field on the opening lap with Bruce McLaren tucked in behind Stewart.

a ban on all but the most modest of aerodynamic aids after the first day's practice, and these had to be mounted to the structure of the car, not on the suspension. In the months ahead there were many interpretations of the new rule, but by the end of the year most cars were running with rear wings with end plates just inboard of the inner edges of the rear tyres, balanced by substantially dimensioned front wings protruding from the nose cone.

No sooner had the wing situation been brought under control than Formula 1's inventive designers were off on a new path — the creation of a series of four-wheel-drive cars, in the belief that they would be able to transmit the abundant power of the DFV engine more efficiently than a conventional two-wheel-drive chassis. Lotus, McLaren and Matra all produced experimental cars with the engine mounted back-to-front and driving through a centrally mounted gearbox and differential, but a combination of excessive weight, mechanical complication and handling difficulties associated with the torque split offset any theoretical advantages of being able to transmit the drive through all four wheels. Had it not been for the advent of wings and their contribution to better traction and cornering power the four-wheel-drive cars might have had a chance, but their development also coincided with a considerable advance in tyre technology, which further reduced the attraction of four driven wheels. Of the cars which raced, the Lotus 63 exploited the concept most fully with the use of small wheels and a wide variety of torque splits (though it won few friends amongst its drivers) while the Matra was the most reliable, finishing all its races (though never threatening to lead). The McLaren was raced only once, while an experimental wide-bodied car designed by Robin Herd for Cosworth was destined never to enter a race, though it served a useful function for a time as a mobile test bed for the DFV engine and its ancillary equipment and services.

Meanwhile, the engine had been quick to find new customers, amongst them Ken Tyrrell, who had been one of the witnesses of its debut that day at Zandvoort; the DFV was to provide him with his passport into Formula 1. Once he had been assured of a supply of engines he was able to call on Matra,

Lotus, Matra and McLaren all produced and raced four-wheel-drive Formula 1 cars in 1969, but with limited success, improvements in tyre technology and the advent of wings combining to overcome the traction problem more effectively than an extra pair of driven wheels. This is the Lotus 63, with its DFV engine reversed and driving through a central differential.

for whom he was operating a works Formula 2 team, and ask them to build him a chassis which would accept the DFV, for Jackie Stewart to drive. As Matra were already designing a car for a works Formula 1 team, which would be using their own V12 engine, it seemed a convenient arrangement to have a separate string to their bow in the form of a Tyrrell-operated Matra International team for which, with Stewart available to lead it, Tyrrell was able to attract sponsorship support from the French petroleum company Elf. Stewart responded to this act of faith by leading works driver Beltoise to a Matra one-two victory in Holland, then added two more victories in his Ford-powered car later in the year to emerge as runner-up to Graham Hill in the 1968 World Championship. A further six victories in the Matra-Ford were to follow in 1969, enabling Stewart to clinch the first of his three world titles at Monza that year.

Bruce McLaren's had been the second of the new DFV-powered teams to appear in 1968 and he had enjoyed a fortunate victory in Belgium to which his new team partner Denny Hulme had added two more successes later in the season and a third in 1969, the year in which the Brabham team also turned to the DFV, thereby enabling Jacky Ickx to claim two Grand Prix victories. Jack Brabham had persevered long and hard with his Repco engines, but the four-camshaft type 860 version, with which he had hoped to reduce his power deficiency compared with the DFV, had proved to be frustratingly unreliable in 1968 and a pair of third places for Jochen Rindt, who had joined the team after three seasons with Cooper, and one fifth for Brabham himself were a poor reward for all their efforts that year.

During the first two years of the Ford engine's Formula 1 career there had been little evidence of any strengthening of opposition from the users of rival power units, although Ferrari's V12, having been given four valves per cylinder, was claimed to be producing 410bhp at 10,500rpm in 1968, when Jacky Ickx scored a lone win at Rouen. This figure was raised to 435bhp the following year with the aid of revised camshafts and reversed ports — the outside exhausts now linked to three-into-one tail pipes — but without any further success for the Italian team.

BRM, meanwhile, had been claiming 400bhp at 10,000rpm for their V12 engine, rising to 450bhp at 10,750rpm in 1969, or some 20bhp more than the DFV was producing by then, but there was little evidence of any power advantage on the track, and both BRM and Cooper, who had switched from Maserati to BRM engines in 1968, were to fare rather less well the following season when, theoretically, they had more power at their disposal. Matra were another team unable to match the performance of the Ford-powered teams, and they withdrew their works cars temporarily after a frustrating 1968 season, while Honda never really recovered from their disastrous French Grand Prix and were also absent from the Grand Prix scene in 1969.

1969 United States Grand Prix

It was a predominantly DFV-powered grid which was assembled at Watkins Glen, therefore, for what almost certainly would mark the 25th World Championship race victory for one of Keith Duckworth's engines. The only opposition to the Ford-powered Lotuses, McLarens, Matras and Brabhams were the lone Ferrari of Rodriguez and a trio of BRMs, and as neither team had won a Grand Prix, or even been the runner-up, for well over a year the chances of an upset appeared to be extremely remote. The discussion before the race, consequently, was not so much about whether a DFV-powered car and driver would win the race as about which of the 14 setting out from the pits would be the victor.

Jochen Rindt, now driving for Lotus, had qualified his 49B for pole position — the seventh time he had started a World Championship race from this coveted place and the fifth occasion since he had joined the Lotus team at the beginning of the year. But this unluckiest of drivers had yet to win a Grand Prix in his five years as a works driver, first with Cooper, then with Brabham and now with Lotus. Only Chris Amon — temporarily retired from the scene — had had a less fortunate record.

Rindt's prospects were considerably improved in the minutes before the start, however, first when Bruce McLaren's engine blew up on the warming-up lap, then when Denny Hulme's McLaren, second-fastest in practice, developed a gear-selection problem on the grid, and finally when an obstruction on the track delayed the start several minutes, during which interval the engines of several other cars overheated.

When the race was finally flagged away Rindt swept into the lead from Stewart, driving his Matra, and Hill, in the second works Lotus, which Graham soon found to be handling unsatisfactorily, causing him to slip down the field. Stewart, meanwhile, maintained the pressure on Rindt — his close friend and neighbour in Switzerland — and on the 12th lap he put his Matra into the lead. Nine laps later, however, Rindt's Lotus was back in front again and his grip on the race was tightened considerably when smoke started to pour from the back of Stewart's car; at the end of 35 laps the Matra was driven into the pit road and out of the race with its engine bathed in oil.

For the remainder of the 108-lap race all Rindt had to do was to pace himself and his car carefully while far behind him an all-Brabham contest between Piers Courage, Jacky Ickx and Jack Brabham himself was fought for second, third and fourth places. Rindt's car was behaving itself impeccably, and despite easing off towards the end of the race the Austrian was able to finish more than three-quarters of a minute ahead of Courage, the runner-up, while John Surtees was able to benefit from Ickx's retirement with engine failure and Brabham's pit stop for a top-up of fuel to bring his BRM into third place — the team's best performance for a year.

However, there was a shadow over the jubilation in the Lotus team as Rindt walked on to the winner's rostrum to collect the $50,000 first prize, which had made this the richest Formula 1 race so far in Grand Prix history. By the time the garland was being placed around his neck Graham Hill was being rushed to hospital for emergency treatment to two badly broken legs, injuries which would bring his career as a works Lotus driver to an end, although he was destined to claim a World Championship point in Rob Walker's Lotus in South Africa three months later at the end of an emotional comeback drive when he was still very weak and in considerable pain.

Hill's accident at Watkins Glen had been precipitated by dropped oil, which had caused him to slide off the track at The Loop on the 89th lap. His car stalled and was reluctant to restart, so Hill climbed out, checked for possible damage, got back in again and eventually managed to fire up the engine and drive back on to the track. However, his car began to handle very peculiarly and, suspecting a deflating rear tyre, he signalled to his pit at the end of his 90th lap that he would be coming in next time round for a wheel change; the stop would also give him the opportunity to have his safety harness refastened. However, his car only travelled as far as the end of the straight. As he braked for The Loop it suddenly flicked out of control, charged into the bank on the outside of the course and rolled several times, Hill being thrown out in the process. It had been a day of very mixed fortunes for the Lotus team.

Almost three years were to pass before Jackie Stewart was able to score the DFV engine's 50th Grand Prix success in a fog-delayed race on the Mosport circuit in Canada — evidence that Keith Duckworth's engine had finally encountered some strong opposition from the 12-cylinder power units. But by 1972 the DFV was well on top again and it would contribute to all but two of that season's 12 World Championship race victories.

Once again the intervening period had been marked by significant changes, not all of them happy ones. The Formula 1 world had lost several more fine drivers, though they had not all been killed in a Grand Prix car — this was still the age when Formula 1 drivers could be seen regularly in other classes of motor racing.

The year 1970 had been a particularly black one, and the death of Bruce McLaren while testing one of his CanAm sports-racing cars at Goodwood had

At the end of 1969 a consortium was formed for the manufacture of a complete range of single-seater racing cars under the March name and Ford did both the company and Jackie Stewart a good turn by purchasing two Formula 1 chassis for Ken Tyrrell to use in place of his Matras, which the French company would no longer allow to be raced with other than their own engine. Above, Stewart is overtaking Brabham on his way to winning the 1970 Race of Champions in his new car, in which he was also shortly to win the Spanish Grand Prix. Below, the March works team leader Chris Amon is holding second place in the Monaco Grand Prix before retiring with his rear suspension adrift.

An epic duel between Jochen Rindt in his very fast but difficult to balance Lotus 72 and Jack Brabham in his more conventional Brabham BT33 was the highlight of the 1970 British Grand Prix at Brands Hatch. Brabham seemed to have the battle won after a see-saw battle, only to run out of fuel on the last lap. It was the second time that year that he had lost a Grand Prix to Rindt in the closing seconds; at Monaco he had crashed at the final corner after locking up his brakes.

Denny Hulme in the middle of a frustrating 1971 season with his McLaren M19. He was to retire from the British Grand Prix with engine trouble and would score points in only four races that year.

Pedro Rodriguez in his BRM hotly pursued by Ronnie Peterson, destined to finish second in his March, Denny Hulme, who would be fourth in his McLaren, and Jean-Pierre Beltoise, whose Matra-Simca would drop out of the 1971 Monaco Grand Prix with transmission trouble.

Jackie Stewart emerges from the Monte Carlo tunnel on his way to victory in the same race with his Tyrrell 003, which is using one of several variations of nose-cone tried that season.

Mike Hailwood had several near-successes at the wheel of his works Surtees TS9B and here he is about to take the lead from Emerson Fittipaldi's JPS Lotus 72 in the 1972 International Trophy race at Silverstone, only to retire later in the race.

robbed the sport not only of one of its most charming personalities but also one of its most technically accomplished and influential people. His loss was followed soon afterwards by the death of Piers Courage in a fiery accident at Zandvoort while racing the de Tomaso which Frank Williams was running for the Italian manufacturer; Courage had emerged as one of the finest of the new generation of Grand Prix drivers. Further tragedy later in the year was to mean that the sport would inherit its first posthumous World Champion because, although it was not known at the time, Jochen Rindt had already scored sufficient points to claim the title before his Lotus 72 went out of control during practice for the Italian Grand Prix at Monza and he suffered fatal injuries in the ensuing accident.

The 1971 season had been equally sad; Jo Siffert, one of the fastest Formula 1 drivers of all, died at the wheel of his BRM during a non-championship race at Brands Hatch, while both Pedro Rodriguez — perhaps the most versatile driver of his day — and Ignazio Giunti — seemingly destined for a rewarding career in Formula 1 — lost their lives in accidents during long-distance sports car races. Then, in 1972, Jo Bonnier was killed at Le Mans to rob motor racing of one of its most influential drivers in his role of President of the Grand Prix Drivers Association, a post which Jackie Stewart was destined to occupy with such vigour in the years ahead.

One of the GPDA's major platforms had been the quest for greater concern for the safety aspects of motor racing, and some progress had already been made on that front, although considerable opposition had been generated amongst circuit owners and race organizers, who claimed that too much was being demanded too quickly of circuits which could not be changed overnight. However, there had been some important moves to reduce the fire hazard, notably by the insistence of rubber bag fuel tanks and an increase in the minimum weight limit from 500 to 530 kilograms to accommodate additional safety equipment on Formula 1 cars. There was also a programme of research into fire-fighting techniques and intensive training facilities for marshals, with Britain as usual setting the pace in this area. By 1972 the weight limit had been raised again to 550 kilograms and a higher specification had been demanded for the fuel bags, which were to be limited in capacity and protected by deformable structures.

There had also been some notable changes in the formation of a typical Grand Prix starting grid with the arrival of several new teams and faces and the departure of others. The most surprising development at the end of 1969 had been the announcement of the creation of a consortium to manufacture Formula 1 cars under the name March. This was followed quickly by the news that Ken Tyrrell would be their first customer, following the decision by Matra not to allow their cars to be run in future with other than their own V12 engine, with which their works team would be making a comeback in 1970 under the Matra-Simca banner. Tyrrell did much to put the March name in the headlines during their first season, usually out-performing the works team and Stewart winning the Spanish Grand Prix in only his second appearance with the new car. But to race a 'customer' car could only be a short-term expedient for the Tyrrell-Stewart combination, and before the end of the year the first Tyrrell-Ford Formula 1 car had appeared; in 1971 its successor would take Stewart to his second world title and give Tyrrell his first Constructor's Cup after Stewart's six victories and a seventh by Francois Cevert in just 11 Grands Prix.

John Surtees had also returned to the Formula 1 scene with his own team, although sadly neither he nor his cars were destined to win a World Championship Grand Prix, despite coming very close on a few occasions. The widespread availability of the DFV engine also encouraged the creation of a number of relatively low-budget Formula 1 cars, including the Tecno, Eifelland, Bellasi and Connew, none of which would make any notable impact on the Grand Prix scene.

The increased opposition to the DFV engine had come from anticipated directions. Ferrari had replaced their V12 with a new flat-12 engine for the 1970 season, which offered improved airflow on to the rear wing, and although this engine had proved troublesome at first, the policy of developing several versions with different cylinder dimensions and valve sizes and angles had been rewarded before the end of the year with four victories from the last five races, three of them by Jacky Ickx and one by Clay Regazzoni. That they had been unable to repeat this performance in 1971 was due more to chassis shortcomings, and especially to problems with tyre vibrations, rather than to any engine weakness, and by the time they had mastered this difficulty the DFV-powered teams had reaped the benefit of more power (though at 450bhp they were still some 40bhp short of that claimed by Ferrari).

BRM were another team to suffer from the tyre problem, which rather undermined the effectiveness of their 48-valve V12 engine, the revised cylinder heads of which had resulted in an improvement in mid-range torque. These cars had been seen at their best on the faster circuits, witness their successes at Spa in 1970 and Zeltweg and Monza in 1971, although Jean-Pierre Beltoise had also driven an inspired race on a rain-soaked Monaco circuit to score a victory there against all the odds in 1972.

Matra's return with V12 engines, reputed to be giving up to 480bhp, had been something of a disappointment for the French team, for although their reliability had been much improved and had frequently enabled them to collect World Championship points for minor placings, they had rarely posed a serious threat, even though Chris Amon had been able to put his car on pole position at Monza in 1971 and at Clermont-Ferrand the following year. Nevertheless, the Matra team could claim considerable credit for exploring new aerodynamic solutions and their wide-bodied car seen towards the end of 1971 had been studied with great interest by rival teams.

Tecno took the bold step during this period of producing a flat-12 engine, but with little reward, while Alfa Romeo's V8 was investigated first by McLaren, who encountered considerable installation problems with it due to its deeper than normal sump, then by March, who persevered with it at greater length before they, too, decided that it was not as efficient as a DFV.

After a period of relative stability in 1970, with cars little changed in profile from the previous year (with the distinctive exception of the Lotus), several interesting new shapes had emerged in 1971. March, for example, had opted for a very bulbous profile for their 711 model, which carried a high-mounted 'Spitfire' front wing over the nose, while Tyrrell designer Derek Gardner had produced a full-width nose in an effort to reduce the turbulence around the front wheels, and Matra had preceded their wide-bodied car with one which would have won no prizes in a beauty competition, but whose severely angled body panels sought to extract the maximum benefit from the air through which it was travelling.

Lotus, meanwhile, had taken a different approach with the car which was destined to win the 1972 World Championship in the capable hands of Emerson Fittipaldi. The Lotus 72 had appeared two years earlier and had caused something of a sensation with its radical wedge-shaped profile, but although it promised much it was to prove a troublesome car to develop to its full potential. However, all was to be well in the end, by which time the

Ronnie Peterson took a clear lead at the start of the 1972 Canadian Grand Prix at Mosport with his March 721G, with Jackie Stewart, Peter Revson and Jacky Ickx leading the chase behind him in Tyrrell 005, McLaren M19C and Ferrari 312B-2, respectively. But Stewart would be in front by the fourth lap and go on to score the DFV engine's 50th Grand Prix success.

now-famous black-and-gold colour scheme adorned the cars. Once again Lotus was breaking new ground in allowing their cars to be called John Player Specials rather than Lotuses, although the more popular designation has invariably been either JPS Lotus or John Player Lotus by those who feel that no sponsor should completely camouflage the identity of the manufacturer of 'their' car.

By the time Emerson Fittipaldi's World Championship-celebrating champagne bubbles had evaporated and the teams had moved on from Monza to Mosport for what seemed likely to be the 50th Grand Prix victory by a Ford DFV-engined car, the evidence of commercial sponsorship of Formula 1 teams had become overwhelming. Apart from the John Player Specials, there were Elf Tyrrells, Yardley McLarens (instead of Yardley BRMs, which were now called Marlboro BRMs), as well as Brooke Bond Oxo Surtees, STP and Politoys Marches and even a YPF Brabham publicizing meat from Argentina. But perhaps more significant on the Brabham front was the team's change of ownership. Jack Brabham had announced his retirement at the end of 1970 after no less than 23 years in the cockpit and had lost little time in returning to his native Australia. He had sold his shares in his racing team to his designer and partner Ron Tauranac, who in turn had soon tired of the hassles of team ownership and, at the end of 1971, had sold the Brabham team to Bernard Ecclestone, once known primarily as a Formula 3 driver in the 500cc days, but more recently as the business manager of the late Jochen Rindt. Only in the years ahead would he emerge as the political powerhouse of Formula 1 and the inspiration behind and ultimately President of the Formula One Constructors Association; for the time being, in Canada, he was the rather more anonymous owner of the car which would finish fourth.

1972 Canadian Grand Prix

Jackie Stewart had had a fairly miserable year by his own high standards and in the defence of his 1971 World Championship he had managed to win only two of the new season's 10 races to date and had picked up points in only two of the others, whereas Fittipaldi had secured his title with five wins, two second places and a third.

It so frequently happens, though, in Grand Prix racing that once the World Championship is won, things start to go wrong for the successful team. It had happened in Stewart's case, and it was about to do so for Fittipaldi, who was destined to finish near the back of the field at Mosport after losing first a nose spoiler, then a lot of time at the pits, and finally two of his gears.

For Stewart, however, this was to be one of his best races of the year, and after starting from the second row he needed only three laps to find a way past Ronnie Peterson's March; thereafter he was never headed, or even seriously challenged. The McLaren team of Denny Hulme and Peter Revson had achieved the most impressive reliability record of any team in 1972, and they had started as pre-race favourites after they had set the two fastest practice times, Revson using his intimate knowledge of the circuit to good purpose in claiming pole position. But both McLarens were to suffer from sticking throttles, a legacy of the considerable quantity of dust and dirt on the circuit after the pre-race fog had lifted and allowed the race to start, very late.

Emerson Fittipaldi, Keith Duckworth, Walter Hayes and Henry Ford II at a celebration party to mark the 50th Grand Prix victory by a Ford-powered car and driver. The engine had also powered the World Champion for the fourth consecutive year, Fittipaldi being the most recent title-holder.

However, only Stewart would be ahead of them at the end of the race.

Peterson went great guns for much of the race, in second place, but after 54 of the 80 laps he tangled with Graham Hill's Brabham when trying to lap it, pushed his car back into the pit road for attention and was subsequently disqualified for entering the area by the incorrect route. Hulme, meanwhile, had been storming his way through the field after his throttle-slide trouble had dropped him to 13th place on the opening lap, and Peterson's exit had put him back on the leader board. Fittipaldi's pit stop then elevated him to fourth place, whereupon he fought a long and gripping battle with Carlos Reutemann and his Brabham, the Argentine driver — who was about to earn his first World Championship points for finishing fourth — adding considerably during the remaining laps to his reputation for being a difficult driver to pass, although Hulme managed to find a way through on the very last lap. Both drivers had moved up a place eight laps earlier when Clay Regazzoni, seemingly set for third place — which would have been the Ferrari team's best result since Ickx and he had finished first and second at the Nurburgring — spun away his place and dropped to fifth, and he might well have slipped to sixth had not Amon's Matra been slowed by a broken exhaust.

It had not been an epic race, for Stewart had been so firmly in command once he had taken the lead, and some of his closest rivals had run into difficulties which had blunted their counterattack, but it had served to put yet another DFV victory in the record book, and with the engine in its latest form showing impressive reliability as well as adequate power, there seemed every likelihood that the domination would continue for at least another season.

1973-1977: The 12-cylinder challenge

It was a happy coincidence that the driver who was to score his first World Championship points in the race which gave the DFV its 50th Grand Prix success should be the one who would give the engine its 75th victory at Zeltweg, two seasons later. Carlos Reutemann had remained a member of the Brabham team throughout this period, but there had been some notable changes of allegiance amongst some of the other leading drivers.

Emerson Fittipaldi, for example, who in 1974 was on his way to his second world title, had moved that year from Lotus to McLaren, while Ronnie Peterson, who had left March for Lotus in 1973, had since been joined there by Jacky Ickx. Niki Lauda, whose Grand Prix career had started in 1971 in a March and had then developed sideways with a spell with BRM, was now making his mark with Ferrari, and Jody Scheckter, who had made a dramatic impact on the Grand Prix scene as a McLaren driver in 1973 — especially at Silverstone, where the famous Scheckter slide at Woodcote had initiated a multi-car accident in front of the pits — was now sharing the driving in the Tyrrell team with the promising Frenchman Patrick Depailler.

Jackie Stewart, meanwhile, had retired from the cockpit to become as successful a businessman as he had been a driver, his exit, following his third world title in 1973, having been made one race short of his planned 100

Denny Hulme gave the McLaren M23 its debut in the 1973 South African Grand Prix, a race the New Zealander almost certainly would have won had he not been delayed by a puncture. The introduction of the M23 was to bring a considerable uplift in team fortunes.

Jackie Stewart entering the famous Karussel on the Nurburgring with his Tyrrell 006. The 1973 German Grand Prix was to mark his 27th and final victory in a World Championship race. A few months later he announced his retirement having withdrawn from his planned 100th Grand Prix following the fatal accident during practice at Watkins Glen of his team colleague Francois Cevert, who had been scheduled to lead the Tyrrell team in 1974.

Grands Prix in the saddest of circumstances following the death in a practice accident at Watkins Glen of his team partner and successor-elect, Francois Cevert.

Earlier in the year the sport had lost its most promising recent Formula 1 graduate Roger Williamson, despite heroic efforts by his friend David Purley to rescue him from his blazing car at Zandvoort, while if Gerry Birrell had not been killed in a Formula 2 race at Rouen he, too, would surely have earned himself a major role in Grand Prix racing in due course. This was another bad period for motor racing accidents, and they had continued in 1974 with the loss in a testing accident in South Africa of Peter Revson, who had moved from McLaren to lead the Shadow team, which had been formed the previous year with American backing. There was also to be another tragedy at Watkins Glen, when Helmut Koinigg, one of several promising newcomers to be given a chance by John Surtees, was killed in the United States Grand Prix.

The considerable number of accidents around this time had focussed attention once again on the need for improved driver protection, and this had prompted renewed efforts to raise the requirements of car design as well as to monitor constantly the protective measures provided by circuits. The GPDA were again active in this field, although there had been a change of spokesman, Stewart having handed over to Hulme following his retirement, while Denny in turn had since passed on the Presidency to Graham Hill. By now, the constructors also had their own body and Peter Macintosh had been appointed Secretary of the Formula One Constructors Association with responsibility for day-to-day administration.

Circuits had also seen some major changes. The Belgian Grand Prix, after an unsatisfactory experiment on a tortuous track at Nivelles, had found a new home at Zolder in 1973 — although an inadequately sealed new surface had put that year's race in jeopardy until the last minute and had led to a return to Nivelles for just one more race in 1974 — while the French Grand Prix had taken place for the first time in 1973 on the Paul Ricard circuit at Le Castellet, between Marseilles and Toulon, which was destined to become a favourite winter testing venue for teams in the years ahead. One month earlier the Monte Carlo street circuit had taken on a completely new look in the harbour area for the Monaco Grand Prix, and by the end of that year the first stage in a major revision of Brands Hatch had been well under way.

In 1973 the flamboyant Lord Hesketh had brought James Hunt into the world of Grand Prix racing to provide it with a colourful new ingredient and, in due course, a new name to add to the growing list of constructors, two other notable additions to which in 1974 were to be Parnelli and Penske. Neither of these American teams was destined to remain for long, nor indeed were Lola — back briefly after an interval of 12 years — and several smaller-scale newcomers such as the Amon, Lyncar, Token, Trojan and Maki, all of them DFV-powered, although the Ensign would become a regular part of the scene. Frank Williams, meanwhile, having picked himself up from the Piers Courage tragedy, had taken several financially painful steps along the path towards establishing himself as a Formula 1 constructor and was currently running his own cars as Iso Marlboros.

An epic battle took place between Niki Lauda in his Ferrari 312B-3 and Jacky Ickx in his JPS Lotus 72D for victory in the 1974 Race of Champions at Brands Hatch. The verdict finally went to Ickx, who took the lead by driving round the outside of Lauda at Paddock Hill Bend and recording one of the most memorable moments of wet-weather driving seen for many years.

Although some of the names and team colours had changed over this two-year period, there had been a considerable measure of conformity in the profiles of contemporary cars. The tall air-intake box had become virtually standard equipment, the intake usually being integrated into an engine cover designed so as to impede as little as possible the flow of air towards the rear wing, which had now been moved rearwards. There was still some divergence of opinion concerning the front of the cars, some being run with full-width noses, while others seemed to respond better to chisel-shaped nose panels flanked by adjustable wings. Radiators, meanwhile, had mostly been moved to either the sides or the rear of the chassis. On the tyre front, Goodyear had had the monopoly since the end of 1972 following the withdrawal of Dunlop, Firestone having departed from the scene two years earlier.

As the fields had grown, so had the length of the Grand Prix calendar, which had been extended to 15 races in 1973 and 1974, three more than in 1972. The power battle between rival engines, however, had tended to diminish, at least temporarily, and the DFV recorded a clean sweep in 1973 when the spoils had been divided between just three teams, Lotus scoring seven victories, Tyrrell five and McLaren two. In 1974, though, there had been a different picture as Lauda's presence within the Ferrari team had given it a new order and purpose under the guidance of the talented Luca Montezemolo, with whom the

Ronnie Peterson was the driver most widely tipped to follow Jackie Stewart as World Champion in 1974, but it was not to be, even though he won as many races as anyone that year. The first of his three victories came here at Monaco, where his JPS Lotus 72D finished almost half a minute ahead of Jody Scheckter's Tyrrell 007.

Mark Donohue was a popular newcomer to the Grand Prix scene with his immaculate DFV-powered Penske PC1, seen here in 1975 at Kyalami, South Africa, where he finished eighth. Sadly, Donohue was to die a few months later as a result of complications following an accident in Austria, which he had appeared at first to have survived with only minor injuries.

Austrian driver was to forge a close understanding. BRM, on the other hand, had ceased to be regarded as a serious competitor by the leading teams, and its survival was beginning to be in doubt.

1974 Austrian Grand Prix

Niki Lauda's first victory in a World Championship race had been delayed until the 1974 Spanish Grand Prix, marking the end of a drought lasting for a year-and-a-half for the Italian team. But since then Lauda and Regazzoni had added two more successes, in Holland and Germany, and had been runner-up on four other occasions before making the journey to Austria. The circuit at Zeltweg seemed to be tailormade for their cars, a thought which was to be given further validity during the final practice period when Lauda claimed pole position alongside the Brabham-Ford of Carlos Reutemann, who had set his best time on the previous afternoon.

The Brabham BT44 had earned considerable praise for its designer, Gordon Murray, on its appearance at the beginning of the season, its compact dimensions and slippery profile promising outstanding performance, but although Reutemann had won with it in South Africa, since then a series of minor mishaps had given him a very thin time, from which he had emerged somewhat dispirited. The fact that he had put his car on the front row of the grid, therefore, seemed to provide further evidence of a personal comeback, the first signs of which had been detected a month earlier at Brands Hatch.

Reutemann judged his start perfectly and rushed away from the line and up the steep incline towards the first curve with Lauda in hot pursuit and the leader's new Brazilian driving partner, Carlos Pace — previously a Surtees driver — taking third place temporarily from Regazzoni. The opening laps were a period of intense pressure as the leading cars circulated nose-to-tail,

Emerson Fittipaldi's best Grand Prix years were as a member first of the Lotus team and then as McLaren team leader and he was to win a World Championship with each of them. Here his McLaren M23 carries the number 1 of the current title-holder as the Brazilian demonstrates his smoothness on the Monte Carlo street circuit, where he was to finish second in 1975 behind Niki Lauda's Ferrari.

Regazzoni moving up a place on the second lap at Pace's expense, and Scheckter in a Tyrrell and Hunt in the Hesketh squabbling over fifth place ahead of Fittipaldi's McLaren and Peterson's JPS Lotus.

The first retirement came after only eight laps when Scheckter climbed out of his Tyrrell, which was stranded at the side of the circuit with a blown engine, then five laps later Hunt stopped for a quick change of tyres on his Hesketh, dropping to near the tail of the field before beginning a magnificent comeback drive.

Reutemann, meanwhile, mindful that he, too, could be consuming rubber too quickly on a circuit which was traditionally hard on tyres, slackened his pace just a little to conserve them, then was given a welcome respite when Lauda fell back behind Regazzoni before dropping out with a sick engine. By this time Fittipaldi had brought his McLaren up into third place ahead of Peterson's JPS Lotus and Pace's Brabham, with Depailler's Tyrrell following in sixth position ahead of Hulme in the second of the Texaco Marlboro-sponsored McLarens.

Pace's progress during the second half of the race was further evidence of the speed of the BT44 when everything was going well. After harrying Peterson's Lotus for several laps he swept past on lap 32 and set about relieving Fittipaldi of his third place, but his fellow Brazilian made things easy for him when the McLaren came to a halt, another engine having fallen victim to the intense heat. Pace's next target was Regazzoni, and he dealt with the Ferrari on lap 40, soon after which the Italian car slowed perceptably before Regazzoni brought it into the pits with a soft rear tyre. He was to lose considerable time before his somewhat disorganized pit crew managed to get him on his way again, by this time down in sixth place behind Brambilla, whose March he would repass two laps from the end.

So now the Brabhams were running first and second, with Pace actually closing on the leader, but not for long, because two laps after taking over second place he lost a circlip securing a fuel line and the bitterly disappointed Brazilian coasted to a halt. Peterson was back in second place again, but he, too, was there only temporarily before a universal joint failed nine laps from the end of the race.

Hunt, meanwhile, who had been making excellent progress on his own account, gained considerably from the misfortune of others and picked up a place a lap over a seven-lap period until eventually he was running in third place behind Reutemann and Hulme and ahead of John Watson, who that season had emerged as a driver of considerable calibre at the wheel of a Brabham BT44 operated independently by Hexagon Racing. Watson's fourth

Tom Pryce, the shy but brilliant Welshman, joined the UOP Shadow team several months after the death of team leader Peter Revson in Kyalami, but Pryce, seen here at Monaco in 1975, was in turn to die in a bizarre accident in South Africa when he was hit by a fire extinguisher bottle being carried across the track during the 1976 Grand Prix. When it came to car control Pryce was in the exclusive Peterson category.

place was to prove his best result of the season, but the day had belonged to Carlos Reutemann in the surviving works car after one of the closest-fought races of the season on a very fast track which had allowed little reward for the timid and little comfort for the wayward.

Remarkable though it might sound, a team which six months earlier had not even existed as a racing entity was to be responsible for forging the 100th Grand Prix success by a car powered by a Ford DFV engine. But the formation of Walter Wolf Racing, to be followed by its surprise victory on its first race appearance in Argentina, was by no means the only dramatic event to have occurred in Grand Prix circles prior to Jody Scheckter's milestone

Niki Lauda was much more than an excellent driver to the Ferrari team. His analytical testing abilities and his determination to succeed gave the team a new sense of direction and made the flat-12-engined cars formidable opposition to users of the V8 DFV engine. Here he leads Ronnie Peterson in the wet early stages of the 1975 Monaco Grand Prix, the first of five Grands Prix he would win on his way to his first World Championship.

Mario Andretti and the Parnelli VPJ4 at Silverstone, where they finished 12th in the 1975 British Grand Prix, having previously picked up points in the Swedish and French races.

achievement in 1977 on the streets of his adopted Principality of Monaco. The period since Carlos Reutemann had secured victory number 75 for the DFV had been one of many more changes and had generated numerous headlines in which the names of Niki Lauda and James Hunt had often loomed large.

Lauda's ability to set Ferrari on the right road had been seen in 1974, but it was in 1975 that everything came good for the Italian team. In securing his first World Championship, Lauda himself had managed to claim five wins out of the season's 14 races and Regazzoni had added a sixth, and only twice that year had one or other of them failed to pick up a World Championship points score. Yet Lauda's most exciting race had been one he had failed to win, beaten by just a second by James Hunt and his Hesketh, who had scored their emotional first Grand Prix victory at Zandvoort after a thrilling battle with the Ferrari leader.

The year 1975 had also been noteworthy for providing more than its share

Graham Hill announced his retirement from the cockpit at Silverstone that year and confirmed the promising Tony Brise as his new leader of the Embassy Hill team. Tragically, both were to die four months later, the victims of a plane crash when returning from tests in the South of France.

The arrival of James Hunt and the Hesketh team on the Grand Prix scene made a considerable impact with the gossip writers. But behind the flamboyance there was talent and serious intent, and Hunt scored a memorable victory in the 1975 Dutch Grand Prix after battling with Niki Lauda's Ferrari most of the way.

of chaos, and three times a Grand Prix had had to be stopped before its full distance, once in tragic circumstances. The Spanish Grand Prix at Barcelona had been soured by a drivers' boycott during practice, a protest against the failure of the organizers to secure the guardrails safely. By the time the race took place nerves had become frayed and tempers had been barely under control and sloppy driving had led to several cars being damaged in the opening laps. But disaster had struck in the most unexpected way when the rear wing flew off Rolf Stommelen's leading car — the recently announced Hill-Ford with which Graham Hill, now running his own team, had replaced his earlier Shadows and Lolas — and the German was launched into and over a guardrail to crash in an area beyond into which unauthorized people had infiltrated, with fatal consequences. The race had been stopped after 29 of the scheduled 75 laps, with Jochen Mass leading.

Torrential rain had been responsible for the shortening of races at Silverstone — now with a chicane at Woodcote Corner — and in Austria. The British Grand Prix had ended with the majority of the field embedded in the catch fences, while at Zeltweg Vittorio Brambilla had been so elated at winning his first Grand Prix that he had spun off and damaged his March on his slowing-down lap as he waved to the crowd!

The year 1975 had brought Mario Andretti back to Grand Prix racing at the wheel of the Parnelli and had witnessed Mark Donohue driving the Penske until the morning of that same day in Austria, when he had suffered a tyre deflation and left the circuit at high speed, injuring two marshals, one of them fatally. It appeared at first that Donohue had survived with only light injuries, but there were complications and two days later this so competent and technically accomplished driver had died.

On a more encouraging note, 1975 had seen the development of two outstanding new talents, Tom Pryce having been signed for the UOP-backed Shadow team and Tony Brise by Graham Hill, after Frank Williams had given him his initial Formula 1 opportunity in that tragic race in Spain. But Brise's career was destined to be distressingly short. There had been a mixture of relief for his wellbeing and thankfulness for what he had given the sport when Graham Hill, its great public ambassador, had announced his retirement from the cockpit that summer, but joy had turned to anguish a few months later when Hill and several members of his team, including his talented new driver, had perished in a plane accident in North London on their return from a day's testing at Paul Ricard in the South of France.

Fortunately, the major Formula 1 accident of 1976 had had a much happier outcome, for Niki Lauda had made a miraculous recovery from what had looked at first to be fatal injuries at the Nurburgring, when the 14-miles circuit had been used for the German Grand Prix for the last time. Lauda had crashed at high speed and had only been rescued from his badly damaged and blazing car through the heroic efforts of other drivers. Prior to the disaster, he had seemed likely to repeat his World Championship of the year before, but although he was to miss only two races, James Hunt, now driving for McLaren, strung together a series of outstanding performances in the remaining races, culminating in a decisive third place in the final event in Japan, to become the first Englishman to win the title for eight years.

Regrettably, 1976 had also been a year of further controversy, with tape measures being brandished at some circuits and rule books given almost over-zealous scrutiny at others, so that the Spanish, British and French Grands Prix all suffered from results being overturned in the post-race scrutineering bay or, in the case of the Brands Hatch race, following a protest against the eligibility of Hunt's 'winning' McLaren to have raced at all; it had been damaged in a first-corner accident which had brought the race to a halt, then repaired in the interval before it was restarted. It was all very confusing to the public and it did the image of Grand Prix racing no good whatsoever.

Also bewildering, not least to its drivers, had been the handling

The Elf Tyrrell team's six-wheeled P34 provided the most radical new design of Grand Prix car for many years when it appeared in time for the 1976 season, but though Jody Scheckter and Patrick Depailler finished first and second in the Swedish Grand Prix and the Frenchman would be runner-up on four other occasions that year, neither of them could find the hoped-for decisive advantage over a conventional four-wheeled car.

characteristics of the most radically new car of 1976, the six-wheeled Tyrrell, with which Scheckter and Depailler had done their best to exploit the theoretical advantages of dual front brakes and small front wheels. They had found it to be an uphillstruggle, however, during which Scheckter's victory in the 1976 Swedish Grand Prix was to constitute the car's only major success in two seasons of racing. Nevertheless, that six wheels had been a concept worth trying was to be confirmed, first when March Engineering had built an experimental car — although in this case the tandem wheels were at the rear — and, much later, when Frank Williams' team developed such a car with a view to racing it in 1982, until the banning of the controversial water ballast tanks rendered the idea less attractive.

Although the Tyrrell had been the headline-stealer, there had been other equally important influences on the Grand Prix scene, one example being the seeming speed with which the Ferrari team had mentally written-off Lauda in the aftermath of his accident. Reutemann had been brought into the team, loyalties had been split, confusion had reigned and, although Lauda had eventually managed to reassert his authority over test programmes, the damage had been done; his days with Ferrari were numbered.

Lotus, meanwhile, had emerged from the doldrums with a new car for the 1977 season with body side panels serving the function of integrated wings, and it had soon become clear that the Lotus 78 was potentially as good as the previous Lotus 77 had been bad. It was the trendsetter which would open the path towards full ground-effects aerodynamics in the years ahead, but meanwhile, despite Mario Andretti's sensitive touch in the cockpit, it was to be plagued with irritating problems which time and again would rob it of likely victory. Nevertheless, once again Lotus were showing the rest the way ahead in racing car design.

There had also been considerable activity on the engine front. Ferrari's competitiveness in 1976 had finally identified the need for a major development programme on the Ford DFV, and as a result Cosworth

Heading for controversy. Having survived a Ferrari-provoked first-corner multi-car pile-up with only minor damage, James Hunt's McLaren was hastily refurbished to take part in the restarted 1976 British Grand Prix at Brands Hatch. After chasing Niki Lauda's Ferrari for 44 of the 76 laps, Hunt found a way past and went on to take the chequered flag, only to suffer disqualification following a protest by the Italian team. This was not the only controversial decision during that very disturbing season.

Engineering had produced a limited series of development engines to various specifications and incorporating the use of magnesium castings, which were to be allocated on a loan basis to the Lotus, McLaren and Tyrrell teams, who were free to use them as they wished. Later, the Wolf team was to join in the arrangement. To develop anything during a busy racing season must always be something of a gamble, and the dilemma for these teams was whether to opt for the improved power and torque and lighter weight of the experimental engines, or settle for the proven reliability of the existing production versions. Not everyone was to guess correctly in 1977.

Further impetus for the quest for more power had been provided in 1976 by the re-emergence of an Alfa Romeo engine on the Grand Prix scene, not a V8 this time, but a purpose-built flat-12 for the exclusive use of the Brabham team. Reutemann and Pace were said to have had 500bhp at 12,000rpm at their disposal at the beginning of the year and 510bhp by season's end (by which time Reutemann had moved on to Ferrari), but a trio of fourth places had been little enough to show for it after they had staggered through a season of unreliability. Only in 1977, in fact, after John Watson had joined the works team following Pace's death in a flying accident, had the Brabham-Alfa Romeos become a serious threat, emerging as front-row cars and, from time to time, race leaders.

An earlier engine development in 1975, which had met with very little success, was the experimental insertion of a V12 Matra engine into one of the Shadows, an exercise which had been quietly forgotten after some persistent trouble with the fuel system. Meanwhile, even more modifications to the BRM V12 engine, the appearance of a new car with a sharply triangular body profile and a change of name to Stanley BRM had failed to restore the fortunes of that so often troubled team, which had bowed out of Grand Prix racing early in 1976. Simultaneously, two new teams had emerged when Emerson Fittipaldi had left McLaren to run his own team with Brazilian backing — and limited success — and former driver Guy Ligier had decided to build a car

No dispute this time. Hunt fought off a strong challenge from Clay Regazzoni to win the 1976 Dutch Grand Prix by a fraction over a second while Niki Lauda continued to make a remarkable recovery from what had seemed at one time to be fatal injuries suffered in his high-speed accident on the Nurburging. Lauda was to be back in action again two weeks later, when he would finish fourth at Monza.

Jacky Ickx striving hard in his Ensign to hold John Watson at bay in the Penske during the 1976 Canadian Grand Prix at Mosport. For the previous seven weeks Watson had been clean-shaven, having honoured a pledge to shave off his beard once he had won a Grand Prix. He gave the Penske team that success in Austria, exactly a year after the death of his predecessor, Mark Donohue.

around the Matra engine and slip Jacques Laffite into the cockpit, a combination which had proved to be both entertaining and effective during its first season, when Laffite scored his best result — second place — in Austria. This was on the day when John Watson's beard had become doomed in honour of a pledge that he would remove it immediately he won his first Grand Prix; he had done so, for Roger Penske, on the anniversary of Mark Donohue's fatal accident and a few months before the American team was to be disbanded. With the withdrawal of Parnelli earlier in the year, American interest in Grand Prix racing from 1977 onwards was to depend to a large extent on the driving achievements of Mario Andretti in the Lotus team; he was not to let his adopted country down, although the World Championship to which he aspired was to elude him for a further year.

Power battle in the 1976 United States Grand Prix at Watkins Glen. Ronnie Peterson and his DFV-engined March 761 resisting the challenge of Jacques Laffite in his Matra V12-powered Ligier JS5 and Carlos Pace in the 12-cylinder Alfa Romeo-engined Brabham BT45. All three cars were destined to retire, the first two with suspension problems and Pace after colliding with Jochen Mass' fourth-placed McLaren.

1977 Monaco Grand Prix

Jody Scheckter's dislike of the six-wheeled Tyrrell P34 had been ill-concealed during 1976, despite his victory in Sweden, so the news that he was moving on at the end of the year had come as no real surprise. It was the destination of his move that had staggered the racing world. Throughout 1976, Frank Williams' cars had been entered as Wolf Williams to signify the financial backing which his struggling team was receiving from Walter Wolf, a naturalized Canadian with oil-industry connections. But Wolf's unbridled enthusiasm for the sport had been tested severely during the year, when the team had failed to pick up a single World Championship point.

Things were to be very different, though, in 1977, for which a brand new Wolf team was to be built around one driver — Scheckter — with a brand new car designed by Dr Harvey Postlethwaite. Peter Warr had been enticed away from Lotus to manage the team, leaving Frank Williams free to concentrate on sponsorship and other business matters — a role he disliked so much that within a few months he was back running his own racing team under the Frank Williams Engineering banner.

The Wolf team were to achieve the seemingly impossible in Argentina when they won their first ever Grand Prix, after Scheckter had started the race half-way down the field. Things had not gone so well in Brazil, where the Wolf

Jody Scheckter on his way to the milestone 100th Grand Prix victory for the Ford DFV engine in the 1977 Monaco Grand Prix. The emergence of a new-look Walter Wolf Racing team built around Scheckter had surprised the racing world, but a first-time victory in Argentina had confirmed the potential of the project. However, leaner times were ahead and Scheckter would move on to Ferrari to win the World Championship, Hunt would replace him only to retire a few months later, then the team would merge with Fittipaldi, which in turn would close down in 1982.

had been one of the earliest retirements, but in South Africa a strong second place behind Lauda's Ferrari had put Scheckter into the lead in the World Championship on a day saddened by the tragic death of Tom Pryce. This so modest but talented a driver had been killed in a freak accident when a marshal had run across the track into the path of his Shadow, carrying a heavy fire extinguisher, which hit Pryce in the head. The impact had killed him instantly, long before his car had crashed at the end of the straight; the young marshal had also died.

With third places in the next two races, at Long Beach (inaugurated the previous year as the venue of a United States West Grand Prix) and in Spain, Scheckter still headed the points table as the teams converged on his adopted home in Monte Carlo for the most colourful Grand Prix of the season. A handling problem had given the Wolf driver a tough time at Jarama, though, and Scheckter — no lover of street circuits at the best of times — was less than enthusiastic about his prospects at Monaco, where Ferrari had produced the best handling car for the previous three years.

First practice served to confirm Scheckter's fears. His own car was still oversteering badly, and sure enough the Ferraris of Lauda and Reutemann were faster, even though they, too, had a handling problem this time. Less palatable to the South African was the news that Ronnie Peterson, his replacement in the Elf-backed Tyrrell team, and Patrick Depailler were ahead of the Wolf in their six-wheelers, but most concerning of all was the speed of the Brabham-Alfa Romeos of John Watson and Hans Stuck. Fresh from some extensive testing at the Alfa Romeo proving ground at Balocco, the Brabhams were not only very powerful, but they seemed to be extremely well balanced and highly controllable.

The second practice period was a washout — literally — and so everything depended upon the vital final hour of qualifying on the eve of the race. Stuck had been the pacesetter up to now, but a dropped valve ruined his chances of improving on his time, and so it was now up to Watson to keep Brabham at the front of the grid. This he did in majestic style and when the times were published his was the only one of the weekend to have broken the 90-seconds barrier. Scheckter had put in a supreme effort until, nearing the end of the session, he had made a slight mistake and lightly damaged the back of his car against a barrier. But at least he was second quickest overall, which meant a clear track ahead of him for those vital first few yards of the race.

Next in line would be Reutemann, Peterson, Stuck, Lauda, Hunt and Depailler — fast starters every one of them — so anything short of a copybook getaway and Scheckter was likely to be overwhelmed in the rush towards the Ste Devote corner, that tricky right-hander which needed to be taken in single file if bumping and boring was to be avoided.

It was the first time that John Watson had started a Grand Prix from pole position, and with the quickest car at his disposal he couldn't have chosen a more appropriate circuit on which to do so. But his rear wheels were lined up on a white-painted road marking and the reduced adhesion contributed to an excess of wheelspin as the race started, and this was all the help Scheckter needed. He made his copybook start and was clearly in the lead before his brakes came on for Ste Devote.

By the end of the lap he was out on his own, as everyone else settled into an order for the pursuit, but Watson was leading the chase ahead of Reutemann and Stuck and it took the Ulsterman only a handful of laps to close the gap behind the Wolf. On the sixth lap Watson attempted to find a way through under braking at Ste Devote, but misjudged it, lost a little time, then set about retrieving it once more. Meanwhile, Peterson had dropped out with brake problems, allowing Lauda up into fifth place behind Stuck, whose Brabham was to come to a halt after 19 laps — exactly quarter-distance — with a small electrical fire. So now Scheckter and Watson were out in front, followed by the two Ferraris of Reutemann and Lauda (soon to exchange places as Reutemann eased his pace in order to conserve his tyres). Next came Hunt in his McLaren, well clear of Mass, his team partner, who was having a fine dice with Andretti and his Lotus, with Depailler locked in with them until his Tyrrell, too, was slowed with brake problems.

Watson, meanwhile, maintained his pressure on Scheckter until half-distance, but then he noticed the first signs of what was to become increasing gear-selection trouble. Inevitably, the gap between the two cars increased and then, on lap 46, it became vastly greater as Watson, hunting for a gear, was obliged to take to the escape road at the chicane leading on to the harbour section of the course. Effectively, his challenge was over, and two laps later his race ended when his transmission seized.

The pressure on Scheckter then lessened considerably, and although Lauda was closing slightly, a quarter of a minute still separated the Wolf and the Ferrari with 20 laps to go. The leader could afford to ease his pace a little without causing too much anxiety in his pit, or indeed in his own cockpit, and so it was inevitable that the gap should begin to come down. But with three laps to go it started to shrink disturbingly quickly and there was a trace of hesitation in the Wolf's exhaust note as the leader went through his gears. It looked as though the Monaco Grand Prix would once again provide a nail-biting finish, especially when Lauda had closed to within six seconds of the leader as they went into their final lap, with the Wolf now clearly in some sort of fuel-feed problem.

Around that final lap, with Lauda sensing that Scheckter was in some sort of trouble, the distance between the two cars could be seen to be closing by the second. But Scheckter was keeping a cool head and asking of his car only what was absolutely necessary. He emerged from the final turn as Lauda's Ferrari was half-way through it, the Wolf accelerated cleanly this time, and though the Italian car continued to close the gap on the run-up to the finishing line Scheckter swept across it still almost a second ahead. He had scored the DFV's 100th Grand Prix success and, interestingly, he had done it with an engine incorporating normal aluminium castings, as distinct from the experimental magnesium-cast engines which had made their race debut that day in the cars of Hunt, Peterson and Andretti. Of this trio, only Andretti had lasted the 76 laps, narrowly beaten into fourth place by Mass after a hard but cleanly fought battle which had been a highlight of the race. Peterson's early brake problems had prevented his new engine from being fully tested, but Hunt's had dropped a valve after 25 laps, ending his pursuit of the Ferraris. The technical post mortem would have to await the return to England (later the decision was taken not to pursue the project until such time as improvements in magnesium casting technology made it more attractive), but in the meantime there was the immediate and pleasurable task of spreading a little champagne in celebration of the DFV's 100th Grand Prix success, almost exactly a decade after its first.

1978-1982: The ground-effects era

In the highly charged and ultra-competitive world of Grand Prix racing it is inevitable that relative team fortunes will fluctuate considerably. An advantage by one will almost certainly be short-lived as rivals race to redress the balance, and it is rare indeed for any one team to enjoy for long the simultaneous availability of the best cars, the best drivers, the best mechanics, the best engines and the best workshop back-up to give them consistent race-winning reliability.

To illustrate the point, one has only to compare the status of two teams — which had once been linked — on the occasions of the 100th and the 125th Grand Prix victories with the Ford DFV engine to see just how far the pendulum of achievement can swing. At Monaco in 1977, Walter Wolf Racing were the team setting the standards, and it in no way diminishes the personal contribution made by Jody Scheckter on that day to say that had his team not done an equally effective job in providing their driver with top-quality support in all the essential areas he would not have had the winner's garland placed around his neck on that occasion.

Williams Grand Prix Engineering, on the other hand, which had made its debut in Spain two weeks earlier with the Belgian driver Patrick Neve in a March, were not even present at Monaco; Frank Williams considered that it was unrealistic to expect to qualify for one of the 20 available grid places with the equipment at their disposal.

Moving on to the 1979 Canadian Grand Prix, it was a very different picture. Williams had always claimed that with the right sort of backing he would get the job done, and true to his word, with the aid of substantial sponsorship support from Saudia Arabia, he had built one of the most efficiently run teams ever seen in Grand Prix racing. Although the elusive first victory had been a long time coming — Clay Regazzoni had made the breakthrough at Silverstone earlier that year — team leader Alan Jones, who had joined Williams at the end of 1977, had followed through with a hat-trick of wins in

Although a series of pit stops put Alan Jones out of the running in the 1978 Brazilian Grand Prix, the new Saudia Williams FW06, designed by Patrick Head, revealed its potential when Jones set a lap time beaten only by Carlos Reutemann's race-winning Ferrari.

The combination to beat in 1978. Mario Andretti began the new season well with an outright victory in Argentina with this JPS Lotus 78, but there was something even better just a few months away — the full ground effects Lotus 79, which Andretti drove for the first time to victory in Belgium. This was to be Mario's World Championship year.

Germany, Austria and Holland and was about to add a fourth in Canada.

As for the Wolf team, it had begun to lose its impetus even before Scheckter had moved on to Ferrari for the 1979 season, as Carlos Reutemann's replacement, where he was to achieve his career ambition of winning the World Championship. James Hunt had taken Scheckter's place, but the fortunes of the Wolf team were about to go into a steep decline, and after failing to collect a World Championship point from any of the season's first seven races Hunt had decided to end his career as a racing driver forthwith. Keke Rosberg had been recruited into the team at mid-season, but still the points cupboard was bare and in Canada the Finnish driver, whose talents had already been marked down by Frank Williams as being of a rare quality, was unable even to qualify his car. The once struggling team had emerged on top and the earlier pacesetter was now struggling for survival and would shortly lose its identity following a merger with Fittipaldi, which in turn would also depart from the scene a little later.

The Williams team had emerged as strong in 1979 as Lotus had proved the previous season when Mario Andretti had duly won that coveted world title. After beginning the season with the promising but previously not always reliable Lotus 78, he had transferred in Belgium to the Lotus 79, which was to prove so superior with its more sophisticated development of ground effects technology that Andretti and Chapman had been able to send rival chassis designers rushing back to their drawing-boards.

In securing his World Championship, Andretti had had magnificent support from Ronnie Peterson, with whom he had developed a close working relationship and personal friendship as the season progressed, and so it had been a particularly bitter blow that his world title had been won on the very day that Peterson had been fatally injured in a multi-car accident shortly after the start of the Italian Grand Prix. One month later, Sweden had lost its other Grand Prix star when Gunnar Nilsson, who had been Peterson's predecessor in the Lotus team, failed in his long and gallant battle against cancer, although not before he had initiated a fund to which the sport would contribute so generously for the benefit of other sufferers.

Nilsson's charity had shown the Grand Prix world to have a heart, and in 1978 another event was to prove that it had both a sense of humour and a sense of responsibility. In the counterattack against Lotus superiority it was, perhaps, predictable that the Brabham team might come up with the most original solution, for its Chief Designer, Gordon Murray, had already demonstrated a considerable degree of ingenuity, witness his experiments less than two years earlier with surface coolers in place of conventional radiators for the Alfa Romeo-engined Brabhams.

His approach to the ground effects problem was, appropriately, far more down to earth. At the risk of over-simplifying an exceedingly complex science,

Mario Andretti and Ronnie Peterson in their JPS Lotus 78s keep close company with Jody Scheckter's fifth-placed Wolf WR1 during the early part of the 1978 Monaco Grand Prix; Scheckter's eventual third place would be the best result from this trio.

the use of ground effects in racing car design can be described as obtaining an increase in adhesion between car and track surface by means of a reduction of air pressure beneath the car when it is in motion; cause a partial vacuum beneath the car and you will tend to suck it towards the ground. Lotus had achieved this by the use of flexible side skirts to prevent air spillage beyond the width of the body and by the careful profiling of the under surfaces to achieve the desired progressive reduction of pressure.

The Brabham solution went much further and owed more than a little to the domestic vacuum cleaner for its inspiration. The team appeared in Sweden with a pair of cars, the rear bodywork of which was fully encased inboard of the wheels save for a vertically mounted fan in the middle which, with tongue firmly in cheek, the team explained was there to provide extra cooling for the engine. Its prime purpose, of course, was to act as a 'sucker' by extracting air from beneath the car, and this it did remarkably well.

Watson and Lauda, who was in his first season with Brabham after leaving the Ferrari team, were only beaten by Andretti in practice, and although Watson retired from the race after spinning off Lauda was able to pass Andretti with considerable ease and went on to score the first Grand Prix success with an Alfa Romeo engine since 1951. Prior to their appearance with the 'fan car' in Sweden, Brabham had been assured by the ruling CSI that it was eligible under Formula 1 regulations — even though the car had not been inspected — but that did not prevent several protests being lodged against it even before the Swedish race had started. When Andretti described afterwards what it had been like being showered by muck and debris from the track which had been picked up by the Brabham and discharged through the fan, more protests followed. A few days later, what could have been an ugly situation was effectively diffused when Brabham agreed to an immediate

Another high-speed sandwich at Monaco in 1978. This time Patrick Depailler and his Tyrrell 008 provide the filling, but not for long because he would break free of the third-placed Brabham-Alfa Romeo BT46 of Niki Lauda, pass John Watson's similar car leading here, and drive on to a comfortable victory.

Niki Lauda at the wheel of the controversial Brabham-Alfa Romeo BT46B 'fan car' which would take him to victory in the 1978 Swedish Grand Prix and provoke a paddock full of protests afterwards. However, diplomacy saved the day and the Brabham team agreed that the fan concept should be disallowed in future, in return for which the Swedish result would stand.

modification of the rule book, which would prevent such cars being used again, on the understanding that the race result at Anderstorp would stand. It was a mature decision, which prevented teams from having to rush off in a new direction fraught with safety implications, not to mention unwelcome complexity and cost.

The other major technological breakthrough of the period was to be much longer-lasting and to have much deeper political implications, so much so that, looking back, it is surprising indeed that the threat posed by turbocharged engines had not been identified earlier or, if it had, why little if anything had been done to control the situation. Perhaps it was because few people expected them to be a long-term threat to the stability of the sport.

Renault had first announced their intention to build a turbocharged $1\frac{1}{2}$-litre version of their Formula 2 V6 engine and use it for their entry into Grand Prix racing in 1976, but it was not until the British Grand Prix the following year that the team had made their Formula 1 debut. Since then there had been two years of intense frustration for the French company as it had learned the hard and painful way how to overcome the two fundamental drawbacks which this form of propulsion seemed to offer — the power lag between the time the driver depressed his accelerator and the turbocharger responded, and mechanical fragility, a problem exacerbated by the intense heat generated by turbocharged engines.

But a breakthrough had occurred at the 1979 French Grand Prix when Jean-Pierre Jabouille had taken his car to an emotionally charged victory at Dijon and Rene Arnoux in the Renault team's second turbo had fought and only narrowly lost a wheel-banging battle for second place with the Ferrari of Gilles Villeneuve. The turbo had slipped into Grand Prix racing through the retention of the '$1\frac{1}{2}$-litre engine with supercharger' clause in Formula 1 regulations, which had been built into the rules over a decade earlier for an entirely different purpose. But the turbo's legality had not been challenged at the time of Renault's original announcement, and the failure to do so at that time was to cost Grand Prix racing teams dear as, one by one, they would be forced to consider taking the turbo route after enjoying so many years of

Riccardo Patrese's driving had been the subject of some criticism by other drivers during 1978, but he was back on top form in his Arrows A1 for the Canadian Grand Prix, the last race of the season, where he finished fourth, close behind the third-placed Ferrari of Carlos Reutemann.

engine stability and consequent containment of costs.

For the time being, however, other problems were of more immediate concern to the Grand Prix circus, which had become just that — a highly organized and commercialized travelling entertainment, moving from one venue to the next around the world and attracting an ever-increasing audience, not just of trackside spectators, but of many millions more through the medium of the television screen, to the delight of major sponsors.

Grand Prix racing had become show business on the grand scale, and the potential rewards were now vast. The formation of the Formula One Constructors Association had meant much more than the creation of an association of team owners and operators. It had led to FOCA gaining operational control of the sport and supplying race organizers with a single bargaining unit, whereas previously they had had to negotiate with individual teams. In return, FOCA was supplying a guaranteed package of cars and drivers — a tidy arrangement, unless you happened to be one of the newer teams who had not been around long enough to qualify for FOCA membership (usually two seasons unless you had sufficient commercial muscle) and therefore were unable to avail yourself of the concessionary transportation costs available to members of the FOCA package.

FOCA's increasing power and influence had been aided, almost guaranteed, by the ineffectiveness of the *Commission Sportive Internationale* (CSI) in its role of official ruling body, but things were about to change. The CSI, later to be reconstituted as the *Federation Internationale du Sport Automobile* (FISA), had a new President in Jean-Marie Balestre, a mercurial administrator in French sporting circles, an accomplished politician and a man with intense energy and ambition. He had been elected to his new post on a platform of restoring power to the governing body and clipping both the financial and political wings of FOCA in particular and of the teams in general. The age of confrontation had arrived, although as Grand Prix racing concluded the European segment of its 1979 programme and headed back across the Atlantic to Canada, with Jody Scheckter its newly crowned World Champion, FOCA and FISA had done little more than probe each other's defences and engage in a few verbal skirmishes; the real battle was still several months away.

1979 Canadian Grand Prix

Jody Scheckter might have clinched the 1979 World Championship when he led Gilles Villeneuve across the finishing line at Monza three weeks earlier, but there was never much doubt as to which was the dominant Ferrari driver once the teams had arrived at the *Circuit Ile Notre-Dame* in Montreal. Gilles Villeneuve was back amongst his home crowd, and every one of them would be expecting this talented French-Canadian to repeat his victory of the previous year; if he let them down it would not be for want of trying.

Alan Jones was the driver most likely to upset the plan. After three straight victories in the second half of the season, followed by a disappointment at Monza, the Williams team leader was determined to prove that, title or not, his had been the driving performance of the season and his the car to beat. The Australian had underlined the competitiveness of his Williams-Ford by claiming pole position with the only lap in less than 90 seconds, more than

The Ligier team switched from Matra to Ford DFV power in 1979 with good effect. After Jacques Laffite had won the first two races of the year, in Argentina and Brazil, it was Patrick Depailler's turn to add a third success in the Spanish Grand Prix which opened the European part of the calendar.

Jacques Laffite was joined by Didier Pironi in the Ligier team for 1980, the year in which they would finish fourth and fifth, respectively, in the World Championship after a season which had brought them one outright victory each, Pironi in Belgium and Laffite in Germany.

six-tenths of a second ahead of Villeneuve, and if Clay Regazzoni, lining up third in the second Williams, could keep the remainder of the field at bay for a few laps the way would be clear for a private dog-fight between the two fastest drivers in the race — the hard-charging Jones against the artistically accomplished Villeneuve.

Yet for all the prospects of a fine race, the main topic of conversation centred on a driver who had arrived with a brand new car and engine, but was now far away in California, busy buying an aircraft. Niki Lauda had walked out of the Brabham team, and out of Grand Prix racing, at the end of the first practice session with scarcely a backward glance. He had decided that he had had enough of driving racing cars round in circles, and from now on flying would be the centre of his interest and of his business life. His enthusiasm for racing had been waning for months, and despite a lucrative contract for the 1980 season, and now a brand new car built around the Ford DFV engine, which promised him a much more competitive year than his past one with Alfa Romeo-powered cars, his heart was simply no longer in it. The abruptness of his decision had staggered the racing world and shattered the Brabham team, although young Nelson Piquet, instantly promoted to team leadership, had lost little time in demonstrating what the Austrian was leaving behind by claiming a close fourth place on the grid with his new car.

As the starting light turned from red to green Villeneuve made a copybook charge from his side of the grid to overhaul Jones and put his Ferrari into the lead before the first corner. Jones tucked his car beneath the Ferrari's rear

Derek Daly's most frightening moment in a 1980 season full of incident. His Tyrrell would land back on its wheels at the apex of the corner, but his and three other cars would be eliminated within seconds of the start of the Monaco Grand Prix. Pironi, Reutemann, Jones, Laffite, Depailler and Piquet were far enough ahead of the action to get through unscathed.

wing to begin what was destined to be a race-long battle between these two as, predictably, Regazzoni resisted some intense pressure from Piquet and the remainder of the field for several valuable laps. By the time Piquet found a way past the second Williams, on lap 8 of the 72-lap contest, the leading pair were well clear of the traffic and slowly but steadily building on their advantage. The performance of the new Brabham, however, was most impressive, and after comfortably outstripping the remainder of the field Piquet looked assured of third place until he was slowed and eventually halted, 11 laps from the end, with gearbox trouble.

Jones, meanwhile, had maintained the pressure on Villeneuve right from the start, but had been prepared to be patient, remaining close enough to keep the Ferrari driver on his toes, but without making any determined effort to wrest the lead from him. The important thing, Jones reasoned, was to conserve his own car and especially its brakes, in preparation for an all-out effort later in the race. It was around lap 45 that Jones went into the attack and soon the two

Rene Arnoux's Renault had started third on the grid, but the power of its $1\frac{1}{2}$-litre turbocharged engine has already taken it ahead of Alan Jones' pole position Saudia Williams within seconds of the start of the 1980 Austrian Grand Prix. However, Jean-Pierre Jabouille's Renault would be first past the finishing line, with Jones less than a second behind it.

Mario Andretti, feeling it was time to move on from Lotus, joined Alfa Romeo for the 1981 season and took an encouraging fourth place behind Jones, Reutemann and Piquet in the season's first race at Long Beach. However, those were the only points Andretti was to collect in a frustrating season dogged with misfortune.

cars were running nose-to-tail. Villeneuve resisted strongly, but on lap 51 he went slightly wide at one of the chicanes. Jones seized his chance, pulled alongside and managed to claim the more favourable line into the braking area for the next hairpin. They took the corner side-by-side, but Jones gained the better traction on the exit and was through.

Scheckter, who had made an early stop for a change of tyres and had since slipped to a full lap behind, now joined Villeneuve in a two-car Ferrari flat-12 counterattack and together they whittled away at Jones' lead, which he had quickly managed to build to 3.2 seconds, until little more than a second separated the first two cars. This was Villeneuve at his most persistent against Jones at his most determined and the two were almost perfectly matched; the gap remained unchanged throughout the vital last lap and Jones crossed the line the victor for the fourth time that year, with Villeneuve a gallant loser after another stirring drive (he would gain his revenge at Watkins Glen a week later). Regazzoni was the only other driver to complete the full distance, a lap more than Scheckter and Pironi (Tyrrell) and two ahead of Watson (McLaren). Meanwhile, the Renault team, who had been fast enough to outstrip everyone else in practice at Monza, only to lose both cars with engine problems, had started seventh and eighth this time, and had made little impression prior to being eliminated before the race had run one-third its distance. The turbo team, Jabouille's French Grand Prix victory notwithstanding, had yet to cause many sleepless nights amongst those whose destiny was still linked seemingly so securely to 3-litre engines.

Riccardo Patrese upset the form book by claiming pole position for the 1981 Grand Prix at Long Beach and leading for the first 24 laps with his Arrows A3. Here he is being pursued on the opening lap by the Williams FW07Cs of Reutemann and Jones, Piquet's Brabham, Cheever's Tyrrell and Pironi's Ferrari, with Andretti's Alfa Romeo tucked in behind Cheever's car.

It took a few weeks short of three years for the tally of DFV Grand Prix victories to grow from 125 to 150, an interval during which the threat to the traditional 3-litre normally aspirated engines by the all-powerful $1\frac{1}{2}$-litre turbocharged power units reached an intensity which placed the very fabric of Grand Prix racing in jeopardy. Only when it was too late to do anything about it, for political reasons, was there a widespread realization of the destructive potential of a formula which permitted two fundamentally different types of racing engine to compete side-by-side, linked by an arbitrary factor of equivalence which was based on cylinder displacement and which bore little relationship to their respective potential power outputs.

The fact that the move towards turbos was confined in the main to the major manufacturer-linked teams, with Ferrari (owned by Fiat) and Alfa Romeo following the Renault lead, whereas the numerically superior and mainly British-based 3-litre teams sought to maintain the financial stability which the availability of an 'off the shelf' engine like the DFV offered them, served merely to widen the divide between the two camps. After a period when there had been a reasonable level of common agreement amongst rival teams on fundamental issues concerned with the conduct of Grand Prix racing, there was now a growing level of discord, a situation which Jean-Marie Balestre was quick to exploit in his vigorous campaign to restore power to where he felt it belonged — at the door of FISA.

This is not the place to dwell at length on the politics of Grand Prix racing in the late-1970s and early-1980s and, indeed, it is a subject which on its own could fill a book of considerable length. It should be sufficient, therefore, to record that it manifested itself in so many ways and so frequently, particularly in the period 1980 to 1982, that it came close to destroying Grand Prix racing as a credible spectacle and as a worthy vehicle for the vast amount of financial investment it had attracted from sponsors.

Ultimately, reason was to prevail, but only after vast amounts of time, energy and rescources had been squandered on counter-productive campaigning and lobbying instead of on genuine efforts to improve the image and public acceptability of the sport.

One proposal which deserved a better fate was Keith Duckworth's contention that Formula 1 should be controlled by a restriction on the flow of fuel, or possibly air, into the engine, rather than on arbitrary piston displacement, but it was destined to fall on deaf ears, at least for the forseeable future. Similarly, a move initiated by Goodyear to ban qualifying tyres was thwarted within months of its inception, and at one stage the American company opted out of the Grand Prix arena completely, at the end of 1980, only to return a few months later and discover that much had changed in the interim, such being the pace of technical development.

One of the darkest weekends of 1980 had coincided with the Spanish Grand Prix, where the simmering power struggle between FISA and FOCA had burst into the open, the scene for conflict having been set at the previous two Grands Prix in Belgium and Monaco, where, acting on team instructions, certain drivers had declined to attend pre-race briefing meetings which had been declared mandatory by the FISA earlier in the year. When the drivers refused to pay their resulting fines, their licences were suspended, whereupon FOCA announced their refusal to race in Spain unless the fines were withdrawn. The organizing club then sought to bypass FISA, FOCA endorsed the move and announced their intention to race under the auspices of a different administration, but Renault, Ferrari and Alfa Romeo elected to take the FISA line and withdraw from the Grand Prix (which by that time had been declared illegal by FISA), fearful of possible repercussions from the FIA which might affect their other motor sporting activities. Thus the stage was set for the first Grand Prix to be powered entirely by the Ford Cosworth DFV engine. The 'FOCA-only' race duly went ahead, but FISA were to have the last word when the FIA endorsed their decision to declare the race an illegal event and therefore ineligible for World Championship points, to the

An ingenious solution which was beaten by the courts. The Lotus 88 incorporated two separate chassis, one to carry the normal running gear and suspension and an inner structure forming a cockpit cell for the driver and body panels, which would be isolated from the shocks inseparable from the rock-hard suspension demanded in the ground effects era. The failure to gain acceptance for a design which he felt offered the sport so much was a bitter disappointment for Colin Chapman. The car was destined never to race.

considerable chagrin of Alan Jones and the Williams team, who had been the winners on the day.

Just as the drivers' dispute had provided the catalyst for the Spanish confrontation, so the events in Spain served as the overture to an ever widening rift between FISA and FOCA, culminating in a complete split before the end of the year and the prospect of two series of races being run in 1981, one by each organization. This ludicrous situation was only resolved after intense pressure from sponsors on the two factions to get together, resolve their differences and draw up a new charter for Grand Prix racing. The result, after a massive cost in legal fees, was the Concorde Agreement, a document of formidable length and complexity and peppered with loopholes inviting exploitation. It was signed just in time for a delayed start to the 1981 season to be made at Long Beach, but the price of getting racing cars back on the track again and witnessing FISA and FOCA spokesmen proffering each other with nauseating quantities of goodwill and affection was a clause which

Heading for the crunch. Nelson Piquet and Alan Jones had clashed verbally on a number of occasions prior to the 1981 Monaco Grand Prix, and neither respected very highly the other's driving ability. The tension could be imagined, therefore, as Jones pressured Piquet's leading Brabham for many laps, well clear of the rest of the field. Piquet kept his cool until lap 54, then got off line while trying to lap back markers and crashed into a barrier. Thereafter Jones looked set for victory until an engine misfire slowed him towards the end and allowed Villeneuve to close the gap and score a lucky victory for Ferrari.

A remarkable combination of mechanical reliability and driving consistency had enabled Carlos Reutemann to collect World Championship points in 14 consecutive races in 1980 and 1981, and for much of 1981 he was the firm favourite to take over the title currently held by his team partner Alan Jones. However, the psychological pressure was to prove too great and Reutemann was pipped at the post by Nelson Piquet in the Caesar's Palace Grand Prix at Las Vegas, where Jones won the race handsomely and promptly retired.

virtually guaranteed the impossibility of putting right any of the imperfections of the document. For the next two years, no changes affecting the performance of the cars could be implemented without the unanimous agreement of all the teams, and with FISA and FOCA now more closely aligned than some of the former FISA-supporting teams felt to be healthy, such unanimity could be ruled out of the question.

In the circumstances, therefore, there was relief that under the terms of the Concorde Agreement sliding skirts along the body sides were already banned and that chassis had to ride with a minimum ground clearance of 6 centimetres. A ban on flexible skirts had been central to Balestre's lobbying over the previous year in an effort to reduce cornering speeds and enhance safety standards. FOCA had conceded this point in return for which they had retained commercial control of the sport.

In the event, the concession was to prove minimal, for Brabham's ingenious Gordon Murray quickly designed a novel hydraulic suspension system which provided the necessary ground clearance when the car was at rest (the only time it could be measured) but tugged the car closer to the ground under the influence of air flow as it gathered speed. It was not working well enough for it to be used at Long Beach, but four weeks later in Argentina its advantage was so great that Nelson Piquet led from start to finish and won with embarrassing ease. An official ruling as to the system's legality was sought, and when approval was given (to the amazement of rival teams) everyone rushed through their own version of the adjustable ride-height concept. Within a month all the major teams were running cars which hugged the track surface, had rock-hard, driver-bruising suspensions to prevent the tips of the solid skirts from wearing away, and which, at the touch of an electric switch, suddenly rose as if on stilts as they approached the clearance-measuring gauge at the entry to the pit road. This was Grand Prix racing at its most ludicrous moment of a troubled period, a situation seen as being the more irrational in that, simultaneously, Colin Chapman's ingenious solution to the conflicting requirements of optimum adhesion of the car and acceptable comfort of and therefore control by the driver — the twin-chassis Lotus 88 in which the driver

Alain Prost's Renault leading Pironi's Ferrari, De Cesaris' Alfa Romeo, Alboreto's Tyrrell, Rosberg's Williams and Mansell's JPS Lotus through the Casino Square on the opening lap of the 1982 Monaco Grand Prix in pursuit of Arnoux's leading Renault, Giacomelli's Alfa Romeo and Patrese's Brabham. Prost would be in the lead by lap 15 and remain there until three laps from the end, when he spun and crashed into a barrier.

was located in an inner cell isolated from the chassis vibrations — had been declared illegal. The fact that every car with driver-controlled suspension on the starting grid was also known to be illegal seemingly did not matter, and despite subtle modifications to satisfy technical scrutineers, the Lotus, even in its 88B form, was destined never to be seen in anger, which is more than could be said of the man who had inspired this clever and potentially effective design.

Fortunately, by the end of 1981 unanimous agreement between all the teams and constructors had been reached on one point — the 'tip toe' suspensions had to go, although the solid skirts, with some changes of specification and dimension, were to remain, which meant that so too must the rock-hard springing, although the introduction of tie-rod suspension linkages helped to alleviate the driver discomfort to some extent.

Meanwhile, the drivers' voices were beginning to be heard once more. There had been a demonstration on the starting grid in Belgium in 1981 following a fatal accident to a mechanic in the abominably narrow and over-crowded pit road, and at the opening race of the 1982 season in South Africa there had been a comic opera scene as drivers camped out on the floor of a hotel during a dispute over the terms of their new licences until some late-hour telephone diplomacy saved the race from imminent cancellation. These incidents, however, were symptoms of a much deeper and growing resentment that throughout all the political manoeuvring and rule manipulating of the recent past the welfare of the drivers had seemingly been ignored, as had been their collective viewpoint on contentious matters, notably in the areas of safety and comfort.

There had been further painful reminders of the dangers of motor racing, even at its most sophisticated level. In 1980, Clay Regazzoni had suffered that most feared of all accidents — the head-on crash at the end of a high-speed straight; that he had survived at all was testimony to the strength of his Ensign's chassis, but his severe injuries were to leave him paralysed and confined to a wheelchair — a sad end to a colourful and entertaining racing career. That same year, another of Grand Prix racing's most genuine enthusiast-drivers, Patrick Depailler, was to lose his life while testing his Alfa Romeo at Hockenheim, having earlier survived crippling injuries in pursuits outside of motor racing. There had also been some miraculous escapes, including two by Derek Daly, who had stepped out of his Tyrrell at Monaco, and again at Zandvoort, following accidents which so easily could have had tragic results, while John Watson similarly emerged from a McLaren which had been snapped in two at Monza in 1981, such had been the force of its impact into a barrier after running wide on a corner and failing to respond to the driver's corrections — a situation which almost certainly would not have occurred in the days of softer suspensions.

The extreme dangers of having to use qualifying tyres from which optimum performance is obtainable for one lap only, having been warmed up slowly on

Marc Surer moves over to allow Riccardo Patrese and Didier Pironi through in what they believe to be a battle for second place at Monaco. Then came Prost's accident and Patrese's Brabham was in the lead, until it, too, spun and dropped back to third place behind Pironi's Ferrari and De Cesaris' Alfa Romeo. When both of these came to a halt on the very last lap. Patrese was left a bewildered but delighted winner!

the preceding lap, and simultaneously threading a path past other cars which may be running on race rubber, or similarly being cruised prior to their all-out fastest lap, was demonstrated in the most tragic fashion during practice for the 1982 Belgian Grand Prix, when Gilles Villeneuve was flung from his Ferrari and fatally injured after it had run into the back of another car and cartwheeled down the circuit. The Grand Prix world was stunned at the loss of its fastest driver, but once again the outcry against these special-purpose tyres and the unacceptable driving risks which they provoke was to be short-lived, and similar incidents later in the season, happily without such tragic consequences, provided a further reminder that nothing had been done to remove this unnecessary hazard.

Equally worrying were the two high-speed accidents to Didier Pironi during private Ferrari tests, which served to remind everyone of the consequences when the 'seal' of a ground effects car is suddenly broken. The Frenchman was miraculously almost unmarked on each occasion, but his luck was to run out during a wet practice morning at Hockenheim when, blinded by spray, he ran into the back of another car (almost a repeat of the Villeneuve accident) and cartwheeled down the track; he survived, but with leg injuries which would keep him out of racing for at least a year and prevent him from becoming the 1982 World Champion, for which role he had emerged as the odds-on favourite.

Meanwhile, two former World Champions had left the sport through retirement. Jody Scheckter had persevered with his Ferrari during its final

The combination of John Watson and the Marlboro McLaren MP4 was strong enough in 1982 for the Ulsterman to claim joint second place in the World Championship with the injured Didier Pironi. Here Watson is competing in the race at Long Beach, where his new team partner Niki Lauda scored a fine victory in only his third race since his comeback. Watson was to come through the field from 17th on the grid to score a spectacular victory at Detroit later in the year to add to his earlier victory in Belgium.

season with the flat-12 3-litre engine in 1980, had failed to become upset by his car's often disappointing performance, and had raised a laugh after his final race at Watkins Glen by undoing his harness and walking down the nose of his car and out of Grand Prix racing, which now had a new World Champion in Alan Jones.

One year later, Jones, having failed to defend his world title from his successor, Nelson Piquet, despite some heroic driving performances, decided that he, too, would retire to a gentler life, in his case back in his native Austrialia; appropriately, he left the scene after completely dominating his final race at Las Vegas, although he would be back within 17 months in search of a substantial sum of sponsorship money which, he hoped, would end his boredom with life on the farm. The 1981 Las Vegas race had been the one at which, by rights, his Williams team partner Carlos Reutemann, with whom he had spent a frosty season after the Argentinian had ignored team orders to allow the Champion through to victory in Brazil, to become the new World Champion. But Reutemann, who had earlier scored points in a record 14 consecutive races, culminating in a victory in that year's Belgian Grand Prix, had added to his score only four times in the subsequent 10 events, and on the vital day his inability to withstand the psychological pressures, which had so often hampered this naturally talented driver in the past, was again his undoing. He, too, was to retire from racing as a member of Britain's most patriotically motivated GP team, a decision he took abruptly after the second race of the 1982 season; a few weeks later his country was in conflict with Britain over custody of the Falkland Islands.

The retirement of two World Champions in consecutive years had been compensated for by the news, late in 1981, that former double title-holder Niki Lauda was to make a Grand Prix comeback, following a test drive with the Marlboro McLaren team and a characteristically rigorous programme of fitness training overseen by his long-time personal trainer Willi Dungl. Lauda, whose airline business had suffered a number of setbacks, was to be paid a lot of money, as much for his name as for his race-winning potential, which was still in sufficient doubt after a two-year lay-off that he agreed to a break clause in case he proved unable to get the job done on the track. He had been staggered at the harshness of the new breed of car when he first tried the McLaren, but he reckoned that within three races he would have revealed his potential, one way or another. True to his word, he delivered his message in the third race, at Long Beach. He won it; Lauda was back, a little mellower, perhaps, but as skilful as ever and with his brain still in top gear.

A less welcome arrival at this time had been the controversial water-filled ballast tanks, ostensibly to cool brakes, but in fact there in order to bring underweight cars up to the minimum limit at weighing-in time. Their widespread use in Brazil had been challenged, the first two cars home were subsequently disqualified, law suits were threatened, courts of appeal were held, terms of reference of the courts were exceeded, and the upshot was yet another crisis, a boycott of the 1982 San Marino Grand Prix by most of the traditional FOCA teams and an open challenge as to the legality of the turbocharged engine under existing Formula 1 rules. This in turn resulted in yet another court hearing at which, despite a formidable case backed by convincing technical evidence that the turbine of the turbocharger did in fact constitute an additional power source, thereby rendering the complete engine 'oversize', the court ruled that the existing turbos were, indeed, legitimate under the rules.

In the circumstances this was a most unfortunate decision, and one is left to wonder whether, in reaching it, the court had misinterpreted the point at issue. At the time there had been a lot of talk about 'getting the turbos banned', but this was not the case at all. Nobody was trying to get turbocharged engines banned (which was just as well because it was far too late to do anything like that). The case being put was that the equivalence for a turbocharged engine should be different from that of a supercharged engine.

One might have thought that there had been an overwhelming case for the court to have ruled that the $1\frac{1}{2}$-litre equivalency for turbocharged engines had been wrongly allowed and that, whilst the $1\frac{1}{2}$-litre limit for supercharged engines should remain, the limit for turbocharged engines should be adjusted downwards to compensate for the additional power source provided by the turbine, perhaps to 1,200cc, with effect from the 1983 season. Not only would this have reduced the overwhelming power advantage of turbocharged engines over 3-litre normally aspirated power units, but quite possibly it would have restricted their power potential to something close to the 550bhp top limit sought by the FISA. Surely it is still not too late to rectify the sin of neglect which has brought about such an acute case of non-equivalence?

Although Renault had led the way in developing a turbocharged Formula 1 car, it was the appearance of the similarly aspirated Ferrari turbo in 1981 which brought into focus the full potential of this type of power unit. The Renault had won races, but its team had known far more disappointments and it had usually been significantly less of a threat on relatively low-speed circuits than on the faster tracks. It was Villeneuve's victories in Monaco and Spain which provided the rude awakening; the first had been inherited, admittedly, after Jones' Williams had been slowed by an engine misfire, but the Spanish success was earned on a circuit where the traditional turbo lag should have been an insuperable problem. Villeneuve's victory had been the result of sheer driving brilliance, a lot of power and minimal turbo lag out of corners; Ferrari had overcome one of the turbo's fundamental problems in just a few months. However, they had yet to achieve engine reliability, and this, coupled with a spate of accidents, had kept them out of the reckoning for the remainder of the season. Nevertheless, spurred on no doubt by the new opposition within 'their' formula from Italy, Renault also began to make some headway on the throttle-lag problem, as well as to find an improvement in reliability. This was all that the brilliant Alain Prost needed to deliver three victories and one second place from the remaining six European races that season.

Alfa Romeo had signified their intention to produce a V8 turbo for 1982 (although this programme was destined to be delayed by a year), while the Brabham team had concluded an exclusive arrangement with BMW to help develop and race a four-cylinder turbo derivative of their Formula 2 engine, which was demonstrated at the 1981 British Grand Prix, but not raced until 1982. Once the alarming spate of breakages had been reduced during a financially painful period of develop-while-you-race acclimatization, the transfer of the Brabham team from Ford Cosworth to BMW power brought a new dimension to the Grand Prix scene in the form of mid-race refuelling stops, although they were not to contribute to the Brabham-BMW combination's sole 1982 victory in Canada. The potential advantages which

A race winner that might have been. The Saudia Williams team developed this six-wheeled derivative of the 1982 Grand Prix car in the belief that it might provide them with an advantage in the 1983 season, but the change of regulations, including a lower weight limit, dimensional alterations, flat-bottomed chassis and the removal of side skirts, caused the project to be shelved. Keke Rosberg is doing the testing.

the current Formula 1 regulations offered to $1\frac{1}{2}$-litre turbocharged engines, meanwhile, had been sufficient to convince the Toleman team, fresh from their domination of Formula 2 racing, to take this route into Formula 1, but the Hart four-cylinder engine had been hampered excessively by a grossly overweight and aerodynamically inefficient chassis during its first season in 1981, when to qualify just to start a Grand Prix had been an achievement in itself. By mid-1982, however, the team had progressed considerably and were to achieve a magical moment during the British Grand Prix, when Derek Warwick outbraked Pironi's Ferrari to run second for several laps, a performance in which Pirelli, another company to have made a recent entry into Formula 1, also made a contribution with a particularly suitable grade of tyre.

However, at the end of the day it was Niki Lauda and his Marlboro McLaren who brought the DFV success score up to 149 Grand Prix victories, but with Rene Arnoux's Renault first across the finishing line in France a week later and Patrick Tambay restoring Ferrari morale following Pironi's practice accident with a convincing victory in Germany, the scene was set for one of the closest finishes in the history of the current Formula 1 and the race which would mark the next major milestone in the continuing DFV saga.

1982 Austrian Grand Prix

Logically, this race should have been a walkover for one or other of the turbocharged teams, for which the ultra-fast Osterreichring, calling for relatively long periods of full-power fourth and fifth-gear driving, seemed to be tailormade. It certainly seemed that way by the end of practice, during which Nelson Piquet had put in a lap at over 150mph to claim pole position for his Brabham-BMW and Riccardo Patrese had secured the next place on the starting grid with his similar car, in which he had been only a fraction of a second slower. Piquet was more than a second faster than Alain Prost, whose Renault was in third place in the line-up, and the fastest non-turbo, Keke

After five years of endeavour, Renault had brought their latest turbocharged Formula 1 car to a high pitch of development by the end of 1982, by which time Rene Arnoux alone had taken pole position no less than 14 times to underline the speed of his cars, even when they were not always reliable. He was to move to Ferrari in 1983, his place at Renault being taken by Eddie Cheever.

Rosberg's Williams-Ford, was more than $2\frac{1}{2}$ seconds slower than Piquet's car and down in sixth place behind the Brabhams, the Renaults and Tambay's lone Ferrari. Only the two Tolemans, hampered by a variety of problems during practice, prevented all the turbo cars from filling the front of the grid, but they, too, were destined to come charging through the field during the first few laps.

Once again, however, mechanical fragility would enter the equation and provide one of the biggest upsets of form of the year and an epic last lap which will linger long in the memory. The early stages of the race were entirely predictable as the two Brabhams shot off into the lead, aided by a light fuel load, Piquet being ahead for the first lap, then being passed by Patrese, the two of them intent on building the maximum possible advantage before making their routine refuelling stops.

Meanwhile, Tambay was already in trouble. At the start there had been trouble in the middle of the grid when the two Alfa Romeos had cannoned into each other and one of them had slewed across into Daly's Williams, all three cars being retired on the spot. Marshals did their best to clear the track of wreckage, but as the field came through at the end of the lap Tambay's Ferrari picked up some debris and punctured a tyre. A slow drive back to the pits and the resulting stop put him more than a lap in arrears and effectively out of contention, although a storming drive back through the field would lift him to a meritorious fourth place at the finish.

Within five laps the two Tolemans were up into sixth and seventh places behind Elio De Angelis' Lotus, which was leading the Ford-powered runners, Rosberg having dropped back a little with a Williams that was not handling at all well with its full fuel load. Both the Tolemans, however, were out of the race two laps later, one with a broken suspension and the other with transmission failure. So now there were only four turbocharged runners remaining with any effective chance, the two Brabhams ahead of the two Renaults. Then, with 15 of the 53 laps completed, Arnoux's Renault came to a halt from fourth place with a broken turbo, which elevated De Angelis and Rosberg to fourth and fifth places, respectively.

Two laps later, Piquet, who had dropped well behind Patrese, brought his second-placed Brabham into the pits several laps earlier than expected and it was refuelled. But Piquet also complained of blistered tyres, which were changed, and the extra delay dropped him to fourth place. Furthermore, after rejoining the race behind De Angelis, it was significant that he was unable to close in on and pass the Lotus. Meanwhile, Patrese continued to increase his margin until he came in for his scheduled refuelling stop after 24 laps, and he was still in first place as he rejoined the circuit ahead of Prost.

The Renault closed right up behind the Brabham as Patrese drove steadily for the first lap or two to warm up his fresh tyres, then the gap increased again. It looked to be all over, but suddenly the leading Brabham locked up its rear wheels and spun backwards off the track and into a tall banking protecting a spectator area. Patrese's race was over and Prost was now comfortably in first place. Thereon, the race became a procession, enlivened only by activity further down the field, such as Tambay's fighting comeback and a hard-charging run by Brian Henton, who had brought his Tyrrell up into sixth place on Patrese's exit, and had then inherited fifth place on lap 32 when Piquet's Brabham expired with a broken engine. But seconds later Henton, too, was out of the race for a similar reason.

By now, Rosberg's Williams, running with a lighter fuel load, was handling much better, and the Finn had been gradually reducing the large gap which had grown between his car and De Angelis' Lotus during the first half of the race. With Pironi out of action, the Finn was now a serious contender for the Championship, and second place was two points more attractive than third. There could be no question of catching Prost, however, who was driving a lonely race at the head of a field that by this time had been depleted to seven cars, Watson having retired his McLaren with a sick engine nine laps from the end.

Then suddenly, with just over five laps to go, a belch of flame blew out of the back of the Renault as Prost freewheeled to a halt on the circuit with fuel injection failure. Apart from Tambay's Ferrari, still a lap behind in fourth place behind Jacques Laffite's Ligier, all the turbos had gone, and a Ford DFV race was on between De Angelis and Rosberg. Whereas the Italian driver's Lotus had been performing perfectly for much of the race, now, just when he needed all the help he could find to fend off Rosberg's hard charge in the highly competitive Williams, he was encountering the first symptoms of fuel starvation. With three laps to go, only 3 seconds separated the two cars. The next time round the gap was down to $2\frac{1}{2}$ seconds, and as they entered their final lap the stopwatch showed only a fraction over $1\frac{1}{2}$ seconds separating them. By

Against all the odds, Keke Rosberg's determination and flair was to be rewarded with the 1982 World Championship in his Saudia Williams FW08, despite the seemingly decisive power superiority of the turbos. Here he is making sure of the title in the car park circuit at Caesar's Palace, Las Vegas.

now, shortage of fuel was causing De Angelis' engine to stammer intermittently, and a mile from the finishing line the two cars were almost nose-to-tail. All De Angelis could do from this point on was to keep a cool head, drive an immaculate line, and ensure that if Rosberg was to get by he would have to take the wide line around the outside of him. The Finn knew that this would be impossible through the long, banked, downhill right-hander leading on to the finish straight so he tucked in behind, tried to get a tow down the hill, then moved out of the Lotus airstream to slip alongside as they raced for the line. Each driver was fighting for his first Grand Prix victory, but that day in Austria it was Elio De Angelis who was to take the centre spot on the winner's rostrum after a winning margin of barely a car's length (Rosberg's turn would come just two weeks later, at Dijon).

It was both tidy and appropriate that the Ford DFV's 150th Grand Prix success should have been recorded by the team which had given the engine its very first success a full 15 years earlier, and for which the DFV had been conceived in the first place. It was fitting, too, that Colin Chapman, who had contributed so much to the conception of the engine, should have had the opportunity on this milestone occasion to fling his cap in the air one more time in his characteristic salute to his winning driver; four months later he would die of a heart attack, and the entire racing world would be stunned.

De Angelis' victory on that hot, dry day in Austria had been the first for the Lotus team for four years, and although it had been against all reasonable odds it had been a reminder that, 15 years on, the DFV was still a potential race-winner, even on a circuit where it had 'no chance'. Furthermore, it would go on to power the winner of two of the remaining three Grands Prix of 1982 and then — after a winter of intensive development into a new short-stroke DFY configuration — it would meet yet another new challenge against the intriguing backcloth of revised Formula 1 regulations calling for the use of flat-bottomed chassis and the removal of side skirts, changes which promised to prolong even further the remarkable career of this outstanding engine.

A smiling Colin Chapman with the JPS Lotus 91, the car which a few months later he would watch score a photo-finish victory in the Austrian Grand Prix in the hands of Elio De Angelis to record the 150th Grand Prix success for the Ford DFV engine and his team's first victory for four seasons. It would be the last opportunity for him to fling his cap in the air in his characteristic victory salute. He died of a heart attack four months later.

1983 and after: A short-stroke strategy

As the 1982 season drew to a close, and despite the fact that the efforts to secure a more appropriate equivalency factor between normally aspirated and turbocharged engines had been unsuccessful, sufficient faith in the future of the Ford DFV engine was being shown amongst several teams for Cosworth Engineering to embark upon a further major development programme.

It was a courageous decision, because 1983 looked as though it would be the most difficult year yet for 3-litre normally aspirated engines, even though the change of chassis regulations, and notably the insistence upon flat-bottomed chassis and no side skirts, suggested that it would be considerably more difficult to put the power down on to the track and that therefore drivers with turbocharged engines might well be unable to use all the power that would be at their disposal.

In the short term, the big obstacle looked to be the acceptance of mid-race refuelling stops as a feature of Grand Prix racing, although this facility was scheduled to be withdrawn at the end of the 1983 season. During 1982 the Brabham team had demonstrated that a set of wheels could be changed and sufficient fuel added for half a race in little more than 12 seconds, and that even if one doubled that time to allow for slowing down and accelerating away again, the advantage in starting on 'sticky' tyres with half-full tanks, then taking on fresh rubber in mid-race, far outweighed the time deficit. It also meant that an excessive rate of fuel consumption was no longer a serious limiting factor.

Only in 1984, when cars would be required to run through a race non-stop and when the limit on fuel tankage would be lowered from 250 litres to 220 litres (to be followed in 1985 by a further reduction to 195 litres) would the full benefit of the most efficient use of fuel be available again to teams in Formula 1 racing.

In plotting the direction of their development programme, therefore, Cosworth had to have regard for the longer-term opportunities, even though it was hoped that customers would derive certain more immediate benefits once the first products of the programme became available in the early part of 1983.

Although high on the list of priorities was the construction of a shorter-stroke version of the engine, as part of the build-up of the programme it was decided to investigate the performance of an alternative camshaft to the DA1 which had been fitted to the DFV engine for so many years. The experimental camshaft, which carries the designation DA12, has a lift of 0.460in, compared with the 0.410in of the DA1, and the angle of the slope is also slightly steeper. When the first encouraging results on the test rig were confirmed in subsequent tests the DA12 was passed into production and has become part of a conversion kit offered to DFV users. Prior to the development of the DA12 camshaft, certain outside DFV builders had been experimenting with their own camshafts along broadly similar lines, but the availability of the DA12 has meant that most of these companies have switched back to Cosworth shafts.

Simultaneously with the camshaft development, Keith Duckworth decided that it would be useful to re-examine the windage of his DFV crankcase with a view to improving the oil scavenging performance and thereby reducing power losses, and in the course of this investigation it transpired that oil was being collected through only one part of the collection slots which had been provided for it, due to an aerodynamic phenomenon within the crankcase. When revised slots were designed and fitted into the case to compensate for this the oil collection performance improved dramatically and several additional horsepower were found as a bonus.

This discovery came about at a time when development of the DFY short-stroke derivative of the DFV was well under way, and it was hoped that the provision of similar new collection slots would offer the same sort of advantage on the new engine. However, this proved not to be the case, and different oil collection arrangements have had to be provided on the short-stroke engine.

The development of the DFY was initiated with two separate programmes running in parallel, involving different cylinder heads. Various bore and

John Watson and Niki Lauda scored a decisive first 1983 victory for the DFV engine by finishing first and second at Long Beach in their Marlboro McLaren MP4/1Cs after starting in 22nd and 23rd places on the grid, an effort which even surpassed Watson's 1982 performance at Detroit.

The first short-stroke DFY engines were delivered in time for the 1983 French Grand Prix, where Niki Lauda, John Watson and Nigel Mansell used them for the first time on the second day of qualifying; all three remarked that their engine felt rather like a particularly good DFV. Apart from the Ford 'ovals' cast into the cam covers, only the painted letters inboard of the rear intake trumpets identifies this as a DFY.

Keke Rosberg and his Saudia Williams FW08C on the new Spa-Francorchamps circuit, which was to host the Belgian Grand Prix for the first time since 1970. The short side pods had proved to be a popular solution by chassis designers to concentrate as much weight as possible towards the rear of the car under the new Formula 1 regulations.

stroke configurations were considered, but in the interests of obtaining a generous valve area it was decided to opt for the 90mm cylinder bore of the 3.95-litre DFL engine in conjunction with a piston stroke of 58.8mm to bring the engine within the 3-litre displacement limit.

The first DFY engines to appear in public were built with cylinder heads the general layout of which followed that of the DFV heads, although in fact the castings were different and the DFY head involved a certain amount of additional machining, notably in the enlargement of the inlet and exhaust ports, as well as some critical extra hand fettling. This head design allows the use of the 1.25in diameter exhaust valves as fitted to later versions of the DFV, but it has been possible to increase the diameter of the inlet valves to 1.42in.

The first DFY engines were to be delivered equipped with Cosworth BD4 inlet camshafts, offering a lift of 0.432in, and DA10 exhaust camshafts, which have a lift of 0.410in and have been widely used in both sports car racing and hill-climb/sprint events, installed in either DFV or DFL engines, and have also had an application in the DFX. Being based on the DFV layout, of course, the valves in this head are angled at 16 degrees.

There was to be no dramatic difference between the performance of the first DFY and that of a fully modified DFV (with the latest cylinder head and crankcase modifications), nor had one been expected. The intention had been to achieve a gain throughout the full rev range rather than to search for maximum top-end power. Although Cosworth have always been most conservative in their power claims, if one takes a figure of 495bhp as being a typical output of a DFV in 1982, the between-seasons changes at the top and bottom ends probably found an additional 15bhp, while the first DFYs came to the line with around 520bhp (the official claim was an improvement of 4 per cent over an advanced-specification DFV). However, the advantages of the DFY run much deeper than that: a combination of a shorter exhaust system and intake trumpets, the use of magnesium alloy for various components, including the inlet manifold and the water pump, plus various head modifications, contribute to an overall weight reduction of 44lb, from 351lb to 307lb.

The first four DFY engines to this specification were delivered just prior to the French Grand Prix — the third of the 1983 World Championship races — two of them going to the Marlboro McLaren and one each to the JPS Lotus and Saudia Williams teams. Frank Williams elected to hold his back for testing, but John Watson and Niki Lauda had their first taste of DFY power in their McLarens and Nigel Mansell sampled the new engine in his Lotus on the Paul Ricard circuit. However, none of these drivers was destined to finish that

The turbos were well on top for the San Marino Grand Prix at Imola, where Patrick Tambay was to score a popular victory in Ferrari number 27. This was the number which Gilles Villeneuve had carried on his car in 1982, when a seemingly certain victory for him at Imola, in what was to prove to be his last Grand Prix, was snatched from him by Didier Pironi in the other Ferrari.

The Ford DFY engine in the second stage of its development with narrow-angle cylinder heads incorporating integral cam carriers. The scavenge and centrifuge oil pumps are compactly packaged towards the front of the engine, these slimline auxiliaries having been produced for fitment to the DFV at the height of the ground effects period of Formula 1 technology. Water is transferred to this side of the DFY through the sump.

race, and the DFY's first result was to come two weeks later, when John Watson came through from 24th place on the grid to finish fifth in the San Marino Grand Prix at Imola, Italy, after another of his characteristic drives through the field.

Meanwhile, the second DFY cylinder head design had been signed off for production at Northampton, with the hope that the first DFYs equipped with these heads might be supplied prior to the Monaco Grand Prix. Unlike the earlier DFY head, this was a completely new and radically different design, offering both a further weight saving and the possibility of greater longer-term development potential. Engine designers seem to hold conflicting views as to the relative merits of different valve angles and combustion chamber shapes, but the Cosworth design team felt that there were certain advantages to be derived from a more compact shape of combustion chamber than was possible when the short-stroke dimensions were combined with the 16-degree valve angle. Accordingly, this alternative head has its inlet valves angled at 10 degrees and its exhaust valves at $12\frac{1}{2}$ degrees. Another significant change from

the earlier designs of DFV and DFY head is that the narrow-angle version incorporates an integral cam carrier and this has contributed towards a further saving in weight of 15lb, bringing the figure for the DFY in this form down to an impressive 292lb.

The programme allows for the further development of the DFY in both versions to be continued during 1983, and it is not anticipated that there will be any significant variation in the power output between the two versions in the short term. Only if and when an advantage of some magnitude is confirmed by one version over the other is it likely that subsequent development work will be confined to that more receptive version.

After the Ford Cosworth family of Formula 1 engines have run their last race and it is possible to look back over the whole spectrum of their achievements, it may well be considered that the short-stroke development programmes initiated during 1982 were the most beneficial to the engines' future career prospects of any since the time when Keith Duckworth designed his ingenious quill shafts as a means of protecting the DFV's gear train from

The only water pump on the DFY (and later DFVs) is located on the left side of the engine with the oil pressure pump and filter housing located immediately behind it. Note the use of twin small Ford 'ovals' on the magnesium covers of the narrow-angle DFY, which has its inlet valves at 10 degrees and its exhaust valves at 12½ degrees to the cylinder axis. This was the first customer engine to this specification to be completed, and it was photographed in the early hours of May 14, 1983.

Considerable use of magnesium has been made in the construction of the narrow-angle version of the DFY, including the front covers for the block and cylinder heads and the cam covers as well as the intake manifolds and the water pump. Shorter intake trumpets are matched to a shorter exhaust system and the overall weight saving means that this is the first Cosworth V8 racing engine to scale less than 300lb. Power output is in excess of 520bhp.

bad vibrations. Some 17 years after that engine's impressive debut at Zandvoort, perhaps it is too late to expect that, even in DFY form, it could ever again enjoy the level of superiority it had once known, but as John Watson was able to prove at Long Beach in March 1983 when he added DFV victory number 153, the V8 engine which had been conceived with a £100,000 handshake, a mountain of faith and a formidable armoury of design brilliance was still a mighty useful power unit with which to go Grand Prix racing.

CHAPTER 4

Living with a DFV

The cost of competitiveness

The vast majority of users of the Ford DFV engine will admit that the experience has been, in the main, a highly successful one, in both financial terms and as regards race results. Indeed, had it not been for the existence of the DFV, most of them would probably have dropped out of Formula 1 long ago, or would not have been able to become involved in it in the first place. Ken Tyrrell, for one, makes no bones about it — it was the DFV which made it possible for him to enter the world of Grand Prix racing.

'When I went to Zandvoort in 1967 it was purely as a spectator. I thought I would like to see the engine run in its first race, but I had no intention of getting into Formula 1 myself — I didn't think such a thing would be possible. Then, of course, the engine was so impressive that on the way home I started thinking — if we could only get our hands on that, there must be a way for us to go Formula 1 racing.'

Ever since he became one of the engine's first customers, Tyrrell has maintained excellent relations with Cosworth Engineering and during Jackie Stewart's years with the team, in particular, there was very close liaison between Northampton and the Tyrrell headquarters in Ockham, Surrey. 'We never became involved with Cosworth on engine development, at least, not in the strictest sense. The only work we did, from time to time, was to run the odd engine which happened to have some non-standard bits in it, although we didn't know it at the time.

'Cosworth have always been very good in this respect. If they wanted to try out something which they thought would be an improvement they would build it into a customer's engine, but they would never tell the customer about it. If it happened to break they would say something like, "Oh, well, one of those things", but more than likely it worked, and so the customer would find that he had a particularly good engine, though he wouldn't know it contained anything special. There was one period — I can't remember which year it was — when we seemed to have an extra special engine from Cosworth. They never told us we had it, we only knew that the car always seemed to go better when we slipped that particular engine in it. At no time did they even hint that it might be a good idea to use it in Stewart's car, and we could easily have put it to one side and simply used it for testing, in which case we wouldn't have known it was much better than normal. It was only a long time afterwards that we discovered, quite by accident, that it was something special!'

There were two reasons why Ken Tyrrell seemed to be a particularly appropriate person with whom to discuss the DFV from an operator's viewpoint; Stewart had an almost obsessive appetite for testing, and while he was part of it the Tyrrell team probably covered far more miles per year than any other user of the Ford engine, while in the more recent past, during the period when the team lacked a major sponsor and money was very tight, it was necessary to run engines for a far greater mileage between overhauls than would normally have been deemed prudent. In both these situations, therefore, the DFV was being severely tested.

'Throughout our experience with the DFV there has been one persistent problem, and that's valve springs. If we have failures at all they tend to be caused by a valve spring breaking and a valve dropping in. There has been no consistent pattern. We may get a failure on one engine at, say, 200 miles, and then we'll have another which we run for several times that distance with no trouble at all. Back in 1981, when we were so short of money, we were regularly running our engines up to around 900 miles instead of their normal 500 to 600 between overhauls. Of course, the engines would lose a bit of power, but you could still test with them. I remember one day while we were doing some testing Jackie Oliver strolled across from the Arrows team and we got talking about engines, and I mentioned that the car we were running that day had an engine with more than 1,000 miles on it. I don't think he believed me then, and I'm not sure he believes me even now, but that engine went on to cover 1,100 miles before we took it out and sent it away for overhaul.'

Ken Tyrrell's sensitivity to valve spring troubles is, perhaps, understandable bearing in mind that in his very first race as a Formula 1 entrant, the 1968 South African Grand Prix, it was a dropped valve which stopped Jackie Stewart when he was running second to Jim Clark's Lotus. Valves have been dropped, off and on, ever since, and inevitably the chances of encountering this problem are inherently greater with a rev-limiter set at 11,300rpm than in the days when the engine ran to little more than 9,000rpm. 'This is why I'm inclined to give Keith some stick over dropping his desmodromic programme', says Tyrrell. 'I know there were some unforeseen problems, and it was obviously going to be a lot more difficult than they thought it would be, but if they'd been able to overcome the problems we'd be running the engine to 12,000rpm today.'

Although there is no conclusive evidence that valve spring weakness stems from a spring being depressed for a long time — it is almost certainly due to some sort of frequency problem causing excitement of the valve gear — the Tyrrell team are not alone in making sure that any engine not in use has its crankshaft turned once every week, an odd number of revolutions, so that the previously compressed springs can be relaxed. On the other hand, a great deal can be done by drivers, if not to eliminate the cause of the trouble, at least to limit its consequences, by having the necessary feel and sensitivity to detect a problem in time. Much will depend upon whether it is an inlet or an exhaust valve, an inner or an outer spring, but a driver with an acute ear and a delicate feel, like a Stewart or an Alboreto to quote two outstanding examples, will know immediately a valve spring has gone and will shut off, whereas others with less feel may well fail to know that anything is wrong until it all goes

'bang'. If they fail to sense the different engine note when the valve is fluffing up and down because only the inner spring is left to try to close it, eventually the head will drop off into the combustion space, the rod and piston will come up and hit it, the piston will break, the rod will go through the side of the block and the repair bill will be a cool £18,000 or thereabouts! Ken Tyrrell had a particularly black weekend in Belgium in 1982 when his bill for two engines badly damaged in the race was £33,000, over and above the normal cost of wear and tear during practice.

Nevertheless, by Formula 1 standards, a DFV team's engine purchase, maintenance, rebuild and replacement costs over a full season, barring any exceptional circumstances, tend to be anything but excessive. One reason for this is the relatively high retained value of a carefully and regularly maintained engine, which has been a considerable encouragement to teams to buy new and trade on at regular intervals. Early in 1982, for example, when the cost of a new DFV was £26,185, a year-old Cosworth-maintained power unit was commanding between £15,000 and £16,000, a figure which, in turn, enabled the less well financed teams to replace their earlier-specification engines with the relatively young examples built to a later specification. At the height of the ground effects era there was a further encouragement to 'trade up' because the cost of converting an earlier engine to one incorporating the full set of slimline auxiliaries was in the region of £3,000.

Its task completed, this Ford DFV has been stripped out of its chassis, still with its exhaust primaries in place, and will be returned for a routine rebuild, an operation which usually involves about 130 man-hours of work at Northampton. Teams keep an accurate record of the mileage of every engine and normally plan for a rebuild at approximately 500 miles, although DFVs have been known to travel more than twice as far on occasions.

Cosworth Engineering have calculated that the average cost to their customers for a routine engine strip-down, inspection, rebuild and bench test is approximately £5,000, a figure which includes both labour and parts and also takes into account the occasional blow-up which, as indicated earlier, can be extremely expensive. A classic example, during the winter of 1980-81, concerned an engine which had been run without water for such a long time that virtually everything was cooked, and as a result it was only possible to salvage just a few of the ancillary pieces. Cosworth submitted a quote for what amounted to almost a new engine — the cylinder block, heads, cams, crankshaft, rods, pistons and one cam carrier all had to be replaced — and the customer gave the go-ahead in the knowledge that he would end up with the equivalent of a brand new engine for about £19,000, several thousand pounds under the current list price. This, however, was a very exceptional case, and Cosworth say that these days there is a very low incidence of self-inflicted injuries on engines operated by the teams they service.

Inevitably, the life of components has varied considerably over the years as additional stresses brought about by increases in power output have been countered by improvements in the specification of the individual parts. Pistons, for example, are usually run for between 500 and 600 racing miles, then changed at the engine's routine rebuild, as are valve springs. The valves themselves, on the other hand, may well last for four or five races, while a set of spring retainers could cover seven or eight races before they need replacing. An engine could go through a full racing season on the same set of bearings, while the small-end bushes will probably last the life of the rods.

Every properly run racing team will keep a meticulously accurate record of

Every DFV returned to Cosworth ends up on the dynamometer after a routine rebuild. Provided the performance figures are satisfactory there will be a final look inside the engine before it is signed off for return to the customer.

the life of each of their engines since its last rebuild and will tend to have a favoured routine for the use of their engines over its planned mileage, although this routine can differ considerably from one team to another. One popular scheme is to slip a new engine into a car after the final timed practice on the eve of a Grand Prix. The new engine will then be used for the morning warm-up and the race itself, and if it is still performing well it will remain in the car for the two days of practice prior to the next race, after which it will be hauled out and replaced with a fresh one during the overnight strip-down and reassembly of the car.

Another theory is that you need a new engine for the second day's practice, with the intention of keeping it in the car for the race and then, perhaps, using it for a spot of testing before it goes for its next rebuild. A third routine, which the Tyrrell team have been known to favour, is to make an engine change between the untimed and the timed practice periods on the eve of the race, the engine being that much fresher for the race than it might have been had it been used for the first, untimed practice on the previous day.

When an engine is returned to Northampton for a routine strip and rebuild, the engineers there will want to know its mileage, the maximum revs to which it has been subjected, whether its temperatures were normal and — if possible — its oil consumption. There will be a file card on that particular engine which will contain precise details of its specification and its history to date — a vital source of information, especially if its specification has undergone any changes since it was supplied new, as is most likely to be the case. Even in the case of a major rebuild involving a majority of replacement parts, such as the aforementioned £19,000 job, an engine will retain its original number — only the information on its index card will change. It can be seen, therefore, that Cosworth will have supplied a considerable number of 'broomheads' and 'handles' over the years, and consequently the number of engines which have been produced in component form exceeds by quite a margin the output of complete engines for which an official DFV number has been allocated.

Originally, all DFV rebuilding work was carried out by Cosworth Engineering, but as the number of engines in use increased and it became impossible to handle all the customer work involved, alternative arrangements had to be made and Cosworth appointed six outside UK companies as officially authorized engine rebuilders, plus one overseas, to whom all components are made available under normal trade conditions. The arrangement has been confined to the seven firms concerned in order to protect their investment in their own rebuilding facilities, although at the time of writing DFV rebuilding work has also become available elsewhere. At the beginning of 1983, the Arrows, Ligier, Lotus, Tyrrell and Williams teams were all having at least some of their stock of DFV engines maintained at St James' Mill Road.

Cosworth normally plan to carry out six DFV rebuilds per Grand Prix, which means a typical annual throughput of some 110 engines counting off-season work. A little over half of the average £5,000 bill will be accounted for by replacement parts — this figure appearing to be considerably lower than the typical cost of materials charged by the majority of outside rebuilders. Conversely, the invoice for a Cosworth rebuild is likely to contain a proportionately higher charge for labour, and the management at Northampton are fairly confident that they devote something in excess of 30 extra man-hours to their in-house rebuilds. It may well be that much of the additional time is spent on inspection and testing, and that this results in a lower materials cost, for nothing is ever replaced unnecessarily.

A typical engine rebuild will account for about 80 hours of an engine builder's own time, to which must be added something like 50 hours by other personnel engaged in stripping down, crack-testing, inspection and specialist services, including those concerned with ancillary equipment, which is always handled by a specialist. Most of this work takes place on the premises, although Cosworth's attention to the ignition system is confined in the main to inspection and testing, both before and after installation on the rebuilt engine; if anything fundamental is amiss on the ignition side the faulty component will be returned to the manufacturer.

It is a full day's work just to strip an engine, and every single component — and that includes every nut and bolt — is washed and scrutinized closely. Only the pistons and valve springs are discarded as a matter of routine. The visual inspection, by a highly experienced engineer, constitutes one of the most vital parts of the whole operation, and it is difficult to put a true value on a pair of highly trained eyes, backed up by a set of sensitive and educated fingers, plus years of personal experience of the DFV's most subtle characteristics and idiosyncracies. Minute particles of metal lodged in a filter, a slight change in the colour or consistency of the deposit on a piston, a miniscule irregularity to the surface of a bearing shell — discernible to the touch though not, probably, to the eye — a slight variation in a bolt's thread formation — these are the sort of tell-tale signs from which the talented inspector can assess with great accuracy the condition of an engine and its component parts and learn so much about its recent history as regards use and abuse. What the eye cannot see, of course, crack-detection equipment may well identify, and this, therefore, is the logical next phase in the strip-and-rebuild procedure.

As far as is practicable, ancillary equipment is refurbished in-house, along with the engine itself, and the combined alternator, distributor and metering unit alone accounts for some four hours of the labour content of a DFV rebuild. It is at the reassembly stage that one of the engine's greatest virtues is most deeply appreciated. This is its foundation on such fine tolerances, a quality which not only has assured such accurate fit of components but has also made the engine so comfortable to work on from an engineering standpoint. Things tend to go together first time.

In rebuilding the engine great care is taken to match and balance components, and consequently at the strip-down stage all parts will have been marked for reassembly in the same pairs or sets. If replacement parts are introduced, they will be selected for their compatability with those to be re-used. A tolerance of only 1 gram is allowed within a set of pistons or connecting rods, for example. These days, the bottom end of a DFV is reckoned to be so tough as to be virtually 'bombproof', but every engine can only be as good, ultimately, as its life support systems, which is why meticulous attention is paid to the refurbishing of ancillary equipment as a matter of routine, the oil pumps alone being the subject of up to eight hours of labour during an engine rebuild. These are complicated mechanisms involving many very small component parts, each of which has to be examined meticulously after stripping and cleaning. Castings are crack-tested, rotors and seals are replaced with new items which have to be matched precisely to their housings,

One of the engine assembly shops at Northampton. Cylinder blocks are carried on tubular steel cradles during the assembly process and components are brought into the shop on shelved trolleys.

and after reassembly there is the rig test, which must be passed before the pumps are ready for the rebuilt engine.

The last four of the 130 hours or so spent on a DFV rebuild at Northampton take place in one of the dynamometer cells, where the engine will be put through its full test routine and its power and bmep, or torque, figures recorded. The yardstick of satisfaction at this stage is not the peak figure achieved briefly over a narrow rev range — something that in another company might be seized upon for publicity purposes — but rather the shape of the curves and their overall quality. Significantly, the talk in Northampton, when the subject of power output is raised, is more likely to be about 'a minimum of . . .' rather than 'we have seen as much as . . .', and appropriately so because what really matters is an engine's total usable power (and torque) over a measured distance, be it a lap (for practice), the length of a Grand Prix, or the full 500 miles between routine rebuilds. Even if the figures on the dynamo are satisfactory the work is still not over. Before the engine can be signed off for return to the customer there is the 'look inside', a final detailed examination to ensure that nothing untoward happened to the valve gear, in the combustion chambers or around the bores during the test. The slightest suspicion, and there will be another strip-down, rectification, reassembly and retest.

Of course, after such meticulous care at every stage in the operation — and an appropriately hefty bill to pay for the devotion and expertize — it is vital that the customer should do nothing to devalue his asset once it has been returned to him. To this end, Cosworth Engineering supply written advice covering both the installation and the operation of the DFV and its derivatives, for water, oil and fuel systems. However, not all teams seem to follow this advice, and some of them pay the penalty for failing to do so.

It has been known for a team to blow up as many as three engines before admitting that the cause was not with the engine builder but with the design of their own oil tanks. Sometimes teams feel they have to make compromises because they are short of space or they are desperate to save weight, so perhaps they alter the method of returning the oil to the tank, or they reroute their fuel system and suffer an occasional misfire, or perhaps they overheat their metering unit because they have cased in their engine too much in the search for ultimate ground effects. These are the sort of things which the leading teams work strenuously to avoid and, perhaps, with their greater rescources, they are better placed to do so.

In an effort to counteract the power advantage of the $1\frac{1}{2}$-litre turbocharged engines there has been an understandable campaign amongst DFV users to reduce the weight of cars to the absolute minimum, and this has led to a widespread adoption of much smaller oil tanks than used to be the norm. Generally, this has worked satisfactorily, but with the reduced capacity great care has to be taken in filling the system and there have been cases of teams, after having made a rapid engine change before a Grand Prix, running into trouble. They couple up the plumbing with the oil pipes still full of air, they then fill the tank, do a couple of laps in the hope of getting rid of the air, then line up on the grid, believing that all is well. But there is still air in the system, and as this is purged out early in the race the oil level drops in the tank, which then may be only two-thirds full. As oil is consumed the level becomes dangerously low and under surge conditions the tank pickup becomes uncovered and takes a big gulp of air, after which there is liable to be a loud bang, because no system can be expected to live under those conditions.

The rapid engine change is forever the bugbear of racing mechanics, which is why the DFV received such a warm welcome amongst paddock personnel, who quickly came to appreciate the convenience not only of its basic concept as a bolt-on extension to the main chassis, but also of its neat packaging, which ensured that it was so much easier to work on in confined spaces and in

Nigel Mansell on his way to fourth place in the 1981 Caesar's Palace Grand Prix in his JPS Lotus 87, the all-enveloping bodywork of which is in marked contrast to the open-ended car which first carried the DFV engine 14 years earlier. As Lotus Chief Mechanic Bob Dance remarks, much of the time taken to change an engine these days is spent stripping off all the panels and ducts in order to reach the engine, then reassembling everything after the engine change.

otherwise less than ideal conditions.

Bob Dance, who leads the Lotus team of mechanics, has lived with the DFV for most of its life and recalls, perhaps just a little wistfully, the ultra-simplicity of working on the DFV's first car, the Lotus 49. 'It was such a simple construction. You could simply pick up this V8 engine with its four mounting points on the front and plug it straight into the monocoque, and at that time, when we were using the ZF gearbox, the arrangement with the bellhousing of the ZF meant that you could plug the gearbox straight on to the engine. It was so simple and straightforward it was unbelievable.

'There was no more bother with taking sections of tubular chassis out in order to get the engine in or out, it was just a case of taking off the gearbox, the rear wheels and the rear suspension as a lump, then the engine as another lump, hop in a new one, and away you went. It has stayed much the same way throughout its life, of course, but the trouble is that the cars have become so much more complicated with the introduction of wide bodies, aerodynamics, skirts and things, that all the paraphernalia of the current cars is now hidden in the bodywork or the aerodynamic underpods. The result of all this is that what was once a quick and simple engine change is now a relatively complicated operation; you've got to dismantle the car before you can get at the engine and all the piping, plumbing, rods and linkages, and it is the dismantling of the undertrays, side boards, skirts (while we had them) and ducts, and later the reassembling of all these things, which has added to the time required for an engine change, as well as to its complexity.'

Nevertheless, even with the relative complication of the recent generation of Grand Prix cars, some remarkably quick engine changes are still being achieved with the DFV, often under very difficult circumstances, as Bob Dance recalls. 'I think our most dramatic engine change was with Andretti in Argentina. We had an engine go in the Sunday morning warm-up, which meant that we had about an hour-and-a-half from the time it exploded to when we had to have the car rolling again. We did it, but only just, and we had to send Mario out just before the pit road was closed in a car which was minus its skirts and some of the bodywork, then we finished off the job on the grid. It was close!'

It was very heartening for Bob Dance and his crew to get Andretti back in the race that day because the atmosphere at the track was incredibly hot and humid — just the conditions in which mistakes are most likely to be made. It is during moments of stress, of course, that the skill and ingenuity of a top racing mechanic is often most clearly revealed. Such an example was to be seen in Belgium around 1974, after one of the Lotus mechanics had had the misfortune to cross a thread in the top of the metering unit, and Bob Dance had to come to the rescue.'Once again the drama came just before the race, and there was just no time to change the unit. We had to try something, however desperate, to get the car into the race, so I decided the only way to get the thread uncrossed was to stick a tap in it. So I wound this tap into the top of the unit, and of course bits of swarf were coming off and going all over the place, but somehow we managed to prevent them from going in any of the wrong places, and to our intense relief we soon had a runner again. I suppose you could call that a fairly rare attack, and Brabham's Gordon Murray, who watched it happening, told me that it was just about the strangest thing he'd ever seen us do and get away with!'

Just as with an aircraft the most critical time is during takeoff (or landing), so with a racing engine it is during start-up, especially in cold weather, when considerable damage can be caused unless proper precautions are taken. The Ford DFV is no different from any other highly sophisticated Formula 1 engine in this respect, and teams have developed routines for painless start-ups, based on the Cosworth rules which are incorporated in some six pages of advice on installing and operating the DFV, but often added to in the light of experience. None is more painstaking, surely, than the routine which Ken Tyrrell and his team have developed over the years.

'You have to remember that one of the problems with a racing engine is that, if it is operating in a cold climate, when you start it up for the first time the scavenge pump will take a big gulp of cold oil and be put under too much load. Now to prevent failure of the pump under these conditions Cosworth have provided a clutch drive so that if there is any overload — which, of course, can equally be caused by some foul material entering the pump — the clutch will slip and ultimately, if anything has to fail, it will be the clutch drive which gives way. Of course, if the pump stops scavenging, the engine will quickly fill up with oil and the next thing you know it's blowing oil out of all the breathers. So, if we have to leave a car overnight, or test in very cold conditions such as in winter at Ricard in a strong wind, we leave a heater underneath the engine so that whatever oil is in the sump, which would otherwise be cold and thick, gets warmed and thinned out.

'Another potential trouble spot is the metering unit, which has very fine clearances — measured in microns — and on a number of occasions in the past we've started the engine up in cold weather and the metering unit has picked up and seized, with the result that it's twisted the quill shaft, which means that you've lost your injector timing. Then, of course, you've got to do an engine change. So we've learned to cope with that by dowsing it; we boil up water before we start an engine from cold and pour the water over the metering unit. We do this all the year round — summer and winter — because we've had this trouble when we wouldn't normally expect it to happen. It may seem a crude solution, but it's effective.'

Bob Dance is also very careful to protect the metering unit before starting up in very cold weather, to prevent it from seizing. 'We like to throw a cover over the back of the car and use a calor gas heater to give things a general warm-up, to get the chill out of the thing as much as possible. There's also another golden rule: if for any reason the engine persistently refuses to start, the answer is to change it. We've seen people waste hours fiddling about when they've got problems. They look at this, they change that, then they try something else, and at the end of it all they're still in trouble. If you can't identify the problem quickly, the chances are that it'll remain elusive, so it's better to cut your losses and change the engine.'

Another golden rule, to which most teams are happy to adhere, is never to fiddle about inside an engine; if there is a problem it goes back to the rebuilder for attention. Trackside engine maintenance is virtually a thing of the past, and with the latest ignition systems it's not even necessary to change plugs — the same plugs are used for a cold start as for the race or practice period. Nevertheless, like most sophisticated racing engines, the DFV will not take kindly to incorrect starting procedures, and as Ken Tyrrell is at pains to point out, most of the problems in the pit road are the result of teams failing to

The same in all but name. The back end of a Saudia Williams will almost certainly be carrying a DFV engine with 'Cosworth' rather than 'Ford' on the cam covers, an arrangement which has facilitated sponsorship support for the team, first by Leyland, BL's commercial vehicle division, and more recently by the Austin Rover passenger car division.

conform with Cosworth's written recommendations.

'Like most teams, when we start an engine from cold we turn the metering unit to full rich, then use a squirt can to supply neat fuel down the intakes. Mike Costin maintains that it's unnecessary to use a squirt can and that he can start a DFV without using one, but although we've challenged him to a duel on this, so far he hasn't taken up the challenge! Of course, you must be very careful indeed in using the can because if you let in too much fuel you'll wash the oil off the bores and damage a piston. So it's something of an art, just like it's an art to know precisely how much throttle you need, and some people seem to have developed it a lot better than others.

'Roger Hill, my Chief Mechanic, is magic when it comes to starting a DFV. He goes through mental agony sometimes when he sees other people making a hash of trying to start an engine, but he'll never interfere — he'll just wince and look the other way because he can scarcely bear to watch. It's a knack, and he's got it. One of the secrets is very accurate control of your throttle as the engine fires and so instead of using the pedal we have a hand lever built into the linkage down in the Vee, so that immediately the engine fires we can snap the throttle shut from its fully open position, then immediately re-open it a little to coax up the revs to the lowest level where the engine will run evenly so as to get some heat into it. Cosworth tell us not to run it under 3,000rpm because of a

12-cylinder opposition. Alfa Romeo's return to Grand Prix racing with a works team was supported by an undeniably powerful 3-litre V12 engine, but the team was to be plagued with unreliability and the closest they came to success was in 1980, when Bruno Giacomelli led the United States Grand Prix at Watkins Glen for more than half the race before being halted with an electrical problem.

possible overload on the nose of a cam, and in fact the engine will usually find its natural speed as it is warming up.

'Restarting the engine when it's warm also calls for a careful routine and if it's at the start of practice or a warm-up you make sure that the driver is all ready to go — properly belted up, comfortable, helmet and gloves on, ready to go out on the track without any further delay. Then one of the mechanics plugs in the air starter — we used to have the starter right at the back, alongside the gearbox, but these days most teams have a Bendix drive on to the flywheel. Someone else will indicate to the driver when the air bottle is plugged in, and then he'll switch on the electric fuel pump and watch his pressure gauge. As soon as he has pressure he'll raise his hand, which is the signal to the mechanic at the back to actuate the starter, without delay, otherwise the engine will be flooded. Now that we have Contactless ignition, which has fixed timing, we've added a retard switch as well — it's not essential, but we find that when we use it the engine starts up like a dream, just like a touring car. At first we had a spring-loaded retard switch, which automatically released itself, but this gave us some trouble, so now we have a simple switch-on, switch-off type.'

Partially blanking off radiators is a commonplace procedure for assisting the warm-up of an engine in cold weather, and because inevitably conditions will be significantly cooler out on the track a driver is unlikely to be sent out until the water temperature has reached 50 to 60 degrees C, while in really icy conditions it is better to wait until water starts to drip out of the overflow through expansion. In cold weather the radiators (and brake cooling ducts) may still be partially taped up for the initial few laps, on the first of which the driver will probably keep to around 6,000rpm, then gradually build up from there at around 1,000rpm per lap. There will be frequent check stops at the pits during this period for temperatures to be taken by probes and tape removed or added as the case may be. These days full instrumentation has largely given way to warning lights, which are unlikely to come on until the water temperature has gone beyond 95 degrees C and the oil temperature around 135 degrees C, the theory being that it is better to give the driver less to worry about until he has a problem which requires a pit stop. (If his temperatures have gone a little high he may well be distracted by the movement in the needles when the problem is not serious enough to affect his racing.)

'When a light comes on', says Jochen Mass, 'you know you've got a major problem — either that, or the light is not functioning properly! The theory is that it should come on in time for you to prevent an expensive disaster, and this is usually the case, although of course sometimes you see the light just as the engine blows up!

More 12-cylinder opposition. In 1981 the reconstituted Ligier team, with Talbot backing and the latest version of the 3-litre V12 Matra engine, brought considerable success to Jacques Laffite, whose victories in Austria and Canada were supported by two seconds and three third places in his JS17, but in 1982 the replacement JS19s were less competitive, Eddie Cheever's second place in Detroit being the only bright spot. For 1983 the team were to return to using Ford DFV and later DFY power.

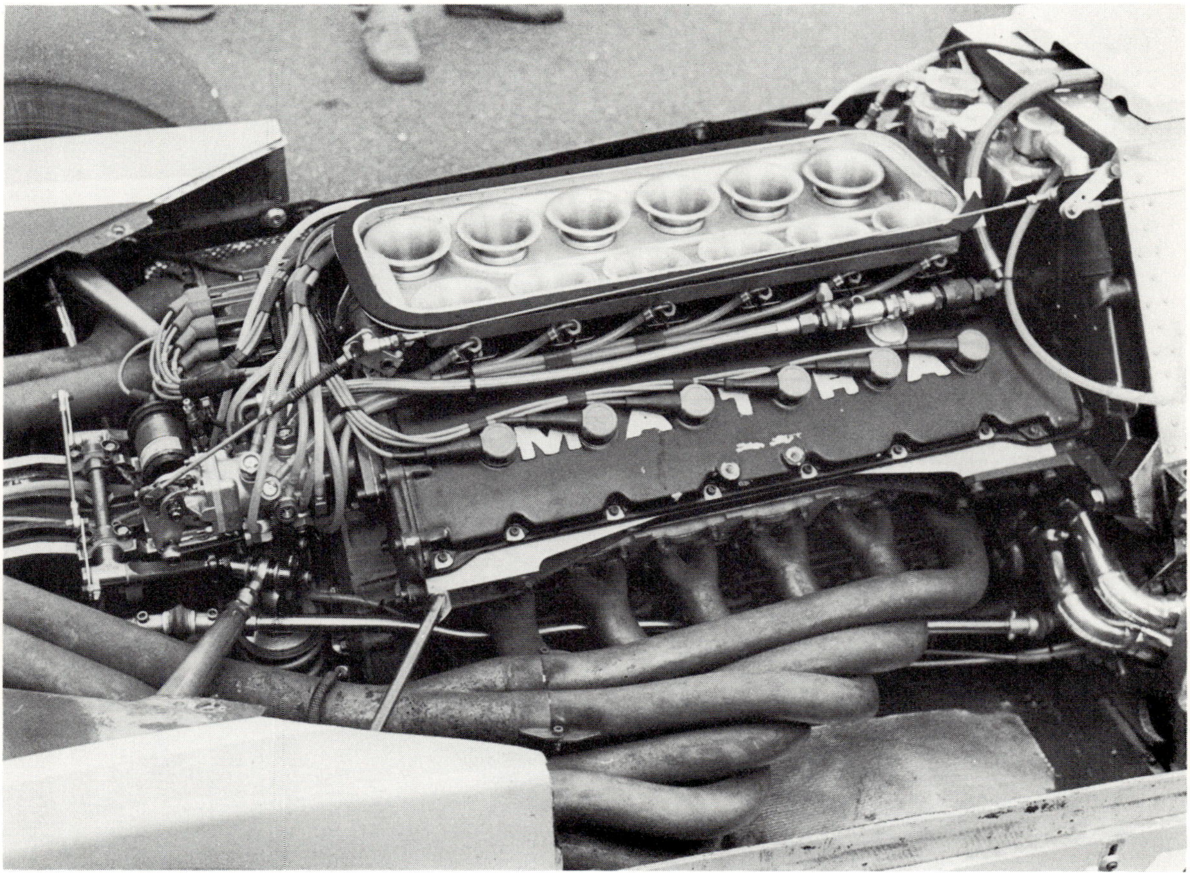

'Of course, the DFV has been a remarkably reliable engine, and the fact that no-one came up with a better solution for so many years proves, I think, that it has been a pretty ideal racing engine. It's light, it's capable of delivering a lot of horsepower and it's proved itself strong enough to last 24 hours, and even to win after 24 hours. Yes, it vibrates a bit, but no more, I would think, than one might expect from a V8. In my experience, it seems to vibrate most around the 7,000 to 7,500rpm mark, then smooths out again near 8,000.

'When you've used the engine for a number of years you develop an ear for it, and you sense straight away when something is not quite right. Then you check your rev-counter and you find that perhaps you've lost a few revs compared with the reading you were getting at that point on earlier laps, like this morning, for example' (we were talking between practice periods at Zandvoort). 'I didn't have a misfire, but the engine just didn't seem to be revving right. This is something you can instinctively feel if the engine isn't getting enough electricity, if the battery power is dropping off. The rev-counter gave me the confirmation that something wasn't quite right, but I knew this before I looked at the instrument. It just didn't feel as peaky as it should.

Turbo opposition. The $1\frac{1}{2}$-litre V6 Renault Gordini turbocharged engine had given the French team many heartaches along the rocky road to reliability, but by 1982 the twin-turbo engine was a potential winner on most circuits. However, it would reach the finishing line first on only four occasions, twice in the hands of Alain Prost, and twice with Rene Arnoux, including a controversial victory in the French Grand Prix after ignoring team orders to let Prost through.

Turbo opposition. Ferrari experimented with both turbocharged and supercharged versions of their $1\frac{1}{2}$-litre V6 engine in 1981 before opting for the turbo, which Gilles Villeneuve took to victories in Monaco and Spain. The 1982 season was to be traumatic, however, with the death of Villeneuve and serious injuries to Didier Pironi after his wins at Imola and Zandvoort, following which the team's Constructors' World Championship, aided by Patrick Tambay's victory in Germany, was a less than usual cause for celebration.

'Of course, not every engine is exactly like the others, and you get slightly different characteristics from engines supplied from different rebuilders. For example, I always think that a Hesketh-built engine sounds slightly different, while some are a bit softer than others and have a different power range. I suppose we all have our personal favourites, but recently I've driven engines from Nicholson, Alan Smith and Race Engine Services and they've all seemed good, though each has had its own special characteristics.'

The clarity with which you can listen to a DFV engine, despite ear plugs and full protective head gear, impressed Derek Daly considerably on his arrival on the Formula 1 scene. 'You can hear everything you need to hear in the cockpit all of the time, and this is very important if there is any weakness up at the top end. For example, you tend to get a fair bit of warning of a valve spring problem because you'll hear it in the airbox or in the injection as a roughness or a hesitation, the beginning of a misfire. Of course, if a valve breaks it's all a matter of luck. You could be fortunate and have the head snap off and it becomes jammed in the cylinder head, in which case the engine will have gone on to seven cylinders; if this has happened late enough in the race you may even be able to complete it, running on seven. More likely, though, the valve

Turbo opposition. The arrival of the $1\frac{1}{2}$-litre four-cylinder BMW turbo in Grand Prix racing by way of the Brabham team resulted in some spectacular blow-ups during their early races in 1982, but a surprise victory by Nelson Piquet in Canada, having failed to qualify for the Detroit race the previous week, marked a turning point. The thirst of this engine was to mark the return of refuelling stops to Formula 1, and Brabham's 1983 car was to be designed around the concept of making the mid-race stop for more fuel and tyres.

head will drop into a cylinder and become mangled as the piston comes up, in which case your first warning of trouble is when bits of metal come flying out of an exhaust pipe!'

Ken Tyrrell recalls one occasion when luck was on his side. 'It was three or four laps from the end of a Grand Prix and it looked as though Jody Scheckter would be picking up a few points. Then the next time he came by the engine sounded awful. In fact it sounded so terrible we knew he wouldn't be coming round again. It was a disaster! But round he came, still making the same awful noise, and he went on like that to the end of the race and collected his points. Of course, when we first heard the noise we knew that a valve spring had gone, but what we didn't know until the engine was stripped down was that the valve head had dropped in and been punched up into the cylinder head and become jammed there. The result was a repair bill of about £7,000 including one new cylinder head instead of one for nearer £18,000 after a major rebuild around a replacement block. It was our lucky day!'

Jody Scheckter retained a high regard for the Ford engine even after he had joined Ferrari for the last two years of his racing career. 'By the time I got involved with the DFV it had been around for several years and been well developed and by then it was incredibly docile. In fact I think you could have dropped one into a saloon car which my wife could have driven with no trouble at all, it was so flexible at low revs. At racing speeds it didn't have any flat spots, and in the rain all you had to do was richen up the mixture one or two clicks and away you went. If you needed to you could run it down to 2,000 revs and if you were careful with the throttle you could accelerate away smoothly without any 'bub-bub-bub' jerking or anything like that. It was amazing.

'In a way I think it has been a big advantage for Cosworth having so many engines in the field, not just because it gave them a better chance of winning, but also because any weakness or fault could be detected and corrected that much more quickly, whereas Ferrari, for example, would only have the feedback from one team. Of course, when I went there they made it very clear to me that I would have more power than I'd been used to with the DFV, but after a test session at Fiorano I wasn't particularly impressed and I said afterwards that as far as I was concerned the V8 Ford Cosworth was more powerful than the 12-cylinder Ferrari. At the debriefing everything I said was being translated into Italian for the benefit of Enzo Ferrari, but I was amused that the translator chickened out and decided to leave out that bit!'

Alfa Romeo joined the turbo teams at the end of 1982 with a $1\frac{1}{2}$-litre V8 which during between-seasons testing proved to be exceedingly powerful but inordinately thirsty. The change of power unit meant that the 3-litre normally aspirated V12 engines used in 1982 could be made available to the Osella team during 1983.

Brian Hart's turbocharged derivative of his four-cylinder Formula 2 engine was adopted by the Toleman team for their entry into Grand Prix racing in 1981, a season hindered by an excessively overweight chassis. A twin-plug version of this engine was to appear in 1983.

Another driver to share Scheckter's enthusiasm for the DFV's tractability in the wet is Manfred Winkelhock, whose first experience of the engine was with the Arrows team in 1980 after a varied background of driving a single-seater in Formula 2, a BMW M1 coupe in the Procar series and a turbocharged Porsche 935 in the German Championship. 'My most vivid memory of the DFV the first time I tried it was that it was so much easier to drive than a turbocharged engine. The combination of immediate throttle response and a fantastic rev band from 6,000 to 11,000rpm, with the engine remaining

smooth once it was on the cam at around 6,500 to 7,000rpm, was amazing to me after the turbo. Of course, in the wet, this combination is even more useful, and the DFV's flexibility means that you can drive it with so much more confidence in traffic, which can be a huge advantage at the start of a race. To me the DFV will always be a fantastic engine and one of my two favourites so far; the other fantastic engine, I think, is the six-cylinder BMW 3.5-litre we used in the Group 4 M1, but of course this was not as strong as the Ford in terms of horsepower per litre.'

The contribution of the Ford engine to the Grand Prix scene has not been confined to what it has achieved for the teams and individual drivers who have used it. The fact that it has been used so widely and has such remarkable stamina has been a major influence in the development of far more sophisticated and comprehensive tyre testing programmes. 'The DFV has been a major asset in our race tyre development programme', says Leo Mehl, who directs Goodyear's worldwide racing tyre operations. 'The fact that it will keep going for 1,000 miles or so at a competitive speed means that we can carry through a day's, or even several days' hard testing without all the hassle of having to break off in order to put a fresh engine in. These days our test programmes are probably three times as long as they used to be because there is so much to be done, and without a really reliable engine we would be badly hindered.

'We endeavour to include three phases into our test programmes. We normally test at a circuit a month to six weeks before we are due to race there and try to get a good look at our race set-up for that circuit. So we will take along perhaps six proven racing compounds for the normal variety of 13in and 15in front tyres and 13in and 15in rears. The objective during the tests will be to reduce the number of selections which we will bring back for the race. Sometimes we manage to do this, and sometimes it's just not possible, but either way that is the first phase of our programme.

'The second phase is to evaluate new tread compounds. We might take along as many as 10 compounds that had never been on a race track before, only tested in the laboratory, and we would aim to carry out comparative tests on all of them against the best of the proven race compounds. It calls for an awful lot of miles, which is why a good, strong, reliable engine is such a vital ingredient of a successful test. Occasionally this phase will throw up something that looks so promising that we might even take it to the next race, even though we have only carried out one test on it.

'The third phase is to test some of our new design ideas. Maybe we want to try a new internal construction, perhaps a new mould shape, perhaps even a differently dimensioned tyre — a little wider, a little rounder, a little squarer, a little stiffer or a little softer. This is part of our basic research, through which we are always trying to look into the future.

'The three phases have to be very carefully controlled to ensure that we end up with good test results with good comparisons. For example, after any sort of delay, and after every one or two hours as a matter of routine, we put a set of control tyres back on the car to see whether the track conditions have changed since we set the control lap time at the beginning of the test. We will always do this if, for example, after bolting on a new compound we are suddenly a second a lap quicker; we have to know whether there was anything else that influenced the time — it's normal procedure, but it all takes time, which is why

Jackie Stewart's enthusiasm and facility for tyre testing was to help Goodyear considerably when the Tyrrell team switched to their tyres in 1971, the year when Stewart was to win the second of his three World Championships. Goodyear's racing boss Leo Mehl claims that the consistency and reliability of the DFV engine has been a major contribution to the establishment of comprehensive tyre testing programmes.

we can ill afford to suffer delays because of mechanical unreliability. Also, we have to wait before the team (or teams) we are testing with are ready to do a job for us. In order to do this they have to be running competitively with a properly set-up car, and whether this takes them a couple of hours or nearly all day we have to wait for them because it is useless testing tyres if you're 2 or 3 seconds slow. Do that and you're going to come away with the wrong answers, and you could well miss something that might have been promising at a faster speed — I'm sure that has happened in the past.

'Ideally, we like to test with several teams simultaneously and have at least three top drivers on hand. This means that if we get a certain result with one of them we can slap the tyres in question on the cars of the others to confirm the result before we rush back home and tear the factory to pieces in order to make the tyres and air-freight them to the next race.

'These days we expect to accomplish a great deal in the course of a typical three-day test, far more than would have seemed possible before several top teams were able to share the same engine. From a technical standpoint, the DFV has proved to be a relatively easy engine to produce tyre for, thanks to its consistent power and rev band, and it has certainly given us less problems than the first-generation turbos before they got rid of throttle lag. In fact, I would go so far as to say that if we could look back 30 years from now I'm sure we'd say that the Ford DFV was the most pleasant — and useful — engine for which we'd ever provided racing tyres.'

CHAPTER 5

Creating a new Indy legend

DFX and the boost factor

Just as the world of Grand Prix racing was transformed by the existence and availability of the Ford Cosworth DFV, so the very different world of what is now known as Indy Car racing was taken by storm by the DFV's 2.65-litre turbocharged derivative, the Cosworth DFX. So dominant was this destroked V8 engine to become, following its introduction in 1975, that the Offenhauser engine, which had been the mainstay of this class of racing for so many years, was to be virtually removed from the American National Championship scene. Steadily and inevitably, the barriers of prejudice against the newcomer from overseas were eased aside and, one by one, teams turned to the engine which, reluctant though they may have been to use it, they could not afford to be without if they were to remain a consistent potential winner.

The success record to date of the DFX is a mightily impressive one. Up to the end of its eighth season (1982) it had powered the winner of 80 Indy Car races and every Indianapolis 500 victor since 1978. It had also provided the horsepower for every United States Auto Club (USAC) and Championship Auto Racing Teams (CART) Champion since 1977. Not surprisingly, more than 90 per cent of entrants in Indy Car events in 1982 were using the DFX engine.

Initial development of the DFX was carried out by the now-defunct Vel's Parnelli Jones team. VPJ started work on the project during the winter of 1974-75, and the first DFX-powered Parnelli VPJ6 chassis appeared during practice prior to the 1975 Indianapolis 500. Both Al Unser and Mario Andretti tested the car, which was essentially one of the team's VPJ4 Formula 1 cars equipped with the mandatory narrower Indy Car-specification wheels and tyres (15in diameter wheels with a rim width of 10in at the front and 14in at the rear) and the experimental new engine.

'There were so many things wrong with that car', recalled Al Unser, 'and it handled so bad. We had a lot of work to do, but I knew we had something in that motor. I told them, "You get it some handling, and these guys will be wondering which way we went!".' It turned out not to be quite so straightforward as that, but an extensively revised version of the car, the VPJ6B, appeared at Phoenix for the first race of the 1975 season and Unser raised a few eyebrows by qualifying it on the pole before going on to finish fifth

The traditional Indianapolis 500 race as witnessed for so many years with 33 mostly front-engined Roadsters heading towards the first turn. This is the 1960 race, in which victory would go to Jim Rathmann, whose four-cylinder Offenhauser-powered Ken-Paul Special started from the middle of the front row.

in the DFX engine's first start. After such a promising debut, the VPJ6B and Unser became the first regular Cosworth-powered combination the following season and on June 24, 1976, he took the car to its first win. The race was the Pocono 500 and Unser completely dominated the day, making up a full lap lost in the pits to prove the DFX to be both fast and reliable.

Later that year Danny Ongais joined the VPJ Indy Car team in the colours of Interscope Racing and thus became the second man to race the DFX. The following year Team McLaren and Penske Racing both joined the DFX ranks and ran the engine in McLaren M24 chassis for Johnny Rutherford (in the works team) and Tom Sneva and Mario Andretti (for Penske), Sneva's 1977 USAC Championship being the first to be won with DFX power.

By the end of that season there were a lot of Offenhauser engines on the market as more teams turned towards the DFX and planned their new cars around the V8 engine. Amongst these was Roger Penske's PC5, which had been built to replace his McLaren M24s, and Sneva used one of the new cars to win his second USAC title in 1978. That year Al Unser had moved into Jim Hall's new Indy Car team to take the wheel of one of Hall's DFX-powered Lola T500s and had won all three of the season's 500-mile events — at Indianapolis, Pocono and Ontario, California — but this great achievement, which has yet to be repeated, still left him a few points behind Sneva at the end of the season.

Since Unser's 1978 victory at Indianapolis the DFX has won all but two of the races staged for Indy Cars (up to the end of 1982), its domination having been sustained through various changes in regulations, notably as regards turbocharger boost pressures, and at the time of writing it seems more securely established as the 'standard' power unit for this class of racing that at any time since the Vel's Parnelli Jones team turned the first page in the new chapter of Indy Car history in 1975.

Although Cosworth Engineering had built up a small batch of short-stroke DFV engines the previous year for Roger Penske, he had had second thoughts about the project, and so these special cranks remained on the shelf until the Vel's Parnelli Jones team expressed interest. The story of the DFX, therefore, really began in the middle of 1974 in Torrance, an industrial suburb on the southern outskirts of Los Angeles, California, where the former Indianapolis 500 winner Rufus 'Parnelli' Jones and the Polish immigrant-turned-Ford dealer Vel Miletich had established their Indy Car 'Super Team' of the early-1970s. Initially the team had run three cars for Mario Andretti, Al Unser and Joe Leonard, but Leonard was badly injured in a crash in 1972 and the team later fell into a morass of evil-handling chassis and mightily unreliable Offenhauser engines.

By 1974 the team were reduced to running 'customer' Eagle chassis and their engine situation was getting steadily worse. At this time the VPJ outfit were also running a Formula 5000 car for Andretti and were about to enter Grand Prix racing with a Maurice Phillippe-designed and DFV-engined car called the Parnelli VPJ4 (Andretti first raced this car in the 1974 Canadian Grand Prix, the same event in which Mark Donohue made his Formula 1 debut in the new DFV-powered Penske PC1).

With the reliability of the DFV so firmly established, it was perhaps inevitable that Miletich should want to investigate the chances of using an

Team Lotus' first crack at Indy came in 1963, when this modified Ford Fairlane engine was dropped into the back of the first Lotus 29, a monocoque-chassis design based on that of the Lotus 25 Formula 1 car.

adaptation of the Formula 1 engine for the Indy Car team, the current state of disarray of which was largely down to engine fragility. 'We were having a terrible time with those Offies', Al Unser recalled. 'We used to puke 'em while we were warming 'em up; the water jackets were the worst part — they used to crack and shift all the time.' The turning point, it seems, came when all but three of a batch of 30 blocks the team had bought failed to pass a specially arranged zyglo and pressure check. Miletich was so incensed by this and by his inability to gain what he considered to be satisfactory compensation that he immediately began to pester his partner Jones and other VPJ personnel with the idea that they should turbocharge a short-stroke DFV.

Despite a number of pre-race teething problems, Jim Clark came close to scoring a first-time victory at Indianapolis. Here he passes one of the traditional Roadsters in his pursuit of Parnelli Jones' leading Agajanian Willard Special, which began to drop oil in the last few laps of the race, preventing Clark from closing the gap on the suddenly slippery surface. But second place put the writing on the wall.

They decided that the project was worth investigating, and two men in the VPJ machine shop were released from other work to become occupied full-time on producing a destroked, turbocharged, methanol-burning version of the engine. They were a highly experienced machinist, Chickie Hiroshima, and a young engine builder, Larry Slutter, and they were to be engaged for the best part of a year on this exclusively VPJ operation.

Unser recalls: 'Everybody laughed at them — they all said it wasn't the way

Encouraged by Clark's first effort in 1963, Ford went ahead with the rapid development of double-overhead-camshaft versions of their V8 engine, specifically for the USAC programme, under the direction of three-times Indianapolis winner Louis Meyer. After another near-miss in 1964, when Rodger Ward's Ford-powered car was beaten by the Offenhauser-powered Sheraton-Thompson Special of A. J. Foyt, everything would come good in 1965.

to go. Everybody they talked to seemed to tell them they were stupid to do it — even Duckworth wasn't able to give them much encouragement.' They even had some doubts themselves, according to Larry Slutter: 'We looked at the Cosworth and we thought, "there's no way this is going to run, the port area is much two small".' But Miletich and his engine men were committed to the project and when eventually they ran the first engine on the dyno they were more than encouraged. 'The first time we ran it', says Slutter, 'it was up more than 50 horsepower over the Offies we had, so we knew right away we had a going piece.'

From that first dyno test in the autumn of 1974 it took Slutter and Hiroshima less than six months to produce an engine that was ready to run in a car. There were a variety of problems to sort out, but Miletich stayed enthusiastically behind the project while his engine men worked almost single-handedly at making the engine a runner.

By maintaining the DFV engine's standard bore of 85.6mm and reducing the stroke from 64.8mm to 57.3mm it was possible to lower the V8 engine's displacement from 2,993cc to 2,645cc to bring it within the Indy Car limit of 2.65 litres. That was the easy bit; making it all hold together was rather more difficult. 'At the beginning the piston problem was probably the most

A confident smile from Jim Clark in the Ford DOHC-equipped Lotus 38 which was destined to take him to victory at Indianapolis in 1965. The engine had originally been developed with centre inlets and side exhausts, but the switch to centre exhausts gave more scope for length tuning.

aggravating of all', recalls Slutter. 'Unfortunately, we couldn't just go to a manufacturer and get a proper piston made at one place. Instead, we had to go to one place to get a forging and have it half-machined, then we had to go to another place to have the pin boss machined, and finally we had to take it to a third place to have it cam ground before we had a good piece. We spent a lot of time and money doing that.'

It took them some time to get the piston configuration sorted out. 'We would run the motor at full throttle on the dyno for about 40 seconds and then back it down to 7,000rpm for 20 seconds, and we would do that for half an hour. Then we'd take it apart and see where the pistons were rubbing and file away at them.' Later, when Cosworth themselves became more directly involved in the project, the situation improved considerably and by 1976 they were producing their own pistons for the engine at Northampton. 'At first', reports Slutter, 'the domes of the Cosworth pistons were too thin and they would oil cake, but when they made a piston with another .100in of metal in the dome the oil caking problem was solved, and we never experienced any problems with the skirt on those pistons.' At first the VPJ team used cams similar to those they had fitted to the turbocharged four-cam American Ford V8 engines they ran in the late-1960s and early-1970s. One of their development problems was in converting the Cosworth engine to accept a much increased water flow rate (from the 38 US gallons/minute of the DFV to 90 US gallons/minute), but the main problem with the cooling system was in trying to cool the exhaust valves and seats — a problem which persisted until a revised layout was developed which enabled the water to flow through the heads and around the valve seats. 'We went without that luxury for the first season', says Slutter, 'but at the time it was still cheaper to run a new cylinder head and throw it away after every race than it was to run an Offy!'

In the early days there was also an oil scavenging problem, which was solved quite quickly. 'That was mostly my fault', says Slutter, 'because I didn't really understand how the Formula 1 air separator pump worked.' Apart from these relatively minor development problems, therefore, the initial conversion from DFV to DFX was reasonably painless, and it was not long before the Cosworth engine was showing itself to have significant advantages over both the four-cylinder Offenhauser and the four-cam Ford-based Foyt V8.

'At that time', recalls Al Unser, 'we had 80 inches of boost and the Cosworth had so much horsepower and was so much smoother that there was no comparison. That Offy shook, and it had a very abrupt feel coming out of the corners so that if you didn't have the chassis exactly right it just broke loose.' 'Another big advantage of the DFX', says Slutter, 'was that it was physically so small. The four-cam Ford tended to lose out because it was top-heavy, but this one had its weight where it belonged.'

The reduced revolving and reciprocating masses and the lower centre of gravity of the DFX also made for a smaller, more responsive package of chassis and engine. 'If anybody ever had an advantage it was me', says Unser, 'with that car and that engine. Once John Barnard had redesigned the chassis and got the car handling it just made the rest of them look sick.' Barnard had taken over the VPJ designer's chair and he was responsible for the modifications which turned the car into the VPJ6B. First of all he designed a new oil system, which enabled him to move the engine back and change the

The famous Wood Brothers pit crew pounce on Jim Clark's Lotus 38 during one of its routine pit stops on the way to its 1965 victory. Ford-powered cars driven by Parnelli Jones, Mario Andretti and Al Miller were also to fill the next three places.

weight distribution system considerably. He also stiffened the front of the chassis and initiated a series of slimmer, smoother bodywork layouts. 'Barnard was good', says Slutter. 'He was the guy that got the whole package working.'

Slutter also gives a lot of credit to Chickie Hiroshima. 'He was a good machinist with a lot of experience. We'd come back from testing with 30 different ideas and he'd calm us down, give us a direction and make things work. He probably saved us a lot of time.' The other principals in the VPJ outfit were Jim Chapman, from England, who was the overall Crew Chief of both the Indy Car and Formula 5000 teams, and Welshman Huey Absalom, who was Chief Mechanic on the VPJ6Bs driven by Unser; both men had already spent five or six years working in the United States, after gaining a lot of experience as fabricators/mechanics in Formula 1 in Europe. 'It was a pretty good combination', says Slutter. 'It was one of those periods when we didn't have anybody fighting anybody else — everybody got along.'

Unfortunately, the same could not be said about the hierarchy of Indy Car racing in the years ahead, and when the DFX engine became something of an innocent pawn in the chess game being played out by the two rival factions, it was time for Ford, who had been prepared to keep a low profile concerning the engine's ancestry, to remind a few people that they had better find a way of getting along if they were not going to destroy Indy Car racing just when its potential was becoming greater than at any time in its long history.

Long before the frustration of entrants with the machinations of USAC had

Further evidence of Formula 1 influence on Indy Car design was to be seen when McLaren entered the USAC scene in 1970. This is their 1971 car, which Peter Revson had just qualified for pole position and which he would drive into second position at Indianapolis, splitting the Ford-powered cars of Al Unser and A. J. Foyt.

Prior to the advent of the Cosworth DFX, the power battle at Indianapolis and elsewhere on the USAC scene was waged between the Ford DOHC engines, which had been handed over to A. J. Foyt when Ford withdrew from direct participation in racing in 1970, and the traditional four-cylinder Offenhausers. Here is Foyt in his Coyote, rolling towards the start of the 1974 race in pole position, with Wally Dallenbach's Offy-powered car beside him. Both were destined to retire, however, and the race would be won by Johnny Rutherford in his McLaren.

caused them to form their separate race-sanctioning organization, however, the growing popularity of the DFX engine and the complexities of developing it against a background of constantly changing ground rules had caused Cosworth Engineering to devote a great deal of time and effort to the project, and in so doing they had the enthusiastic support of Ford, even though it was the 'Cosworth' name which had appeared on the cam covers.

'Indy Car racing had been undergoing similar problems to those which had afflicted Formula 1 some years earlier with the Coventry Climax withdrawal', recalls Walter Hayes. 'The Offy's days were ending and it was the end of a great period, but whereas certain people were going around saying "this stock block", or "that stock block" as a way for the future, others — and notably Penske — could see the sense in having a true racing engine rather than a modified production engine which, though it might be considerably cheaper to buy in the first place, would end up by being a lot more expensive if it were to be developed into a reliable race-winner.

'Gradually his point of view prevailed, and so the question came up as to what the engine should be called. One of the influences was that there were some people in the United States who wanted to run it, but who had contractural arrangements which precluded them from going with a Ford engine — for example it would be very difficult for a Chevrolet dealer to do so — and another factor I had to bear in mind was that Ford had pulled out of motor sport in the United States at that time so that all the company's engineers and rescources could be put to work on the emissions and associated

Bobby Unser heading for second place at Indianapolis in 1974 in Dan Gurney's Offy-powered Olsonite Eagle. Only 12 cars would be running at the end of the 500-miles race that year, and seven of them would be Eagles, four in the top six places, while Unser would become USAC Champion.

regulatory programmes which were so heavily preoccupying the industry. A kind of puritanism had swept the country, and whereas I was completely happy about what we were doing in Europe, I didn't think it was really a very good idea to play games in the States in an area of racing with which, at the time, I had little first-hand knowledge.

'So not only did I agree to the change of name, I actually suggested to Keith that he call it a Cosworth in the United States in order that this could facilitate the growth of the sport as much as possible as well as increase the rescources of his company. You see, through the DFV engine Cosworth Engineering had grown dramatically, and by this time they had something like 185 employees on the payroll — very fine employees, too, every one a sort of genius in his own way — and all of them were dependent upon the continuing success of and demand for the DFV. What were they to do if anything happened? Keith had built one of the finest machine shops in Britain — he did a lot of prototype machining for us and we used to put as much specialist machining we could his way to maintain a financial throughput into the company — and it was important that he should, if possible, broaden his motor racing base, on which his reputation had been built. So I was really very delighted when the turbo opportunity came along.'

Turbocharging had arrived on the Indy Car scene as early as 1965, but only in a very tentative way, and it was not until two or three years later, at a time when gas turbine-powered cars were stealing most of the headlines, that the exhaust-driven turbocharger began to play an important role in this branch of the sport. Arriving at just about the same time as a new wave of knowledge concerning chassis design and aerodynamics (a direct spinoff of Formula 1 experience), the effect had been to dramatically increase lap speeds on the oval circuits.

The gas turbines were considered to be a major culprit in this respect and were effectively legislated out of contention, but after restrictions in fuel usage and in wing dimensions in 1973 had failed to reduce speeds to an acceptable extent and two horrific accidents at Indianapolis, claiming Salt Walther and Swede Savage, had provided a further reminder of the perils of unbridled speed, a further effort to restrict cars was made for the 1974 season. This took the form of a further restriction on fuel consumption (down from 340 to 280 US gallons at Indianapolis) and on wing width, but perhaps of most significance, a boost restriction was applied to turbocharged engines, on which a pressure relief valve was to be introduced to restrict the inlet manifold pressure to 80in of mercury, or in other words, approximately 50in of mercury over normal atmospheric pressure. As a 1in column of Hg requires a pressure of approximately 0.5psi to sustain it, the 80in rule meant, in effect, a maximum boost pressure of some 25psi.

It was at this point that the DFX engine entered the scene, but just as the DFV's competitiveness had been influenced by subtle changes in Formula 1 rules throughout much of its life, so was the Indy Car rule book to become a movable feast. The pop-off valves were to be adjusted to give a maximum of 75in Hg in 1976, a change which the rulemakers said would be 'frozen' for five years, but a few months later they decided that the limit would revert to 80in in 1977! There were also bewildering changes in precisely how and when the

The beginning of a new era in USAC racing. Mario Andretti carrying out some circuit tests in 1975 with an early DFX engine installed in the back of the Vel's Parnelli Jones team's Parnelli VPJ4. Larry Slutter, later to join Cosworth Engineering, and Chickie Hiroshima were responsible for the initial conversion of what had started out as a short-stroke Formula 1 engine to turbo-charging under USAC rules.

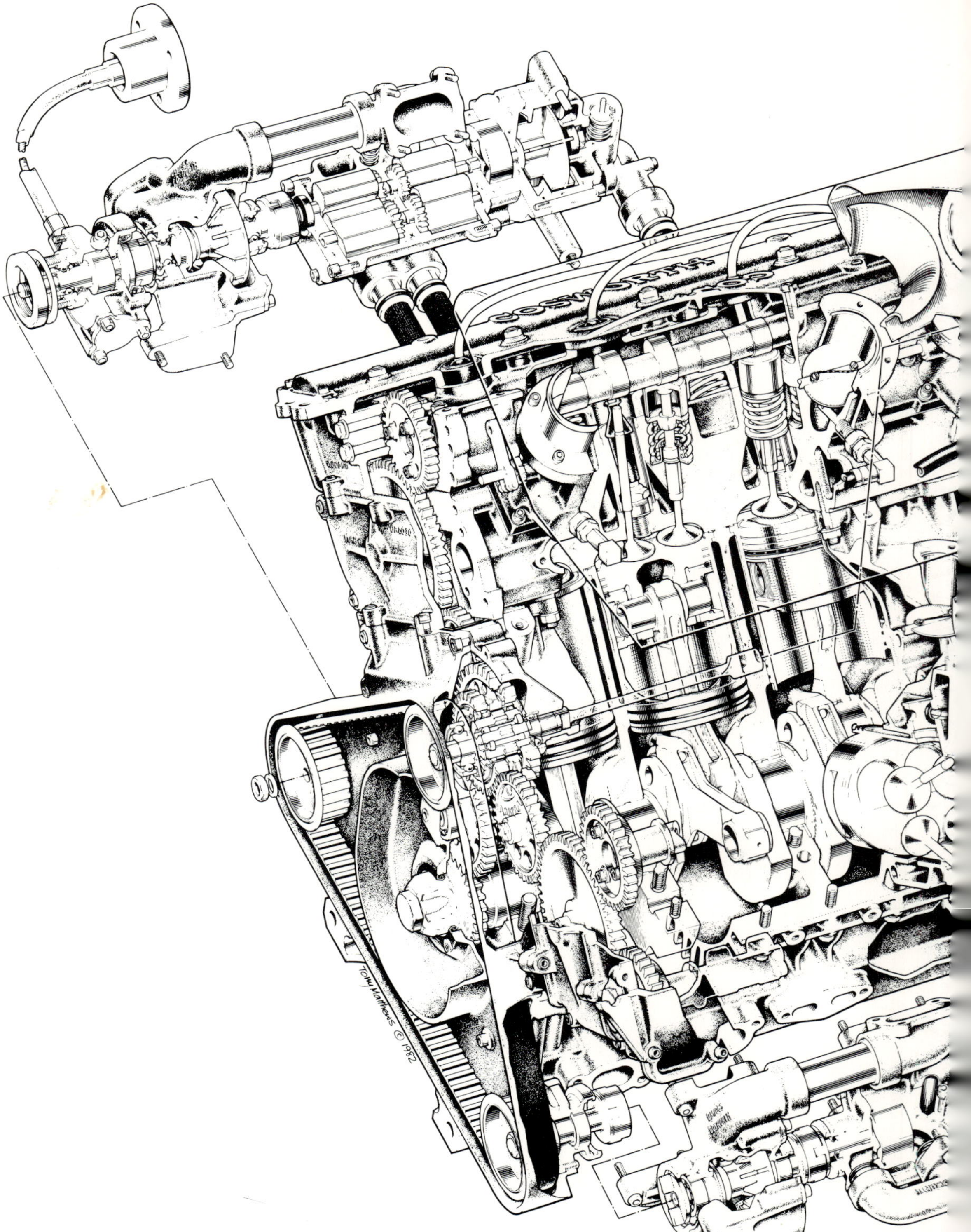
Tony Matthews © 1982

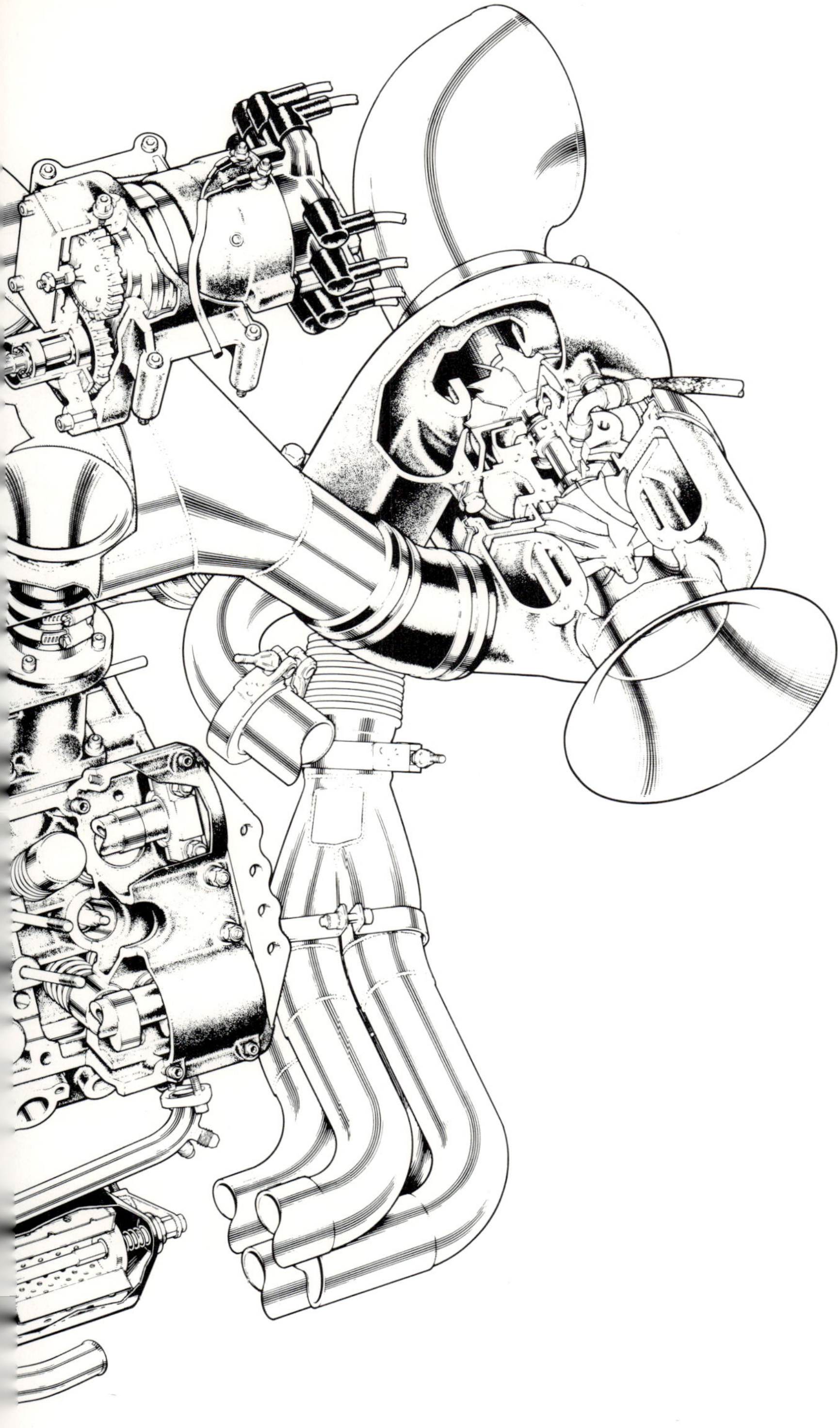

The engine that has transformed Indy Car racing. This is the 1982 version of the Cosworth DFX as drawn by Tony Matthews, in which form it produces well over 700bhp with the boost pressure restricted to 48in of mercury.

individual regulations were to be applied; some years the pop-off valves were required both for qualifying and for the races, whereas in other years they were not required during the races. Meanwhile, there was a fairly well orchestrated campaign by a vociferous minority who were dedicated to the re-emergence of stock-block engines at the expense of the 'exotic European-built' DFX.

To put this in perspective, one has to remember that the famous Indy Establishment had for long represented the pinnacle of parochialism in the world of big-time motor racing. Theirs was essentially an all-American activity, performed by an all-American club, and they were tremendously proud of that fact. So it had gone greatly against the grain when, in 1961, an Australian based in England had arrived on their doorstep and shown them that their famous and beloved Indianapolis Roadsters had their engine planted at the wrong end of the chassis. Then, when Jack Brabham and his Cooper-Coventry Climax went away, to be replaced in 1963 by a Scotsman in a Lotus-Ford, who not only finished second but actually came close to winning (as he was to do in 1965), it was as though the Queen had moved into the White House. The only consolation was that Jim Clark's Ford four-cam V8 engine had been designed, built and developed entirely in the United States.

It was Dan Gurney who had been mainly responsible for forging this particular link between Lotus and Ford. Gurney had been so impressed with Colin Chapman's latest monocoque-construction Formula 1 car that he was convinced that a similar design, suitably adapted and powered by a competitive engine, would be a potential race-winner at Indianapolis. He invited Chapman across to take a look at 'The Brickyard', and while there he introduced him to some top Ford personnel. The meeting was most timely, for Ford were embarking upon the establishment of their all-out performance image and a serious Indianapolis involvement fitted into this strategy very neatly.

A deal was struck wherein Lotus would design, build and operate a team of purpose-built cars and Ford would supply the necessary engines. Jim Clark and Gurney were the nominated drivers for the team's first appearance at Indianapolis, in 1963, for which Ford produced a specially developed version of the 260 cubic inch Fairlane engine, with the displacement reduced to 255 CID. Although it featured an aluminium cylinder block and head castings it was a relatively simple engine by racing standards, still retaining pushrod overhead valves and running on gasoline through carburettors rather than with injected alcohol fuel. Nevertheless, it came close to being an Indianapolis winner first time out, Clark being all set to overtake Parnelli Jones a few laps from the end when Jones' car started to spray out oil and turn the track into a skating rink.

Clark had to settle for second place that year, but Ford were so encouraged by this that they pressed ahead with the development of their double-overhead-camshaft derivative of the V8 engine, initially with centre intakes and side exhausts, then with the intakes between the camshafts and the exhausts emerging from the centre of the Vee, where there was more scope for length-tuning. This was the engine which Clark was to use for his famous Lotus victory in 1965, and which would also power Graham Hill's Lola into the winner's circle the following year; it would continue to be at the forefront of Indianapolis-style racing until the advent of turbocharging brought the Offenhauser back into the picture. With the subsequent retirement of Louis

Meyer, who had been responsible for the Ford engine build programme, followed by Ford's curtailment of their direct involvement in motor racing towards the end of the decade, the four-camshaft Ford engine passed into the hands of A.J. Foyt, in whose workshops development was to continue into the 1970s. Whilst its conversion to turbocharging was not entirely successful in the days of unlimited boost pressures, when the 80in Hg limit was imposed for

Al Unser would give the DFX engine its race debut in the back of his Parnelli VPJ6B at Phoenix in 1975, when he would finish in fifth place, but he would be back again in 1976 for an outright victory in the Bobby Ball 150 to add to his earlier successes in the Schaefer 500 at Pocono and the Tony Bettenhausen 200 at Milwaukee that season. Here he is at Phoenix running inside his brother Bobby's Offenhauser-powered car.

Al Unser taking a tight line at Phoenix with his DFX-powered Parnelli VPJ6B, which designer John Barnard had turned into a highly competitive runner, aided by the low centre of gravity of the Cosworth engine.

Although Al Unser had a highly successful 1977 season, finishing runner-up to Tom Sneva in the USAC Championship, he was out of luck in the Tony Bettenhausen 200 at Milwaukee, where his Parnelli VPJ6B is seen here running with short-track bodywork and wings.

safety reasons this by now venerable engine came right back into its own and in 1977, before the DFX began its domination, Foyt added a sixth Indianapolis victory for the Ford four-cam engine to the five it had scored in 1965-67, 1969 and 1970.

It was from beyond the shores of the United States that many of the advances in Indy Car chassis design at that time had emanated, and indeed many of the cars contesting USAC races were actually of European origin. It had been a very bitter pill to swallow, therefore, when a British racing engine, the Cosworth DFX, had arrived to complete the transformation of what had been such a traditionally nationalistic USAC scene, just when the widely used Offenhauser was running out of breath. The majority of professional racing team owners, however, are nothing if not realists, and several of the Indianapolis stalwarts could see the commonsense of adopting a power unit which, whilst undeniably more expensive than a stock-block off the shelf, was not only likely to be a lot cheaper in the long run through its superior reliability and performance, but would be almost certain to win the vast majority of the races in which it was entered; the only question which seemed to be in any doubt was which chassis and which driver would take the DFX into the winner's circle.

By the summer of 1978 the political wrangling between USAC and the major entrants had reached such a pitch that the majority of the latter had decided to form themselves into an entrants' association, and by the following winter they had taken the decision to promote and stage their own series of races. The direct USAC-CART confrontation was now well under way, and in the rhetoric which was to follow the DFX engine tended to be drawn into the picture alongside CART's 'rich, undemocratic owners', whereas USAC described their own posture as being for the 'little guy', who would only be able to afford Championship (Indy) Car racing if normally aspirated 5.8-litre Chevrolet stock-block V8s were allowed to be competitive. At this point, USAC announced a drastic reduction in manifold pressure for turbocharged engines, starting at 50in Hg in 1979 and dropping to 48in Hg in 1980. Under the revised rules the Offenhauser was allowed more boost (because it was a four-cylinder engine rather than a V8) but even at the 60in Hg it was allowed it had breathing problems and it developed insufficient power to beat a DFX running with 48in Hg, so its early departure from the scene became inevitable.

For a while, there was a threat to the DFX's domination from Chevrolet in the form of an all-aluminium version of their well developed 358 CID V8, and in fact Mike Mosley won a race at Milwaukee in June 1981 with an AAR Chevy-powered Eagle. But the more conservative boost allowed under the revised regulations had enabled the DFX to achieve impressive reliability and longevity, and the prudence of opting for a high-mileage pure race engine in preference to a comparatively shorter-life stock-block power unit was soon to be seen in various teams' balance sheets. Although the reduction in boost pressure from 80in to an eventual 48in Hg had been made with certain political undertones, there was no real conflict between USAC and CART on this issue, and when CART ran their Indy Car Championship in the summer of 1980 the 48in boost pressure limitation was retained and it seems likely to persist for some years to come.

Larry Slutter, for one, was happy to see the reduction in boost pressure, which he says has made the DFX a lot happier. 'We would have had to spend a lot more money making it as reliable as it is today if we still had 80in, he says. These days it is common practice to put as many as 800 miles on a DFX

Al Unser's victory in the 1977 California 500 at Ontario, with his Parnelli VPJ6B fitted with 6C bodywork, marked the third win for a DFX-powered car in a 500-mile race, Tom Sneva having added another success at Pocono with his McLaren M24 to Unser's victory there in 1976.

between routine rebuilds, despite the increased revs (up to 11,000rpm is regularly used during qualifying), the raised compression ratios and the longer-duration cams which have followed the reduction in boost.

The majority of engine builders agree that the most vulnerable part of the DFX has been the gear train at the front of the engine. This is because an engine runs at or close to its maximum revs for so much of the time when racing on the fastest oval tracks. The sustained high revs also put a lot of strain on valve springs. However, Slutter says that DFX blocks, crankshafts, cylinder heads, liners and valves will all run 3,000 miles with only periodic inspections, while pistons will usually run for 800 to 1,000 miles without problems. These days the majority of engines run with Cosworth crankshafts, connecting rods and pistons, although there are some DFX engines in use with either TRW or Mahle pistons, Carillo rods and Moldex cranks.

It was an unusual experience for the initial development of a Cosworth racing engine to take place outside the factory, but it was necessary, if only for political reasons, for Cosworth Engineering to maintain a low profile with the DFX in the early stages and allow American technology to be applied to the engine within the United States. At first, so far as Cosworth were concerned, the engine was simply a short-stroke DFV, and no claims were made as to its suitability for USAC or any other sort of racing. It was just hot-tested at Northampton in normally aspirated form and with a suitably low compression ratio, then shipped across for conversion.

Inevitably, a lot of the parts had to be replaced. For example, the gudgeon pins and pistons were inadequate for a turbocharged engine, and as it was not

The Cosworth DFX engine came back to England in 1978 when most of the top USAC drivers took part in races at Silverstone and Brands Hatch which counted towards that year's Citicorp Cup National Championship. Here is Tom Sneva finishing second to team partner Rick Mears in his Penske PC6 at Brands Hatch, having previously finished third behind A. J. Foyt and Mears in the rain-shortened Silverstone race.

The final adjustments are made before firing up a DFX on the Penske brake. Unlike in Formula 1, the majority of the top teams competing in CART/USAC races either have their own in-house engine building and testing facilities or have long-standing arrangements with nearby specialists.

possible to fit suitable gudgeon pins in the existing connecting rods, the rods also had to go. The problem of heat around the exhaust valve seat has already been referred to, and there were also some head sealing problems. But when the VPJ team had put in some new valve seats and incorporated a different head sealing arrangement the engine began to look quite promising in its converted form, which included Hilborn fuel injection, for which Hilborn produced a special intake manifold.

As other teams began to see the potential of the turbocharged engine, a brisk market suddenly opened up for secondhand DFV power units for conversion, which was good news in Northampton because this in turn created an increased demand from the Formula 1 teams for replacement engines. Nevertheless, it soon became apparent that the level of interest in the DFX had reached such proportions that there seemed a real danger that it might be legislated against, so Cosworth decided that it was time to act in order to protect their investment.

While the debate about future regulations was building up into what increasingly looked like becoming a conflict, Cosworth representatives crossed the Atlantic and collected about 20 non-returnable deposits for engines, to be manufactured in Northampton, but to a specification which had yet to be precisely defined. It was a tremendous act of faith by the teams who responded, and it meant that the people who had identified the engine's potential and the good which ultimately it could do for this category of racing would henceforward have a considerably stronger voice in the political debate.

It was at around this time that Larry Slutter, who had been so closely involved in the early conversion work in transforming a DFV into a DFX, accepted an invitation to become Cosworth's man in the United States, and one of his first tasks was to enable Cosworth to build the DFX in England, based on American technology, by shipping across from the United States the cranks, rods, injection equipment and all the other American-built material which had become virtually standardized on the locally assembled DFXs.

Having put the engine into production in this form, Cosworth immediately set about upgrading the detail specification in several areas, to improve both drivability and performance, and this has been an on-going programme ever since. In particular, they applied a considerable effort to the further development of the Hilborn fuel injection system, in the course of which modifications were made to several components, including some of the valves, and various replacement components were fitted, including new injectors and a different sensing valve.

However, it is fair to say that Cosworth were never really happy with this fuel system, which was entirely mechanical in operation and was, in effect, a tap system whereby the fuel supply was turned on or off with seemingly little regard to boost, speed or throttle opening, under the influence of a 'brain', which was intended to calculate how much fuel was needed. Cosworth's main dissatisfaction with the system was that it was not possible to modify the fuel delivery at one engine speed and boost without altering the delivery at all the other speeds and boosts as well, and you only needed the system to run weak, as it was inclined to do at times, and you could have a melted piston very quickly indeed.

In the end Cosworth decided to develop an entirely new fuel system for the DFX. Like the Hilborn, it was a constant-flow system, but incorporating a diaphragm which sensed the pressures in the plenum and intakes and was controlled through a three-dimensional cam. An immediate benefit was easier starting due to the increased accuracy of the fuel metering, whereas with the earlier system it was all too easy to wet the plugs if the engine failed to fire up immediately. Unlike the DFV engine, with its combined high-pressure electrical and mechanical fuel pump, the DFX relies on a mechanical pump which is actuated immediately the engine is turned over.

Cosworth's revised system, which was to become known as the monovalve in the United States, did away with the eight individual butterfly throttles in the intakes by locating a large single butterfly throttle upstream of the straight injector trumpets, directly after the compressor. This arrangement was used throughout 1981 and 1982, but not without some operational problems at first, mainly because most teams found it difficult to get the engine running smoothly, especially when leaving the pits during a race. This was because of the inherent lack of power of the single butterfly system at part-throttle compared with the eight butterfly system — no amount of adjustment will cure the problem, so most teams have learned to live with it. However, one outcome has been a further development on the inlet slide, and some latest-specification engines have been equipped with a slide throttle system with a cast plenum chamber on the top, which is aimed at improving throttle response and general drivability.

In retrospect, it was probably fortuitous that the early development days of the DFX engine had coincided with the time when the regulations allowed 80in of Hg, for it meant that everyone had lived dangerously, with prodigiously high power outputs, and had tended to learn an awful lot, awfully quickly — although sometimes very expensively! In those days, outputs of the order of 900bhp had been claimed regularly, and it only needed a race to be run for a considerable distance under the yellow flag, when consequently less fuel was being consumed, for drivers sensing victory to turn up the boost when the green was shown again and achieve even higher outputs. Under these circumstances, as much as 1,000bhp has been claimed from the 2.65-litre engine!

There had been widespread relief, therefore, when the regulations had been changed, eventually to be stabilized at 48in of Hg, although since that time the task of ensuring acceptable engine reliability has changed rather than disappeared altogether. These days there is a determined effort by teams to push up revs in order to obtain more power at the lower level of boost, and this has meant that whereas in the earlier days revs were kept down to around 9,000rpm or a little above, today the DFX is being run with DFV cams at DFV-type speeds, namely at around 11,000rpm. Whereas horsepower dropped to below 600bhp when the rules were first changed, the higher compressions and improved valve gear had lifted outputs towards the 700bhp mark by 1981 and they are continuing to rise well beyond that figure.

Mention has already been made of the need to improve the cooling of the exhaust valves, and this meant doing away with the original DFV-type cylinder heads and producing heads in which the exhaust valves were placed further apart. However, the valve size remained the same for some time, even after the Formula 1 engine had been changed to larger diameter valves, and it is only more recently that the larger valves have been fitted to the DFX, although of course they are still spaced further apart than in the DFV engine. Conversely, it was the considerably greater blow-by experienced with the turbocharged DFX which precipitated the development of the larger oil scavenge pumps which have subsequently been adopted on other engines.

Another change came about as a result of Cosworth's eventually successful effort to woo the American teams away from the Mallory magneto, which had been a mainstay of racing engines in the United States for so many years, and on to either the Contactless or the Lucas capacitive discharge system of electronic ignition. The change has facilitated the use of rev-limiters and has also overcome another problem in that the output of the magnetos was so high that electrical interference made it very difficult to test as it was virtually impossible to use any electronic instrument near them. Initially, there were a few problems resulting from the changeover to electronic ignition, but in the main these were caused by inadequate wiring, and there is now a general acceptance of the fact that because of the very high currents required for short durations to charge the capacitor it is necessary to fit some very substantial wires between the battery and the ignition set in order to make it work satisfactorily.

It is fair to say that the DFX has not always been the easiest of engines to start, particularly in its earlier days, but experience has led to the evolution of operating procedures which have overcome most of the obstacles. For example, although it is not essential, a number of teams insist that the first step before firing up a DFX is to heat the engine oil (50 grade as compared with the 40 grade used in the DFV), usually by placing an electrically powered wand into the oil tank. The intention here is to avoid possible damage to the main bearings, and although the risk is much reduced these days with the use of freer-clearance bearings following the reduction in boost pressures (the bearing clearances have remained unchanged since 1977), in the days of 80in of Hg, when narrow-clearance bearings were the norm, great care was required to avoid turning the bearings in the block.

Once the oil temperature has reached 25 to 30 degrees C the spark plugs are removed and the engine is turned over a few times to generate some oil and fuel pressure, whereupon the fuel valve is turned on and the engine turned over a few more times until fuel begins to appear through the spark plug holes. Whether magneto or electronic ignition is used, it is possible to fire up a DFX engine on race plugs, although more often a set of warm-up plugs are used. Although Bosch plugs have appeared on the Indy Car scene in recent years, Champion plugs remain the most widely represented, their 504V being used for warming-up and sometimes for racing on slow tracks and the 504 being the essential race plug for the faster tracks.

Unlike Formula 1 machinery prior to 1983, Indy Cars are not equipped with on-board starters and so they tend to arrive in the pit road from the paddock with external starters and battery carts being towed along behind them. It takes a lot of turning to get a narrow-clearance, methanol-burning, turbocharged engine running freely, and this requires not only a powerful starter, but also a very powerful electrical charge. The physical job of clambering beneath the rear wing and plugging in the heavy starter is not too uncomfortable when the car is cool, but the mechanic involved usually has a hot and exciting few seconds in getting a car away again after one of the impressively brief Indianapolis-style mid-race pit stops.

As with most racing engines, a lot of damage can be done if a driver tries to go too hard too quickly, and most team managers insist on several slow laps of a high-speed oval in order to get the oil temperature up to its proper operational reading. Penske Racing's team manager, Derrick Walker, for example, recommends that his drivers should see at least 70 degrees C before 'standing on it hard', he likes a normal running temperature of something in excess of 80 degrees, and he sets 95 degrees as an operating maximum.

Mario Andretti is one of the relatively few drivers to have had racing experience with both the DFV and the DFX engines, and he is certainly the most experienced of this select group. He says that compared with the DFV, which from the standpoint of driver feel seems to give out relatively modest horsepower, 'though the engine is very responsive, has a very good power

Johnny Rutherford at the wheel of his McLaren M24B on the newly renamed Brands Hatch Indy circuit, where he finished third behind Sneva, two places better than he had managed at Silverstone, where Gordon Johncock just beat him into fourth place with his Offenhauser-powered Wildcat. The public relations-consciousness of the American drivers greatly impressed the local press corps, but the crowds were disappointing and the experiment was not to be repeated.

curve and feels to be giving usable horsepower from 8,500rpm', the DFX can only be described as 'a bit of a beast', particularly on a road course.

'Trying to use full power and use it effectively is a real struggle when there's no way you can drive smoothly because there's no progression. As far as what's at the end of your foot is concerned, well, it's a bomb at 8,000rpm and it's a bomb at 11,000rpm. The way the extra power comes in just knocks you out of shape when you're road-racing one of those things', he says, with more than a trace of admiration for its horsepower. 'In the rain — and maybe not having any trick rain tyres has something to do with it — but *man*, it's a terror!

'When they first cut back the boost, the top end of the DFX came down quite a bit. But all that has been made up with cams and compression ratios and with the kind of horsepower we have now it's definitely a stout engine. You can really feel the horsepower, whereas when we first started running 48 inches we were down to about 650bhp and that was a little too docile . . .

'Both the DFV and the DFX are real vibrators because of their 180-degree cranks, and as far as smoothness and progression are concerned they're nothing like a 12-cylinder Alfa or Ferrari, though they do give you a very efficient feel. Yet on a super speedway like Indianapolis or Michigan the DFX operates fairly effortlessly at 11,200rpm. It must be that the harmonics are just right at that range because it feels like it could go on forever, and of course a lot of times it does!'

In one respect, the development of the DFX has followed a complete circle in so far as the engine, which started out as a very lightly modified DFV, and then became the subject of a series of more radical alterations based on then-current thinking in the United States, has subsequently emerged with a lot more DFV-inspired pieces in its specification. This came about following the reduction in boost pressure and when Cosworth realized that their 'production' DFX, which was giving around 585bhp, was being more than matched by one or two engines being built up on the other side of the Atlantic.

Keith Duckworth reasoned that following the significant drop in boost pressure it might be beneficial, in planning the DFX's further development, to consider it not simply as a turbocharged engine, but rather as a normally aspirated engine which is required to operate in an increased density atmosphere. Applying that philosophy, the people at Northampton then set about producing what was, in effect, a blown DFV, with the engine's intake and exhaust systems, tuned pipe lengths, cams and so on, all very similar to those which had been used on the Formula 1 engine. The result of these developments during the winter of 1980-81 was a gain of around 90bhp, while the modified fuel system, incorporating a Cosworth metering unit and a Hilborn pump, also improved the general engine management and led to some gain in fuel mileage.

More recently, in Cosworth's on-going performance-improvement programme for the DFX, emphasis has been placed on the development of even more precise fuel management systems incorporating electronic sensors and timers. Instrumentation to record instantaneous consumption of fuel and whether or not total consumption to date is within the required limit is now seen as essential equipment for the future within a formula in which tankage is related to a theoretical consumption of not more than 2.8mpg (US). This programme, which is being directed towards both engine management and the provision of driver information, is being carried out in conjunction with a continuing search for compressors capable of delivering increased rates of volume and flow.

The effective conversion of the DFX into a normally aspirated engine with tuned exhaust lengths (there has been a change from short to long exhausts) has led to continuing research into further alternative tuned lengths of intakes and different plenum systems, which all affect the performance of turbocharged engines considerably. However, despite the tentative move towards slide throttles, the single butterfly arrangement has by no means been abandoned, and notwithstanding the increasing use of road circuits for the Indy Car series, on which the slide throttles might have been expected to offer an advantage through a more immediate and accurate response, the feedback from teams seems to suggest that the difference is only marginal between the two systems. On the large ovals, where response and speed changes are much less critical, the single butterfly arrangement offers the benefit of a relatively modest, but nevertheless useful, increase in power.

Cosworth's project engineer on the DFX is Paul Morgan, who is based in Northampton, but since the formation of a wholly owned subsidiary company in the United States, customer liaison has mostly been routed through Cosworth's premises in Torrance, California. This company came into being after Larry Slutter was taken on to the Cosworth strength, initially to source components for engine assembly in Northampton (at first he worked out of a room in his home), but gradually the Torrance operation has been extended to embrace technical liaison as well as engine and component supply.

The initial premises were quickly outgrown, and Cosworth are now in much more commodious accommodation nearby, with the option to acquire the remainder of the building should business continue to expand to justify this. A staff of six now operates there — four engine builders, a parts specialist and a secretary — so that a limited amount of customer overhauls can be undertaken, although in Indy Car racing the policy of major teams all running their own engine build facility or putting their work out to long-established specialist race engine rebuilders, which began in Offenhauser days, has largely been continued. This is why, although Cosworth like to supply a new team's engines direct from Northampton to ensure that they start off with units built to specification, thereafter it is relatively rare for the DFXs to cross the Atlantic again for routine rebuilds.

The bulk stores of DFX pieces, however, are held at Northampton, only a relatively small shelf stock being maintained in California because the air freighting system ensures that a wanted part is never more than two or three days from arriving at Torrance, having cleared Customs. A few long-standing customers continue to order direct from Northampton, where Jack Field, who used to be responsible for selling Cosworth products in the United States in the early days, is in overall charge of sales, but the vast majority of users look to the Torrance facility to satisfy their requirements. The Cosworth base there also has wider implications than just servicing Indy Car racing and it has enabled the company to exploit other areas of the specialist racing market, notably in the supply of pistons. It would appear that a significant foothold has already been achieved in this expanding market, and there seems little doubt that those extra square feet of factory space could be put to good use should the decision be taken to acquire them.

The DFX's revised 1981 specification, which provided those valuable extra 90bhp, and the proof that the engine in that form was capable of winning straight out of the box, came just in time, because even amongst those who were making such effective use of it there was still that undercurrent of resentment at having to pay a considerable sum of money for what was still regarded as a foreign engine. Had the DFX not achieved such impressive and consistent power and such remarkable reliability at that time, the campaign to legislate it out of contention might well have gathered more supporters; in short, it needed to win out of the box, and keep on winning, simply to ensure its continued acceptance, however grudging that acceptance might be.

It is doubtful whether the campaign for a change to a stock block-based formula will ever die completely, because such a move will always have superficial attractions. It is only when the true cost is worked out that the idea becomes less attractive to those who have to balance the books. Furthermore, that total cost cannot be confined simply to the price of converting a stock-block engine into an equally consistent race-winner, because to provide reliable, race-winning power has been only a part of the DFX's achievement.

Perhaps its greatest contribution of all to Indy Car racing has been to facilitate its restoration as a major sporting spectacle after a period during which its health was in a parlous state. It has done this by putting at the disposal of potential entrants an engine which can be bought, slapped into a chassis, fired up and used to win races without the need for additional expensive development. The other necessary ingredient has been supplied by chassis manufacturers, often British-based and notable amongst whom more recently has been March Engineering, who have similarly provided a vehicle which

No fewer than 17 of the 33 cars which qualified for the 1982 Indianapolis 500 were Marches, most of them 82C models and all of them Cosworth DFX-powered. This posed picture at the factory in Bicester features almost the entire March staff and celebrates the completion of the 1,000th car to be built since the company's formation in October 1969. It is a March 83C, earmarked for A. J. Foyt in the year in which he was to aim for a fifth Indianapolis 500 victory.

could be purchasd off the shelf with the reasonable expectation that it could carry a driver to victory.

It has been primarily the existence of competitive chassis and engines which has encouraged people into Indy Car racing who otherwise could not have contemplated participating, due to the excessively high cost of developing their own equipment. Their presence, in turn, has created the relatively large fields of comparatively evenly matched cars and drivers which are so essential for high-quality, open racing. The new standards of professionalism displayed by CART could not have been effective had they not been founded on such a reliable technical base, for promotion without the promise of close competition is, in the end, a futile exercise.

Compared with Formula 1, Indy Car racing is a significantly more personality-dominated and exploited sport, where the promotional emphasis is centred on drivers rather than on their cars. Few would argue against the desirability of this, for the mass market will always respond more readily to sportsmen and sportswomen than to their equipment. Nevertheless, in the Indy Car field it is the equipment which has produced the personalities, by bringing exciting new talent to the fore as a result of the increasing number of opportunities to drive competitive cars.

An interesting by-product has been the growth of non-American drivers in this class of motor racing, a trend which is likely to be extended as the CART series continues its expansion beyond the traditional oval tracks on to circuits where international experience in other classes of racing can be so beneficial. In several respects, therefore, the once great divide between Formula 1 and the traditional form of Indy Car racing has been narrowed, and this, surely, can only be a good thing at a time when international communications through the media's use of satellites is offering the prospect of vast new audiences for sports previously supported by mainly parochial enthusiasms.

At the time of writing, Indy Car racing is in a better state of health than at any time in recent years, after an anxious period when it could so easily have been sunk without much trace. Credit for the turnaround should rightly be shared by many people in positions of influence, for although the debates have been acrimonious at times as forceful personalities have aired often diametrically opposed views, ultimately an element of realism and reason seems to have prevailed, encouraged by the knowledge that what has emerged in the last few years under the banner of Indy Car racing is worth protecting and promoting.

Even those who were most violently opposed to the decision of key entrants like Roger Penske to form themselves into a collective voicepiece and ultimately into an independent race sanctioning body seem now to accept at least the motivation for their move. A car owner's star event has always been Indianapolis, where the publicity is intense and the rewards for success are high. But in order to do a good job there an entrant has to run a highly professional team with highly trained personnel and comprehensive workshop facilities, which cannot possibly be supported on the back of this one event. Furthermore, no team can remain fresh when it is only extended once per year, which is the other major reason why it was essential to generate a renewal of public — and through it media and commercial — interest in the other traditional races in the calendar which, for the most part, might have been quite long in history, but were woefully short of people coming through the turnstiles.

CART's major achievement has been to give Indy Car racing a genuine series image, with the public spotlight turned on it for several months of the year, not just during the month of May. During 1982 there was some real evidence that the wounds inflicted during the course of battle with USAC and the Indianapolis Motor Speedway had begun to heal, that the futility of arbitrary rule changes — which largely precipitated the dispute in the first place — had been recognized as the major cause of dwindling support by entrants and public alike.

Most of all, the attraction of a series sponsor in PPG Industries, the automotive paint and glass manufacturer, had given the Indy Car races a visible cohesion, and it was a considerable encouragement when, shortly after a change in command at Indianapolis in 1982, it was announced that in 1983 the famous 500-miles race, which alone had remained on the USAC calendar of events during CART's formative years, might even become a points scoring round of the CART's Indy Car World Series.

Less pleasing, however, was to be the news, later in the year, of some divergence of opinion between CART and USAC on the fine print of their respective rules. Just as in Formula 1, where the fatal accident to Gilles Villeneuve while practising for the 1982 Belgian Grand Prix had added impetus to a campaign to legislate some of the speed out of Grand Prix cars, so the pre-qualifying accident at Indianapolis which had killed Gordon Smiley, followed by the fatal crash by Jim Hickman at Milwaukee, had prompted general agreement that something had to be done to reduce speeds — and especially qualifying speeds — on the ovals.

CART's solution was to announce that side skirts would be banned in 1983, chassis would be flat-bottomed and body sidepods would be raised an inch above the chassis baseline, the rear wing overhang would be reduced by 5in and the engine boost pressure would remain at 48in Hg. It was unfortunate, therefore, that USAC's subsequently announced revised rules differed in two fundamentals — the sidepods were to be 2in above the chassis baseline and the boost pressure was to be reduced to 45in Hg (with a similar reduction of 3in, from 58 to 55in, in the case of 3.42-litre stock block turbo engines). Leaving aside the fact that the reduction in boost pressures can be seen as another move calculated to increase the relative competitiveness of the normally-aspirated stock block engines, the variation in chassis rules between the two bodies was a reminder that the process of reconciliation still had some way to go.

Nevertheless, a new wave of sponsorship interest for the 1983 season, at a time when the United States was still in the grip of an economic recession of considerable proportions, was seen as an encouraging pointer to Indy Car racing's prospects. The DFX engine, with seven full seasons of successful participation behind it, had become a widely understood power unit on the Indy Car scene, as a result of which it could be maintained efficiently and cost effectively. It had already shown considerable versatility in its adaptability to changing boost regulations, and there was the intriguing thought that its already impressive reliability could well be improved upon even further should the legislators ever decide on the need for a further reduction in lap speeds and seek to achieve this in a sensible way.

This does not mean a further reduction in boost pressure, which would merely encourage teams to use even higher rev limits (these are already running beyond the 11,000rpm mark where valve gear limitations become critical) but rather a limitation on intake air, which could mean that it would no longer be beneficial to rev the engine beyond, say, 10,000rpm. Such an engine, running at a moderate boost pressure, ought to prove exceedingly reliable and would be an even greater attraction to potential entrants who have yet to move into this class of racing. Such a development would undoubtedly find favour with both Cosworth and Ford, and it is difficult to perceive of any valid objections by teams who wish to remain competitive whilst simultaneously containing or even reducing costs. Whether the legislators can be convinced, however, must remain to be seen, but it would seem to be an area for debate worthy of consideration.

CHAPTER 6

A matter of endurance

DFL and the C100 saga

Apart from the obvious differences in cost and performance per litre, there is one other particular area where the requirements of a racing engine differ from those of a high-volume power unit intended for road use. Whereas the production power unit usually requires an element of design flexibility to ensure that it can be adapted to a variety of applications — perhaps even extending from sports cars to commercial vehicles — ideally a racing unit should be purpose-built, not just for competitions, but specifically tailored to a single racing formula, to the exclusion of all others. There should be no compromises if the maximum suitability for a precisely defined purpose is to be achieved.

Keith Duckworth, therefore, was less than ecstatic when he heard that certain teams were proposing to use his Ford DFV engine for endurance races and that these would include the 24-hours event at Le Mans. 'If they had wanted a 24-hour engine I would have designed them a 24-hours engine', he is quoted to have remarked at the time. There is little doubt that at the back of his mind were two matters of concern. The first and more serious was that there was a reasonable chance that the engine would fail to last 24 hours, even at the somewhat lower levels of stress which endurance racing normally involves, and that should this be the case the failure in such a highly publicized event as the Le Mans classic would reflect adversely and unfairly on his company. The second worry was that, even if it held together, the DFV would be called upon to compete against endurance racing engines which had been developed for that specific purpose; it would be rather like a sub-4-minute miler being entered for a marathon and being expected to be the first to break the finishing tape.

It was the fundamental change in endurance racing regulations for the 1972 season, when a limit of 3 litres was imposed on sports cars to help reduce lap speeds (the Le Mans record had been raised to almost 152mph the previous year in a 5-litre 12-cylinder Porsche 917), which brought about the sudden interest in the Ford DFV as a long-distance power unit. Despite his misgivings, Duckworth and his colleagues at Northampton responded to the challenge, and tests with engines equipped with softer camshafts, a reduced compression ratio and a more conservative rev limit were soon giving encouraging results.

Derek Bell working hard at the wheel of the Gulf GR7 of the oil company-backed team operated first by John Wyer and, after his retirement, by John Horsman. Considerably more success was earned by these Ford DFV-equipped cars than came the way of Ford's own F3L coupes which had been built to accept the same engine a few years earlier.

Although inevitably DFV-powered cars were to compete in other events in the endurance racing calendar, ranging in duration from 5 to 12 hours, the spotlight shone most brightly at Le Mans, where the opposition was at its most formidable. It was therefore somewhat ironical that the Matra Simca sports car team, the growth of which had stemmed from the frustration of being unable to mount an effective challenge to the Ford DFV-powered teams in Formula 1, was to rule the roost at Le Mans during the first three years of the Ford engine's presence there. However, when the French team withdrew following the completion of their hat-trick of victories (with Henri Pescarolo in the winning car on each occasion), DFV-powered cars stepped in decisively in 1975 to fill the first three places, the Gulf-Mirage of Jacky Ickx and Derek Bell beating the Ligier-Ford of Jean-Louis Lafosse and Guy Chasseuil, with Vern Schuppan and Jean-Pierre Jaussaud finishing third in the second of the Gulf team's cars.

The following year, a DFV-powered Mirage and a Lola finished second and third, respectively, behind the winning Porsche, but the engine's second outright Le Mans victory had to wait until 1980, when team owner Jean Rondeau, sharing one of his Rondeau M379Bs with Jaussaud, beat a strong Porsche contingent to win the race overall as well as take first place in the Index of Thermal Efficiency competition, which related performance to fuel consumption.

The Le Mans organizers have a long history of interest in the promotion of fuel efficiency, and their campaign gathered considerable momentum in the aftermath of the oil crisis of 1973. Their pre-occupation with the subject during this period was one of the reasons why, for a time, their classic race was to be run outside the official FIA endurance racing World Championship, but the parting of the ways did nothing to diminish the status of Le Mans as the premier long-distance event in the calendar. Indeed, without this event as an anchor pin, it was the FIA series which was to suffer, and after its sharp decline it took another fundamental change in formula and the restoration of the French classic into the official fixture list to restore public interest to a reasonable level.

The influence of the *Automobile Club de l'Ouest* was to be seen clearly when the proposed new Group C regulations were published, for in the traditions of the Le Mans race fuel efficiency was to loom large; indeed, it was to become the central issue. Endurance races would no longer be regulated primarily according to the engine displacement of competing cars, but rather by the rate at which they consumed fuel.

As Keith Duckworth had for long been emphasizing the weaknesses of basing racing formulae on arbitrary limits on engine displacement (he had also reminded those who would listen of the pitfalls in attempting to express so-called equivalences between turbocharged and normally aspirated engines by means of a mathematical factor related to engine size), the new Group C

Derek Bell on his way to victory at Le Mans in 1975 with the Gulf GR7 he shared with Jacky Ickx. This was their first Le Mans success together, but others would follow, though not with Ford-powered cars.

rules for endurance racing held certain attractions to him as an engine designer/builder. They made it possible, for example, to consider a long-distance derivative of the DFV without the constraint of the 3-litre limit, which meant that a larger cylinder bore or a longer piston stroke, or both, could be envisaged in the scheming of an engine which would achieve the most satisfactory level of performance and reliability at a rate of fuel consumption commensurate with what was permissible under the new rules.

An oversize DFV was not an entirely new concept. Such engines had been running for a number of years in branches of the sport where they were permitted and seemed to offer a performance advantage. In particular, they had been seen in action in British hill-climb events, where additional mid-range torque could be of considerable benefit in punching a car out of the tight corners which abound in this type of event, and where a tenth or even a hundredth of a second per mile saved could mean the difference between success and relative failure. The DFV engine had also been used in both standard and non-standard displacement forms to power modified production-based cars in club races and sprints, a slightly incongruous adaptation, perhaps, but nevertheless one which had revealed a versatility far beyond the intentions of its designer. These early examples of 'stretched' DFVs, however, were mainly the work of outside builders, and it was not until the new opportunity provided within the orbit of endurance racing was examined that Cosworth and Ford seriously considered the development and manufacture of a larger-displacement derivative of the DFV.

Two programmes were to emerge from the various discussions which ensued, and it is important that they should not be confused, even though they were interrelated in some respects. The first was to be the development and productionizing of what we now know as the DFL engine, a programme which would involve the testing of engines in alternative displacements which initially would be run in normally aspirated form, with the idea that they would be adaptable to turbocharging at a later date. The second and separate decision was to build a small number of cars designed around the new Group C rules, which would become mobile testbeds for the further development of the DFL engines in their various forms and be used as a basis of a Ford team to compete in German Championship events as well as in selected races in the International endurance-racing calendar. The Ford C100 programme will be discussed in more detail later in this chapter.

As had been the case with the Formula 1 DFV engine, the contractural arrangements between the Ford Motor Company and Cosworth Engineering concerning the DFL programme were straightforward and to the point. Once again the sum involved in purely cash terms was £100,000 (which represented a lot less, of course, in 1980 than it had in 1966), and this was to be supplemented by technical support in the form of engineering services to Cosworth such as computer time, finite element modelling programmes and modal analysis.

In return for this contribution towards expenses, Cosworth were to initiate the development of both a 3.3-litre normally aspirated derivative of the DFV incorporating a standard stroke with an increased bore and a 3.6-litre derivative, which would retain the standard bore, but with an increased stroke. Then, if these two developments proved satisfactory, Cosworth would develop a 3.95-litre version, incorporating the increased bore and the

The first Ford C100 was developed out of a design which had to be schemed before the finalized Group C regulations had been agreed, and consequently considerable dimensional alterations were needed once the delayed rules had been published. The C100 designation referred to the 100cm height regulation demanded in Group C. This car was first raced at Brands Hatch in 1981 under the previous Group 6 rules.

increased stroke.

The engines were to be suitable for Group C racing (which implied an acceptable level of fuel efficiency) and for a period of three years the Ford 'oval' would appear on the cam covers of the engines. There was also an undertaking to manufacture and make available to a team nominated by Ford a number of 3.3-litre engines and to service them, beyond which Cosworth would be free to make and sell any versions of the DFL to any customer for any purpose.

At one stage in the discussions consideration was given to the possibility of both the Ford and Cosworth names appearing on the engines, but when they were published the regulations expressly excluded such an arrangement because under Group C the engine had to bear the name of a manufacturer of cars which were homologated in either Group A or Group B. (For the DFL engine's FIA recognition form, Ford nominated the Escort XR3 as an example of one of their Group A cars.)

There was a seemingly interminable delay in the framing and publication of the Group C rules in their final form, which meant that the DFL programme

The C100 in 1982 guise with long-tailed bodywork. The car was initially run with the Ford DFL engine in 3.3-litre form, but 3.9-litre versions were provided in time for Le Mans, where the additional vibrations caused failure of the crankshaft dampers after the cars had run promisingly during the early hours of the race.

had to be started without the benefit of knowing precisely what the requirements would be as regards fuel efficiency. Although pleased that a major racing formula was being based on such a criterion, Keith Duckworth was considerably disappointed when, eventually, the rules were published and found to be so lenient in this important respect. 'The regulations, which fixed the minimum weight at 800 kilograms, allowed 100 litres of fuel to be carried and permitted fuel stops at intervals of less than an hour at Le Mans — 25 stops in the 24 hours — suggested to me that it would be possible to run a 700bhp engine in Group C, whereas I had been hoping that the rules would have encouraged the use of engines giving around 500bhp. It occurred to me that the users of 1½-litre turbocharged engines in Formula 1, who seem to represent a powerful lobby in rules negotiations, had swayed the decision and that the colossal rate of fuel flow permitted was probably based on the consumption of a 1½-litre turbo when raced flat-out.' The announcement of the rules was to cause the three-engine element of the DFL agreement to be revised.

'The first stage of the programme was relatively straightforward in that the 3.3-litre displacement was achieved by combining the DFV's stroke with the bore of our four-cylinder 2-litre BDG Formula 2 engine. This meant that we could use BDG pistons in the DFL, which simply required some bigger liners and for the block to be bored out a bit. However, as development continued we made an improved piston for the DFL and also made a small change to the cylinder liners.

'For a long time I had been saying that if we were to become involved in Group C or any other fuel-economy formula we needed to have a longer stroke, and so the 3.3-litre engine was only an interim measure. I then got down to making the longest-stroke crank that I thought was possible with the standard block, and this gave us an extra half-inch which, with the larger bore of the 3.3-litre, offered us a displacement of 3.95 litres. However, I had been hoping that the longer stroke could be used with the standard bore and that the resulting 3.6-litre engine would be most suitable for using up the amount of fuel which the regulations would permit. You must remember that if you are to be successful in a fuel economy-related formula, you must first ensure that you are able to use all the fuel, and then you must ensure that you consume it efficiently.

'It was immediately very clear to me that my proposed 3.6-litre engine wouldn't use anything like enough fuel, and that even with the 3.95-litre displacement available with the aid of the larger bore the DFL in normally aspirated form would still prove to be too economical for the rules as published for 1982 and 1983. These virtually dictated the necessity for turbocharging, but of course there was no possibility of doing this within the time cycle at our disposal; turbocharging had to be another step along the way.

'Where the rule makers slipped up is that they failed to appreciate that in Group C racing a given engine will be so much more economical than it was, or would have been, in Formula 1 with full ground effects. The lack of, or markedly reduced level of ground effects means that an engine in a Group C car will spend a much lower percentage of its race time running at full throttle, and therefore its rate of fuel consumption will be much lower. Experience has confirmed that even driving a normally aspirated DFL Group C car flat-out all the way it cannot be made to use all the available fuel if the engine is running at peak efficiency. The rules mean that you can go up and up on your power range because you can only use it for a smaller proportion of the time.'

It had been envisaged that the normally aspirated DFL in 3.95-litre form would deliver around 570 to 580bhp, although in its early days the output fell a little short of that, 540 to 550bhp being nearer the mark. However, the slightly reduced horsepower was of minor concern compared with the engine's considerable vibration characteristics. In view of the increased stroke and the retention of the same conrod length the secondary out-of-balance of the DFL is 50 per cent greater than that of a 3-litre DFV, which means that the loads on the engine mountings when the engine is mounted solidly are also 50 per cent higher. The shaking of components mounted on the engine or transmission is similarly increased. However, not all of the problems encountered by users of the DFV in 3.95-litre form can be attributed to the higher degree of shake; in many instances a major contributory factor has been the less than adequate way in which the engine loads have been fed into the various chassis, and certain of the problems might well have occurred had the cars concerned been fitted with a 3-litre DFV engine. Lack of familiarity with a flat-plane V8 racing engine and its inherent vibration characteristics was to a large extent responsible for the less than satisfactory reliability record of cars during the first full season of the DFL in its 3.95-litre form, but the lessons were quickly learned and the later chassis showed the benefit of the experience gained.

It was cruel misfortune, however, that the most significant step taken to minimize the vibrations should inadvertently have been the indirect cause of the most disappointing retirements of DFL-powered cars from the 1982 Le Mans race, involving two cars from each of the Ford and Rondeau teams. The longer stroke of the 3.95-litre engine indicated the need for a crankshaft damper, an item which had not formed part of the specification of the standard-stroke 3.3-litre DFL. Working closely with Holset, Cosworth experimented with a wide variety of damper sizes, types, materials and rubber compounds before selecting a design and specification which achieved satisfactory results on the test rigs. But once again, it seems, the long Mulsanne straight at Le Mans, on which engines are often called upon to run through seemingly critical rev bands for prolonged periods of time, was to reveal a problem not experienced elsewhere.

One after the other, the four cars concerned, after running competitively and seemingly in good health, suddenly stopped. Although the problem remained obscure at first, subsequent inspection revealed that the crankshaft damper had failed and in doing so had severed the ignition trigger wire immediately behind it. During a later investigation the conclusion was reached that in addition to the damper's normal rotary motion the engine was imposing on it a fore-and-aft oscillation so that, whereas the outer ring stayed still, the bonded rubber centre was being made to work longitudinally (for which it was not designed at that stage) until eventually the damper lost its integrity and the ring broke loose and cut the ignition trigger. In the subsequent redesign, the damper was allowed a measure of fore-and-aft movement and the hub was located more securely. 'One of the contributory factors of our damper problems', explained Keith Duckworth, 'was that whereas it had always been assumed that the damper should have been cooled, this had not been done at first, and then we had changed from one batch of dampers to another on which we had not completed sufficient testing. However, in the course of the redesign we greatly increased the mechanical integrity and subsequently carried out several hours of testing without encountering any troubles.'

As already mentioned, the normally aspirated DFL had been legislated against by the liberal fuel rules, and whilst the engine continued to be available in this form and, along with the 3.3-litre version, continued to play a part in the endurance racing scene, the mainstream of development at the end of 1982 was concerned with its conversion to turbocharged form, using Japanese IHI turbo units. A variety of different schemes and layouts were considered, involving single or twin turbos and single or twin intercoolers, but the advantages of a single turbo with one intercooler seemed to be considerable. In a formula where chassis constructors have been slow to get cars down close to the weight limit the saving of weight and the much simpler packaging offered by a single installation cannot be underestimated, especially as with the DFL it was the intention to use only a moderate 'blow' with a variable boost pressure. The target output was in the region of 700bhp at 8,000 to 8,500rpm.

The conversion to turbocharging meant that for the first time with the DFL engine there would be a need for a more sophisticated engine management system, and Cosworth became involved in a joint project with Micro Consultants, another company within the Group, in the development of electronic control of ignition and boost levels, as well as on the provision of fuel-flow indicators and information for the driver and pit crew to determine the correct driving style during a race.

Simultaneously, Ford and Cosworth jointly tackled the problem of secondary vibrations on the V8 engines. 'Ford helped us with an analysis of the vibrations', says Duckworth, 'when they came up and instrumented a DFL and a DFV on the testbed. This showed that it was our secondary out-of-balance which was markedly greater at the engine mounting points, which was very useful to know because I was worried that we might have block weave and equally high amplitudes of other orders of vibration which might be causing the trouble, so that even if we balanced out the secondaries we might not be any better off.

'Those results definitely showed that the secondaries were by far the most likely cause of our mounting troubles and the difficulties of hanging anything

Manfred Winkelhock at the wheel of one of the C100s which were operated from Germany throughout much of 1982 in collaboration with the Zakspeed organization. The cars were also used for the German Championship races.

on to the engine, so we have since been experimenting with secondary balancing systems to reduce the vibration levels. We are using Lanchester-type shafts, although the solution is not without its difficulties because owners of DFL engines are anxious that we shall be able to carry out conversions for them, and this imposes further difficulties on the already very great problem of mounting the shafts within the space available.'

A great deal of development activity was taking place around the DFL engine, therefore, as the 1983 racing season was about to start, but simultaneously Ford announced a sudden change of plan concerning the second element of their endurance racing involvement, namely the decision not, after all, to operate a team of Ford C100s in 1983 events other than those concerned with the German Championship. Instead, the cars would be made available as required for such further development of the DFL family of engines as Cosworth might find useful. There would not, therefore, be an escalation of the Ford v Porsche confrontation initiated in 1982 as a reminder of the famous Ford v Ferrari battles of the 1960s. The reasons for the decision were complex in so far as they formed part of a new competitions strategy, the details of which will not become fully visible until the mid-1980s or even later.

The Ford C100 project had been born out of the decision by car designer Len Bailey and endurance racing entrant Alain de Cadenet to produce a car embodying ground effects aerodynamics and other Formula 1-developed technology which, in the short term, would comply with the existing Group 6 regulations governing that class of racing, but would be convertible to the proposed, but yet to be fully revealed, Group C rules. Bailey, of course, had a long history of involvement with Ford, dating back to the days of the GT40, whilst similarly de Cadenet had been a regular participant in endurance racing with Ford-powered cars. With Ford's expressed interest in the concept of

Group C in its promotion of fuel efficiency and the opportunity it afforded for the exploitation of advanced aerodynamic concepts — both areas which translate naturally to the passenger car field — the adoption of the Bailey-de Cadenet project was a logical step towards the establishment by the company of a full Group C team once the regulations had been finalized.

The original intention, after the completion of the Bailey-designed car, was that its subsequent development would continue in Britain in collaboration with a private team, but these plans were shelved and the car was taken to Ford's competitions department in Cologne, Germany, where this work was continued. It returned to England later in the year, however, to compete in a race at Brands Hatch, which it led comfortably until the car's lack of a gearbox oil cooler resulted in a transmission failure.

Bailey's work on a proper C100 (the name of which was coined from the 100mm limit on roof height, just as the Ford GT40 had indicated the 40in dimension of earlier regulations) was hampered by the delay in the finalization of the new rules, and he withdrew from the project early in 1982 when the car, based on a Hesketh-manufactured aluminium chassis tub, became the responsibility of Ford in Germany.

Meanwhile, a replica of the works car, but built around a monocoque tub fabricated in honeycomb material by TC Prototypes, had been taking shape in Britain for de Cadenet to race, but after the aluminium-chassised car had

A display of DFV components providing another reminder of the meticulous care which Cosworth Engineering takes over the detail work of their products and the surface finish which is applied to them.

proved disappointing, the de Cadenet car was adopted as the second-generation Group C design and taken to Germany where the programme was thereafter to be managed from the Zakspeed headquarters at Niederzissen, under the personal control of Erich Zakowski.

Klaus Ludwig and Manfred Winkelhock became the team's regular drivers, to be joined for Le Mans by Marc Surer and Klaus Niedzwiedz, but although the C100 was to win two German Championship races, outright success in any of the classic endurance events was to elude the team, although it was to come tantalizingly close at the Nurburgring, where the C100 was leading comfortably until a gear case problem caused the differential carrier to move and eventually to damage the crownwheel and pinion.

At this point, Formula 1 car designer Tony Southgate joined the operation, charged with the task of designing a 1983 version of the car as well as overseeing the further detail development of the 1982 C100s. The first of the new cars, which were intended ultimately to appear with both short-tail and long-tail bodywork, was completed in February 1983 and underwent its initial circuit tests at the Paul Ricard circuit in the South of France, equipped with a normally aspirated 3.95-litre engine. However, Karl Ludvigsen, who had been in overall charge of Ford's competition activities during the C100's short career, announced that it would not compete until the development of the turbocharged version of the DFL engine — by then at a fairly advanced stage, but still requiring further time at Northampton — had been satisfactorily concluded. A few weeks later, after Ludvigsen had moved to another assignment within Ford and Stuart Turner had taken control of Ford's European competitions activities, it was announced that the C100 would not be appearing on the endurance racing scene after all in its latest guise, although the car would feature in the German National programme. One of the 1982 cars, however, was soon to be taken over by the British driver Martin Birrane, with the intention that it would be used for a combined programme involving selected endurance races and events in the newly created Thundersports category in Britain, which marked the return of high-powered sports cars to the National calendar.

The Ford decision to withdraw from the endurance racing scene, coupled with the fact that several potential users of the DFL engine were having considerable difficulty in raising sufficient sponsorship to support their planned 1983 programmes, caused Cosworth to re-examine their position with the DFL and to call a halt to the further development of the turbocharged version. During the winter period, some difficulties had been encountered with the exhaust system, and although these had been largely overcome it had always been clear that the successful development of a turbocharged DFL would be an expensive exercise, and so it was proving. With the Ford team no longer a customer and others in various states of financial difficulty, it was apparent that the potential market for the turbo DFL no longer justified its considerable development and manufacturing costs.

However, the winter work had not been entirely in vain and attention was turned back towards the normally aspirated engine, which still had a role to play in the 1983 endurance racing scene, and whose competitiveness was likely to be considerably enhanced in 1984, when the maximum fuel tankage in Group C was due to be reduced from 100 to 85 litres. One element of the development programme which was unaffected by the abandonment of the

The crankshaft damper recessed into the front face identifies this as a 3.9-litre version of the DFL engine. The use of the Ford 'oval' on the cam covers was another identification of a DFL until similar covers started to appear on the Formula 1 DFY and certain DFV engines in 1983. The DFLs have been equipped with the slimline auxiliaries which were developed for use in Formula 1 at the height of the ground effects period.

turbocharged version was the use of balance shafts to help reduce the level of vibrations.

The conversion involves the external mounting of two shafts, one above the other and geared together, which are located below the exhaust ports alongside the front half of the block. The shafts, which run at twice engine speed, are driven from the crankshaft by a rubber belt, and although their mounting lugs were welded in position on the development engines, the intention is to incorporate the mounts into the block casting. Even without the balance shafts, however, the latest specification crankshaft damper seemed to work extremely well when it underwent prolonged tests in the first of the 1983 C100s, so with the shafts added it seems likely that in future Group C chassis manufacturers making use of the 3.95-litre DFL engine will have a much easier installation job.

Right from the start of DFL manufacture, Cosworth have issued explicit installation recommendations, particularly in respect of oil, cooling and fuel systems, but unfortunately motor racing tends to breed proud people, not all of whom take kindly to being told how to do their job. Failures due to incorrect installation procedures used to be quite commonplace during the early years of the DFV in Formula 1, and a similar pattern has emerged in the endurance racing world, although undoubtedly the existence of so much expertise within today's Formula 1 teams has been of considerable benefit to Group C people who, in the main, have worked quickly and sensibly to sort out their problems.

Sometimes these can be caused in the most unlikely way. For example, at one stage during 1982 the Ford C100 team encountered some mysterious losses of engine power and found some inconsistencies of behaviour of one engine against another. It was not until the engines had been removed from the cars and returned to Cosworth for inspection that it became clear that the trouble was not with the engines themselves — although they were in a terrible state — but with the cars' air filtering system; the engines turned out to be the dirtiest that Cosworth had ever seen. The loss of power was because they had been internally ground by a mixture of sand and dirt, all as a result of an aerodynamic phenomenon which had caused grit and garbage to be scooped

Keith Duckworth examining a DFL in course of assembly by engine builder Terry Moss. This example has been fitted with the latest magnesium throttle slide covers.

up into the air inlet of the intake system in such a quantity and density that the filters had proved quite inadequate. With the relocation of the intakes and a filter modification the problem was cured.

Manfred Winkelhock, who was involved in the C100 project from its inception until the end of 1982, is one of the few drivers able to offer a direct comparison between the DFL in both 3.3-litre and 3.95-litre forms and the 3-litre DFV. 'My first experience of the DFL was at Brands Hatch in 1981 when we ran the engine in 3.3-litre form. Compared with the DFV, which I have always thought of as a fantastic engine, the DFL felt perhaps a little bit stronger, but of course the extra power was hidden because the C100 was so much heavier than a Formula 1 car. Whereas with a Formula 1 at that time you aimed to be down to well under 600 kilograms, with the C100 we were scaling nearly 900 kilos that year. That engine you could rev to around 9,500rpm, and although it vibrated a bit more than the DFV, I didn't think it was too bad.

'The first 3.95-litre I drove was at Paul Ricard, and that really was a bit of a disappointment. In fact, it felt as though it had less power than the Formula 1, though I'm sure it had quite a bit more really. But the biggest problem was the vibration, especially around about 8,000rpm — it was very pronounced there, and it even affected my breathing. We were using a rev range from about 6,000rpm to 9,000rpm, but it only started to feel really strong at the very top end.

'Then they started to change a few things and the engine became better. The compression was reduced a little bit and this seemed to make it vibrate less, and soon we were getting 9,500rpm, which was much better, although we were still only seeing about 540bhp. But there was still more to come, we knew that, and we could see that if we could get something nearer to 600bhp without turbocharging we could have a terrific long-distance engine because the DFL was so good on fuel. When I finished second behind Mass at the Norisring, when his Porsche had no fuel left at the end, I still had 25 litres in the tank, so even with quite a lot more power the DFL will still be well within the fuel consumption limits for 1983, and by then more will have been learned about aerodynamics, too, which will also help the engine indirectly.'

A lot of aerodynamic and installation lessons had been learned by the time Tony Southgate had schemed his 1983 version of the C100, and following the car's initial runs in France he was confident that even with a normally aspirated engine it could give a good account of itself during 1983. Then came the news of Ford's withdrawal from direct participation, and with it the prospect that the new cars (in addition to the prototype there were sufficient component parts in existence to assemble four or five more) would see service only as mobile testbeds. But as the last words of this book were being written negotiations had begun which might yet result in these cars being seen in action after all, most probably in new colours, perhaps even with a new name on the side, but quite certainly with a Ford DFL engine tucked in behind the driver. The story isn't necessarily over yet . . .

CHAPTER 7

A rewarding partnership

Fruits of the Ford-Cosworth connection

What have Rolls and Royce, eggs and bacon, Crosby and Hope, gin and tonic and Marks and Spencer in common? The answer is that they have been good for each other, and have almost certainly achieved more in combination than they would have done had they remained apart. Much the same can be said about the Ford Motor Company and Cosworth Engineering. Each of them would have progressed very satisfactorily without any association with the other, of course, but not only would motor sport have been much the poorer and far less adequately equipped, but both Ford and Cosworth themselves would also have lost a great deal.

As is almost inevitably the case when a large multi-national corporation forges a link with a small entrepreneurial company, it is the beneficial effect on the smaller operation which is the more immediately visible. This is certainly so in the case of Cosworth who, during the years of association with Ford, have progressed from employing a handful of people in modest North London workshops to having a staff of approximately 275, divided between Engineering and Manufacturing Divisions in Northampton, Research and Foundry Divisions in Worcester and the North American satellite based near Los Angeles. Along the way they have become part of a publicly owned conglomerate specializing in high-technology engineering, although Keith Duckworth remains both Chairman of the Board and a Director of the holding company.

Whilst it would be an exaggeration to suggest that this remarkable expansion has been achieved entirely on the back of Ford (one has to remember, after all, that Cosworth started to make a name for themselves with their work on Coventry Climax and Fiat engines prior to the introduction of Ford's 'Kent' power unit), there is no doubt whatsoever that it was the inherent quality of the latter family of engines and their consequent suitability for performance tuning and modification which provided the vital bridgehead from which Cosworth were able to conduct their further expansion in an orderly manner.

The quality of their work in this field had ensured that news of their reputation had travelled quickly within the competition field, and this reputation grew steadily when it became clear that their products were

The Cosworth forge, which came into being in order to safeguard the supply of high-quality forgings for the DFV and other racing engines, has since become the hub of a most successful commercial operation — the manufacture and sale of Cosworth forged pistons, in which the company is now a world leader.

achieving success across the broad spectrum of their customers, not just in the hands of a favoured few. In a field of endeavour well known for exaggerated claims leading to operational disappointments, Cosworth's policy of quoting performance figures conservatively, of refusing to release an engine or a component until it had met their own stringent in-house test standards, and of backing up their products with a meaningful customer liaison service which included advice on installation, the provision of ancillary services and operating procedures, had quickly won them many loyal friends.

In a sense, therefore, they had already placed themselves at the front of the queue when the time came for Ford to consider the possibility of embarking upon a Formula 1 engine with an outside specialist. Keith Duckworth and his colleagues, of course, were already well known to those of Ford's engineers who had been concerned with competition matters, for they had worked closely together on a number of projects. Their engineering skills were never in doubt, their ability to achieve consistency of quality had already been proven, and their understandable pride in turning out a good job seemed to provide the final assurance that whatever the difficulties that might be encountered in exploring new territory, they would find a way of overcoming them, if only to protect their own reputation.

The immediate success of the Ford DFV engine was to accomplish so much more for Cosworth Engineering than simply to confirm their status within the competition world. Although a measure of public awareness of their name beyond motor sporting circles had already been achieved through their association with Ford's sophisticated public relations programmes, which in the mid-1960s had been heavily engaged in promoting their Total Performance image on the back of competitions achievements, it was the Formula 1 engine which was to carry the Cosworth name into the front page headlines. This was the engine which ensured that the company would expand quickly but safely, that it would prosper and be able to diversify into areas of engineering beyond the confines of motor racing. It was also the engine which would make Keith Duckworth, in particular, a very wealthy young man, as in fact Walter Hayes had envisaged, and indeed as he had hoped, for such a thing was inevitable if the whole project was to achieve its anticipated success for both companies.

'I have always believed that the wisest manufacturers develop friendships with interesting technological people or bodies outside of their own company', says Hayes. Apart from the fact that this keeps you in the forefront of technology (remember that although big companies have enormous resources, quite a lot of funny little inventions tend to come out of funny little companies — a lot of new thinking comes that way, particularly in motor sport) these little companies don't have the huge overheads of the big companies. Four or five years ago we worked out that it cost us $29,000 per

Hand finishing one of the valve seats in a four-valve cylinder head. Although a great deal of machining of components is carried out on computer controlled machinery it is often the hand work afterwards which is responsible for those vital last few bhp.

employee in Europe whether he or she worked or not — it was the cost of getting each of them into an office — and one of my friends in another large company in London calculated that the space being occupied by each of their wastepaper baskets was costing them £90 per year.

'So small companies can get things done more cheaply, and often more quickly, but if you have this kind of relationship with them you must make sure that they stay rich and profitable; it may be all very nice having a relationship with a mad inventor (and I'm not suggesting that Keith is one of those!), but it's not terribly helpful if at the end of the week he can't pay the rent. Therefore, one of the critical issues with the DFV engine, right from the beginning, was that after the initial batch, which were to be supplied to Lotus, any subsequent engines would be sold by Cosworth, and if there was any profit in them, they would keep it.

'I made it very clear from the beginning that all we wanted was absolutely first-class customer service, absolutely first-class parts, and of course absolutely first-class engines and therefore, because this would cost a certain amount of money to establish, we would extract no money whatsoever from the engine. Now a lot of people wouldn't have done that. They might have wanted 5 per cent or 10 per cent on each engine, or maybe they would have set up an organization of their own to start selling the bits and pieces. We could have worked something out with Duckworth along those lines, but we didn't think it was the right thing to do.

'So you can say that the DFV is an engine which made Keith a millionaire, and so it should have done because he deserves the credit, but it was also a very important part of the deal that it should do so, a fact which no-one else seems to have spotted. As the market for the engine was opened up and expanded, Cosworth prospered, and soon Keith had his helicopter, which gave him a great deal of pleasure as well as being a very useful form of transport for him. This was very gratifying because he had worked desperately hard on the design and initial development of the engine and had shown a certain physical frailty at that time when the many hours he spent at his drawing-board affected his sight for a short while: I was extremely concerned about him. Just because he's a slow-speaking Lancashire chap who looks to be taking things very easily, he gives the impression that there's no turmoil inside him, but I happen to believe that there is, in fact, quite a lot of turmoil inside him and that he's probably a little tenser than most people realize.'

Duckworth's eye strain may have been aggravated by the fact that his months at the drawing-board coincided with a period when he went on a strict diet, and his health improved once the design phase of the DFV programme had been completed. But like most of his colleagues, he continued to put in extremely long hours as the arrival of the Formula 1 engine committed his company to ever more demanding responsibilities. He seemed to take it all in his stride, but in 1973 he was to suffer a heart attack, which not only curtailed his flying activities in so far as since then he has had to sit beside another pilot, but it also caused him to take a number of steps over the next few years to safeguard the long-term future of the company.

In 1974 he was introduced to Alfred Vickers, formerly Managing Director of Jensen Motors, and he persuaded him to act as a consultant to Cosworth Engineering as a means of strengthening the company's management team. In due course Alf Vickers was to take over full-time as Managing Director of

An operator at Northampton setting the controls for the automatic machining of a cylinder head. Loading of individual machines will be planned a minimum of four months ahead while the overall operation of the Manufacturing Division can be geared to forward programming of up to 16 months.

Cosworth to the considerable relief, one suspects, of the other Directors, who have never tried to camouflage the fact that they are much happier, and probably more productively employed, when being concerned on a day-to-day basis with engineering matters rather than with company administration.

By that time the company had grown to such a size and complexity that efficient administrative systems in all departments had become essential, yet one of the major ingredients of Cosworth's success was that it was still motivated by the entrepreneurial flair which had been with it from its earliest days. Keith Duckworth, Mike Costin, Benny Rood and Bill Brown had each contributed a special talent in a particular area which had been both compatible with and complementary to those of his three colleagues. The result was a tight and highly efficient team, but it had accomplished so much that the whole enterprise needed now to be more formally managed if it were not to lose its direction.

The transition from a small to a medium-size operation is almost always a difficult one in the growth of a company, and continued expansion invariably means sacrifices as well as benefits. Each member of the original Cosworth team had something to lose as well as much to gain, but the person liable to be most deeply affected by the further growth and diversification of the company was Bill Brown, who had carried much of the burden of administration during Cosworth's formative years. Bill was a person of wide interests — powerboating being just one of them — and had always enjoyed the challenges and the stimulation of the small-company environment. With Cosworth continuing to expand and becoming involved in new ventures he decided that perhaps it was time for a personal change in direction, as well, and so he elected to go out and 'do his own thing' in pastures new. In this he has since been very successful, and his former colleagues, understandably sorry to lose him at the time, are pleased that some of his subsequent activities have enabled him to maintain contact with Cosworth on the engineering side.

The continued growth of Cosworth, meanwhile, had given Keith Duckworth cause to re-examine his own position within the company. 'Cosworth Engineering had become a large company, of which I was by far the major shareholder, and it struck me that should I have died in that situation it was probable that my executors would have had to sell my interest in a forced-sale situation and, perhaps, into hands which might not have been sympathetic to the objectives of the company and of the people involved in it. I felt, therefore, that for Cosworth Engineering to become part of a large public company, provided it was allowed to be run on its own, was in its own best interests and those of its employees, and the opportunity for this to happen came about in February 1980.'

During that month Cosworth Engineering became a wholly owned subsidiary of United Engineering Industries (UEI), a holding company which over a number of years has bought out a collection of entrepreneurial firms, mainly in the advanced engineering and electronics fields, all of which have continued to be run independently of each other under their original management. 'Another advantage of the new arrangement is that obviously it gives us access to more funds should we need them to diversify into other major activities, while possibly it also allows for better use of the funds which we have created in the past.'

By no means all of Cosworth's engineering drawings take place on Keith Duckworth's personal drawing-board. This is the design office at St James' Mill Road, where the staff work in appropriately light conditions on the first floor of the block adjacent to the administration building and where the quality of their pencil work matches the best in the world. The poster on the far wall celebrates the first 100 Grand Prix victories by the DFV engine.

Not all of Cosworth's successes have been achieved on the race track, and the company has been involved in the development of a marine version of the DFV as well as in the design of a centrifugal hydraulic clutch for powerboat racing. This is Jackie Wilson at the controls of Chris Hodges' catamaran in which he set a world record in the unlimited engine capacity class at 123mph. Later, Wilson and Brett May, obliged to run their DFV-powered boat in the inboard class of the Parker Dam endurance race in Arizona, finished some 80 miles in front of their nearest class rival.

Cosworth's achievements in the motor racing world continue to be mainly responsible for keeping the company name in the public's eye, but the Cosworth contribution to motor sport covers a wider area than most people realize, the provision of racing pistons for Chevrolet engines and of cylinder heads for Opel's Manta and Ascona rally cars being just two random examples of a wide ranging involvement in the competitions field which has grown from the reputation established through the Ford-Cosworth connection.

These days a great deal of the company's business comes from the mainstream of the motor industry. Ford have directed a constant flow of specialized engineering projects towards Northampton throughout the years of association between the two companies, while many other car manufacturers have trodden a similar path in the acquisition of anything from individual components to a comprehensive design, prototype build and development service of a major unit such as a cylinder head, or even of a complete engine, to be followed up in some instances by a series-production contract for the product in question.

The acquisition of the former Hepworth and Grandage forge and its installation at Northampton opened the door to a seemingly ever-expanding market for forged pistons, for which the production cycle has been speeded up to the point where a batch of, say, 400 can be put through in five working days. Another major area of expansion has been brought about through the foundation of the Research and Development Division at Worcester, incorporating a high-technology foundry, where some 35 people are employed. This has enabled all major castings to be manufactured in-house and has brought about the development of a special Cosworth sand-casting technique which Duckworth feels a lot of people are ready to accept as being the future method of casting cylinder heads. 'The accuracies that we can manage to hold on aluminium casting are greater than those that can be held on gravity die-casting and most of the other processes, while our definition and flatness and the material properties that we can obtain by our techniques of controlling the metal are vastly better than what is possible from normal casting techniques. We have been successful in casting parts for the aerospace

Keith Duckworth and his colleagues have put the versatility and convenience of helicopters to excellent use for a number of years. Duckworth's first machine, which he used to pilot himself, was a Brantley, but this has since been replaced by this Allison turbine-powered Hughes 500C, which can carry up to four passengers.

industry that the rest of the world has failed to cast, so on precision and on properties of the material you could say we're pretty well beyond equal.'

Some 230 of the total Cosworth workforce of around 275 people are employed in the Engineering and Manufacturing Divisions at Northampton, however, where Cosworth have some 54,000sq ft of space under roof on a $4\frac{1}{2}$-acre site stretching on both sides of St James' Mill Road. Approximately two-thirds of the output which finds its way from Manufacturing, into the inspection and quality control departments and then on to the stores is earmarked for outside customers, the remaining third being the requirement of the Engineering Division, which is responsible for the production and rebuilding of racing engines. This is where the meticulous inspection carried out by the engine builders as a matter of routine can provide a valuable additional monitor of the Manufacturing Division's quality-control performance.

As these words are being written, Cosworth Engineering are poised to celebrate their first 25 years of trading. During that period they first outgrew their original modest workshops in Friern Barnet, from where, apart from Duckworth himself, only one of the original employees — Bill Pratt, now Production Manager — has remained with the company throughout. The first move was to Edmonton, still in North London, where the company took over the premises in which the original Lotus Elite took shape prior to Lotus' move to Cheshunt, in Hertfordshire. Cosworth had grown to a staff of some 38 people before it was time to move again, this time to Northampton, where Duckworth wisely acquired far more land than was needed initially, but which has since been largely built upon (it has been necessary to rent further land close by as an employees' car park).

Despite all the changes, however, and the diversification, there is still ample evidence of the pioneering spirit which pervaded those earlier premises, and one senses that Duckworth, Costin and Rood, in particular, have changed little over the years, even though their responsibilities have grown so dramatically. There is also no lessening in their mutual regard.

'Mike is one of those brilliant people who has a natural talent in various directions', says Duckworth. 'He has superb reactions and balance and everything else, which I personally believe could have enabled him to become a World Champion racing driver.' (This is a view shared by many people, including the author, who witnessed on several occasions the apparent ease with which he would take an occasional day off from being an engineer to climb into a racing car and calmly 'blow off' all the seasoned regular drivers who had been racing all season.)

'Secondly', says Duckworth, 'Mike is a natural engineer. Although he might not have been particularly highly educated as an engineer, he happens to know what will and what will not work. In other words, he's a practical engineer, but it goes much deeper than that. He seems to have some quite uncanny sixth sense as to whether things will work or not. He's probably not particularly inventive as such, whereas I possibly am inventive to a degree, but Mike can tell me where my invention is not going to work before we've even made it!

'If he doesn't like something, I believe he's right 95 per cent of the time, and if he likes something, again he will be right 95 per cent of the time. This is an astonishing general ability to comprehend — just to be able to look at the idea and say "It's wrong", or "I like that", or "I don't like it". If he doesn't like something, although he might not be able to say exactly what it is he doesn't like, you can be pretty sure that there's something in there that's wrong.

'Therefore, Mike is the bloke who, if you've got an idea about something, can tell you that you're daft before you've spent much time on it — and that is an infinitely valuable thing. He has an intuitive grasp of engineering matters, allied to the practical ability to construct anything, all of which puts him in tremendous demand. It means, for example, that he has moved away from being in charge of development to being a useful sounding board for me on design and for other people on development, while not having to be directly involved in either. He's also in general charge of all quality control aspects and rectification schemes. He will decide whether something will or will not do from the output of the machine shop, which of course has been expanding so much over the years, and this means that he has to spend more of his time looking at bits and sorting out new manufacturing processes. If you have any difficult manufacturing problem other than machining, he's the person to call for to look at things like welding or brazing processes, surface treatments, heat treatments and — particularly these days — casting techniques.

Mike Costin's official designation is Deputy Chief Engineer, which may seem inadequate in view of his versatility, but is probably logical when Keith Duckworth's is Chief Engineer (Chairman). Duckworth says that he still hogs the position of Chief Engineer because he doesn't regard the title of Chairman as of any relevance in the context of what he does for the company. The third surviving member of the original managerial quartet, Benny Rood, is listed as Industrial Engineer in the corporate structure, although Chief Production Engineer might be a more accurate indication of his particular area of responsibility.

From running his own machine shop it was a logical step for Benny to move in-house to run the Cosworth facility, but as the company has expanded so his

An aerial view of the original Cosworth building in St James' Mill Road, Northampton. In the foreground is the administration block, with the sales counter immediately behind the double doors, and the research, development, prototype engineering and racing engine assembly and test facilities taking up much of the covered space on this side of the road. Extra land has had to be leased at the rear for staff car parking.

spheres of activity and influence have become more specialized. Although lacking a formal engineering education, like Mike Costin, Benny Rood has a great feel for what is and what is not possible, as befits someone who once produced and raced his own Rood-Velocette motorcycles and was responsible for the Hogan-Rood two-stroke hydroplane engines which emanated from a base in Essex. He is the person his colleagues turn to when they have to sort out how to machine something that is very difficult to machine. He is very adept at this, and is also very clever at making special-purpose machines, which are in widespread use at Northampton.

'We convert quite a lot of standard machines to numerical or computer numerical control', says Duckworth, 'for automatic operation, and this is Benny's area. He's obviously involved in the purchase of new machinery as well as making sure that it will do the job we require it to do, and do it efficiently. He will oversee the modification of any machinery as needs be, and on the general production engineering side he will suggest how best we can make something, then he'll make sure that the machinery will work properly in that way. Like the rest of us, he's very much an ideas man — he can visualize things very clearly and come up with practical solutions.'

Alf Vickers' arrival on the scene has led to the creation of an organizational structure through which, to an outsider, Cosworth Engineering appears to operate in a highly efficient manner and with a forward loading of machinery programmed anything up to 16 months ahead. 'I think you could say that Mike, Benny and I are not particularly strong on managerial talent, actually', says Duckworth. 'We are all such enthusiastic engineers for getting the job

Keith Duckworth's foresight in acquiring much more land than was originally required has since paid off handsomely. Cosworth's manufacturing facilities are now sited across the road from the original buildings, with the forge located in the separate unit on the right. Since this picture was taken the gap between the two buildings has been built upon and Cosworth now have 54,000sq ft under roof at Northampton.

done that our organizational capabilities have not been well developed; in fact I would say they are underdeveloped! That's certainly very true of me; I know the theory of it, but I'm capable of wrecking any organization in 10 minutes flat anyway! I think Mike agrees with the principles of organization, but sometimes it gets in the way of actually getting the job done, while I'm not sure that Benny even agrees with it!'

I sense that Keith Duckworth himself has to suffer the consequences of divided loyalties. He, too, does not like organizational structures to get in the way of what he considers to be the important things in life, yet he is too analytical a thinker to be unaware of their value, particularly to a company which has grown to the current size of Cosworth. As for his asset value to the company, his inventiveness speaks for itself, but this is only one element of his total contribution, and on its own it would have been insufficient to even begin to get the job done.

It has been supported by many other attributes, including an above-average ability to see things from more directions than most people can manage, and this gives him a fair chance of getting through to the root cause of the problem by the end of the day. He admits to being a deep thinker in analysis and to enjoying just trying to think and picture how things work. He sees himself using a combination of knowledge obtained from both formal education and from what he calls the school of life to see how things are and to picture how they are likely to work, over a wide range of subjects.

'I would say that if you can think well from first principles you can derive answers, or come to a good understanding of the relationship of cause and effect. I would describe this as commonsense, which is not in fact all that common. I would also describe it as intelligence, as distinct from being knowledgeable. In this field one seems increasingly to require quite a lot of knowledge, but the problem then is that you also need a good memory because there's no point in having experience if you can't remember what it was. My memory is still good, although I sense that it is beginning to look over-full, so perhaps it is not half as good as it used to be!

'I sense that the increasing amount of knowledge and hard experience has tended to make me less decisive on engineering matters, and design is far more difficult because I now have so much more idea of all the problems that can be reached. At the time of the DFV I had a sufficient lack of knowledge — probably the optimum amount of knowledge — which meant that I could think my way through most of the pitfalls and avoid them by the thought process. I had not reached the stage of having so much experience of torsional vibration problems, to take one example, and all the other things which have happened since, which cause me now to look at everything in so much depth that I find myself saying "Wait — this could happen, or that could happen". I don't know whether they're actually going to happen or not, but in attempting to design out something that has only a slight chance of happening simply slows the process down.

'I am probably now at the stage where, when I am designing something, I try to design out a problem which has only a 5 per cent or less chance of happening anyway, and that therefore it would be much better not to think about it because I'm quite adept at sorting out the problem should it in fact arise. If I were only able to think of fewer things in the first place and accept that if a problem occurred it could be sorted out quickly in development it might be much better, but now I tend to have so many things that I can see could possibly happen that I hesitate at the design stage, and therefore I am much slower because I am preoccupied with things that might not happen anyway, which is a waste of time.

'On the other hand, I see in other people a tendency to fall into so many holes, which means that you are immediately in a state of the triumph of development over design, which is expensive. It costs nothing to rub things out on a sheet of paper, but once you are into metal you are almost obliged by time and circumstances to make a compromise that retains as much of the hardware that you have as possible, whereas in a lot of cases you should probably have started again.

'From a business point of view, I think that a combination of commonsense and an ability to analyze things clearly allows one not to make things which are commercially invalid, and therefore this enables one to make sure that one's company survives without too much problem. I think that from a commonsense point of view I am probably suitable to be a Company Director because at Boardroom level I can, in fact, cover a wide range of subjects, provide some clarity of thought and comment and say, perhaps, "Someone seems to be forgetting the odd main issue here", and so on.'

Duckworth is not by nature an egotistical person, but he would be inordinately unresponsive if he did not take some pleasure in the fame and recognition which his long association with Ford has given him. Cosworth Engineering have never believed in spending a fortune on public relations, preferring in the main to let their products do the job for them, but the Ford connection has given them an association with one of the most sophisticated and skilfully managed public affairs teams in the business, and there has been an automatic rub-off for Cosworth from much of the promotional effort which Ford have made in the motor racing field.

At the same time, Ford's use of competitions in general and motor racing in particular has been directed along fairly clearly defined lines, which do not necessarily run parallel to those adopted by other car manufacturers with a direct competitions involvement. The use of an association with motor sporting achievement as one of, but not the only, pillar on which to build a Ford Total Performance image, has already been referred to, and this was accomplished most effectively during the 1960s.

Since then, however, there has been a subtle change of emphasis, and Ford's continued involvement in the sporting scene, whilst still offering considerable marketing potential, which has been utilized to the full, has had more deep-rooted rewards. In particular, it has played a mainly hidden, but nevertheless immensely important role in bringing the company's engineering teams into contact with areas of high-technology engineering and sophisticated research which have been developed in many instances within the aerospace industry and have subsequently been drawn into the top echelons of the motor racing world.

There are many who claim that there is no relevance between a road car, even a high-performance road car, and the modern breed of single-seater to be seen in a Formula 1 Grand Prix or pounding round the 2½-miles oval at Indianapolis, but this is far from the case. The development of new materials, the methods by which they are formed or fabricated, the study of their performance and properties under conditions of high stress and their influence on vehicle design and form are just some of the areas of common interest, and Ford's close association with the most technologically advanced areas of motor racing has helped to stimulate the interest of their own engineers and to considerably enhance the quality of their own in-house research and development programmes. Indeed, it is doubtful if there is a car manufacturer anywhere in the world in the early-1980s which is committed to spending more on advanced R&D programmes or which enjoys so many fruitful associations with small, specialist entrepreneurial companies of the type which they pioneered with Cosworth Engineering in the 1960s. In short, Ford's policy of maintaining close liaisons with leading specialists in the competition field has not only helped to define a product image and to sell more of the product to a wider and in the main more affluent market, it has also provided the momentum for creating an even more technologically sophisticated design base for future products. The traffic, however, has not been all one way, and Cosworth Engineering, not to mention various racing teams, have been the beneficiary in the recent past of a number of R&D programmes which have been initiated within Ford and which have been directed specifically to enhancing performance or efficiency on the race track.

That famous Ford-versus-Ferrari confrontation at Le Mans in the 1960s apart, it has not been Ford policy to spend vast sums on motor sport, and even the Le Mans operation turned out to be a very cost-effective exercise in so far as most of the money was spent up front, whereas the exposure was spread over several years. European budgets, however, have always been slim by comparison, and much of the money has been directed towards technology rather than buying things. The £100,000 going-in fee for the Formula 2 FVA and Formula 1 DFV engines, of course, has been widely quoted as representing the motor racing bargain of all time, but of course Ford's real commitment went considerably deeper than that, for just as a wise sponsor of a racing team sets aside a further sum of money (perhaps half as much again) to make sure that the sponsorship works properly, so Ford was to do much behind the scenes thereafter to maximize the effectiveness of their investment in Cosworth Engineering and Keith Duckworth.

There was the occasion, for example, when Jackie Stewart, having won the World Championship in one of the DFV-powered Matras run by Ken Tyrrell, suddenly found himself out of a drive because the French company would no longer permit anything other than a Matra engine to be used in the chassis. 'I was staying at the Hilton in London', recalls Walter Hayes, 'and I remember quite clearly Stewart coming up the stairs looking terribly worried by it all and asking me what he should do.' The upshot of that conversation was that Hayes bought a pair of March chassis so that Jackie could stay with Tyrrell.

Shortly before, Max Mosley had introduced Hayes to the other members of the newly formed consortium who were to manufacture March racing cars. 'I managed to save them from a fate worse than death because I remember I asked them what they were going to sell their Formula 1 chassis for, and when they told me I said that they'd go bust if they did, so they'd better put the price up. I think I said it ought to be at least £9,000, but whatever it was they thought it was an enormous amount of money, but since then Mosley has frequently said that it had been the salvation of March. It was another example of making sure that the little ones stay in business.'

That such a modest sum as £20,000 or thereabouts could so positively influence the career of a top Grand Prix driver seems almost unbelievable in these days of multi-million dollar team budgets, but it meant that much could be done to influence events, even with relatively slender resources. 'It meant that it was sufficient for me at that stage as the Ford Motor Company's man running the programme to be a kind of occasional marriage broker cum midwife of the whole motor sporting scene, as and when it was necessary, but without doing much more than pushing. For example, we managed to help young Rolf Stommelen on his way because we felt we wanted a German name or two on the scene, then of course we gave assistance to Emerson Fittipaldi, whom we had started off in Formula Ford and watched closely as his career developed.'

So far as Grand Prix racing was concerned, Walter Hayes' policy was to do what he could to enhance the environment in which the Ford DFV engine was being used and thereby ensure that motor sport as a whole remained healthy. 'I have always thought that as long as there is Wimbledon, tennis will be healthy, that if there is an America's Cup, then yachting is alright, and that therefore the same thing should apply in motor racing. As long as there was a prosperous and buoyant Formula 1, the whole structure would be in that much better shape.'

Nevertheless, he soon found himself looking at a rapidly changing world in which the sums of money involved were escalating out of all proportion. 'We were moving towards the era of the million dollar driver, and so it was no longer a case of saying OK, we'll help you to replant your garden and put a few flowers in it because they were liable to reply that that was fine, but what about my yacht marina? Aspirations as well as incomes had changed dramatically. You know, I knew a great deal about the income and resources of Jim Clark because I played a fairly large role in the affiars of that highly talented young man — I know just how much he earned in his lifetime — but of course he died just when motor racing was becoming a big sponsor game and everyone decided to raise their sights.

'Thereafter it was a very different scene, besides which there were various other things I wanted to do with our budget — for example the Safari Rally in East Africa, which could never be a cheap exercise — and, remember, our expenditure, which I wanted to keep to around a million dollars a year in terms of programme money, was to cover not just the UK, but the whole of Europe. When Ford of Europe was created in 1967 to co-ordinate the activities of the 15 individual Ford companies already located in Europe there was the opportunity to both streamline and expand the competitions activities and to encourage a greater level of co-operation between companies running their own local programmes, all of which cost money. So there were times when our budget was spread fairly thinly, especially when inflation in Europe became a significant factor and effectively reduced our spending power.'

Nevertheless, against this background of rising costs, Ford's competition influence and involvement continued to expand. At first, much of the activity had been British-based, but soon after the formation of Ford of Europe, Hayes, who had been appointed one of its Vice Presidents, flew over to Germany, spotted a little factory which was not being used and pinned a note on the door. It read: 'Do not touch, by order. This has been reserved as the new headquarters of Ford Motorsport in Germany. (Signed) Walter Hayes'. He then flew home again, but a new era had begun in which Ford's competition activities would henceforth have two centres, each of which would be responsible for its own programmes, but would also provide such technical and logistical support for the other as might be required from time to time.

The British operation was put under the direction of Stuart Turner, and when he later moved into Public Affairs his deputy, Peter Ashcroft, assumed control of the competitions department. In Germany, Jochen Neerpasch was appointed to run the newly formed unit in its early days, and when he left the company he, too, was to hand over the reins to his number-two, Mike Kranefuss, who was to take on considerably wider responsibilities in due course, first in Europe and more recently in the United States.

Early in 1983, Stuart Turner moved back into the competitions arena with overall responsibility for Ford's European-based activities just as it appeared that the company might be taking a more global viewpoint in planning its competition strategy. The success of the Ford of Europe concept in dovetailing separately operated competition programmes so as to simultaneously satisfy local needs and provide the best possible overall coverage within the territory has become well established and it seems now to offer a blueprint for a similar degree of collaboration and co-ordination on a larger scale. The establishment of a European-style competitions base in the United States, embracing both in-house facilities and close liaison with outside specialists, has already provided the opportunity for a considerable measure of co-operation and interchange of engineering and ideas between Ford personnel on each side of the Atlantic, and there seems to be little reason to believe why the concept should not be extended in the years ahead to embrace all of Ford's major territories in which a significant level of competition activity is present.

Much of Ford's future competition programming, inevitably, will be built around the use of suitably modified high-performance derivatives of mainstream products, but the achievements of the past 16 years make it unthinkable that there will not also be an on-going involvement with the top echelons of single-seater racing. No action by a major car manufacturer in the racing world has ever come close to matching the significance of Ford's decision in 1966 to contribute a desperately needed Formula 1 engine to Team Lotus.

Looking back over those 16 years it is clear to see that virtually everything has changed except the engine, and yet that engine was the catalyst of this extraordinary period of change. Its timing was impeccable, and its arrival coincided with the end of one era and the beginning of another; the Gentlemen had completed their innings, now it was the turn of the Players. The Ford-Cosworth association had produced a piece of machinery the nominal value of which was a modest £7,500, but its true worth was incalculable in that it was to provide the foundation on which the new structure of Grand Prix racing would be built. It was to make World Champions of men who might otherwise have remained in the spectator terraces or, at best, indulged in a modicum of club racing with no realistic hope of progressing far beyond the minor formulae. It was to open the door to teams which otherwise could not have contemplated a progression into Formula 1, and Grand Prix racing would have been much the poorer without them. It was to bring a level of long-term stability to the top category of international motor racing which it had previously never enjoyed, and which in turn was to ease its transformation from a relatively narrow-interest activity into the world of high-technology show business. It helped to foster many latent talents, such as the all-round professionalism of Jackie Stewart, the entrepreneurial abilities of Bernard Ecclestone and even, in a convoluted way, the political skills of Jean-Marie Balestre. It also, of course, spawned further engines which would transform in scarcely less significant a manner that most traditionally American form of motor racing of which the Indianapolis Motor Speedway has for so long been the hub, and it would bring about a renewal of the Ford presence on the endurance racing scene as well.

Much had been hoped for when Colin Chapman had invited Walter Hayes to dinner that evening in 1965 and Keith Duckworth's name had inevitably been drawn into the conversation, but the new Ford-Cosworth link which was to result from that initial meeting was destined to achieve so much more than its participants could possibly have envisaged. The whole of motor sport should be grateful for the day that Ford and Cosworth helped to put Lotus back on top in Grand Prix racing; more than 150 victories later, and with the rumble of turbos on the tracks, it is remembered as a moment of profound inspiration and as an act of faith which deservedly has been repaid so handsomely on so many occasions.

Appendix A

Ford DFV World Championship race winners

1967

Dutch Grand Prix — Zandvoort	Jim Clark	Lotus-Ford DFV 703
British Grand Prix — Silverstone	Jim Clark	Lotus-Ford DFV 703
United States Grand Prix — Watkins Glen	Jim Clark	Lotus-Ford DFV 707
Mexican Grand Prix — Mexico City	Jim Clark	Lotus-Ford DFV 704

1968

South African Grand Prix — Kyalami	Jim Clark	Lotus-Ford DFV 803
Spanish Grand Prix — Jarama	Graham Hill	Lotus-Ford DFV 704
Monaco Grand Prix — Monte Carlo	Graham Hill	Lotus-Ford DFV 814
Belgian Grand Prix — Spa-Francorchamps	Bruce McLaren	McLaren-Ford DFV 805
Dutch Grand Prix — Zandvoort	Jackie Stewart	Matra-Ford DFV 812
British Grand Prix — Brands Hatch	Jo Siffert	Lotus-Ford DFV 809
German Grand Prix — Nurburgring	Jackie Stewart	Matra-Ford DFV 812
Italian Grand Prix — Monza	Denny Hulme	McLaren-Ford DFV 819
Canadian Grand Prix — St Jovite	Denny Hulme	McLaren-Ford DFV 819
United States Grand Prix — Watkins Glen	Jackie Stewart	Matra-Ford DFV 817
Mexican Grand Prix — Mexico City	Graham Hill	Lotus-Ford DFV 803

1969

South African Grand Prix — Kyalami	Jackie Stewart	Matra-Ford DFV 817
Spanish Grand Prix — Montjuich	Jackie Stewart	Matra-Ford DFV 802
Monaco Grand Prix — Monte Carlo	Graham Hill	Lotus-Ford DFV 811
Dutch Grand Prix — Zandvoort	Jackie Stewart	Matra-Ford DFV 940
French Grand Prix — Clermont-Ferrand	Jackie Stewart	Matra-Ford DFV 938
British Grand Prix — Silverstone	Jackie Stewart	Matra-Ford DFV 812
German Grand Prix — Nurburgring	Jacky Ickx	Brabham-Ford DFV 939
Italian Grand Prix — Monza	Jackie Stewart	Matra-Ford DFV 946
Canadian Grand Prix — Mosport	Jacky Ickx	Brabham-Ford DFV 926
United States Grand Prix — Watkins Glen	Jochen Rindt	Lotus-Ford DFV 921
Mexican Grand Prix — Mexico City	Denny Hulme	McLaren-Ford DFV 933

1970

South African Grand Prix — Kyalami	Jack Brabham	Brabham-Ford DFV 948
Spanish Grand Prix — Jarama	Jackie Stewart	March-Ford DFV 054
Monaco Grand Prix — Monte Carlo	Jochen Rindt	Lotus-Ford DFV 934
Dutch Grand Prix — Zandvoort	Jochen Rindt	Lotus-Ford DFV 945
French Grand Prix — Clermont-Ferrand	Jochen Rindt	Lotus-Ford DFV 929
British Grand Prix — Brands Hatch	Jochen Rindt	Lotus-Ford DFV 901
German Grand Prix — Hockenheim	Jochen Rindt	Lotus-Ford DFV 901
United States Grand Prix — Watkins Glen	Emerson Fittipaldi	Lotus-Ford DFV 052

1971

Spanish Grand Prix — Montjuich	Jackie Stewart	Tyrrell-Ford DFV 053
Monaco Grand Prix — Monte Carlo	Jackie Stewart	Tyrrell-Ford DFV 077
French Grand Prix — Paul Ricard	Jackie Stewart	Tyrrell-Ford DFV 066
British Grand Prix — Silverstone	Jackie Stewart	Tyrrell-Ford DFV 077
German Grand Prix — Nurburgring	Jackie Stewart	Tyrrell-Ford DFV 077
Canadian Grand Prix — Mosport	Jackie Stewart	Tyrrell-Ford DFV 066
United States Grand Prix — Watkins Glen	Francois Cevert	Tyrrell-Ford DFV 091

1972

Argentine Grand Prix — Buenos Aires	Jackie Stewart	Tyrrell-Ford DFV 077
South African Grand Prix — Kyalami	Denny Hulme	McLaren-Ford DFV 096
Spanish Grand Prix — Jarama	Emerson Fittipaldi	Lotus-Ford DFV 101
Belgian Grand Prix — Nivelles	Emerson Fittipaldi	Lotus-Ford DFV 097

French Grand Prix — Clermont-Ferrand	Jackie Stewart	Tyrrell-Ford DFV 066
British Grand Prix — Brands Hatch	Emerson Fittipaldi	Lotus-Ford DFV 097
Austrian Grand Prix — Zeltweg	Emerson Fittipaldi	Lotus-Ford DFV 082
Italian Grand Prix — Monza	Emerson Fittipaldi	Lotus-Ford DFV 115
Canadian Grand Prix — Mosport	Jackie Stewart	Tyrrell-Ford DFV 100
United States Grand Prix — Watkins Glen	Jackie Stewart	Tyrrell-Ford DFV 091
1973		
Argentine Grand Prix — Buenos Aires	Emerson Fittipaldi	Lotus-Ford DFV 115
Brazilian Grand Prix— Interlagos	Emerson Fittipaldi	Lotus-Ford DFV 130
South African Grand Prix — Kyalami	Jackie Stewart	Tyrrell-Ford DFV 131
Spanish Grand Prix — Montjuich	Emerson Fittipaldi	Lotus-Ford DFV 115
Belgian Grand Prix — Zolder	Jackie Stewart	Tyrrell-Ford DFV 066
Monaco Grand Prix — Monte Carlo	Jackie Stewart	Tyrrell-Ford DFV 139
Swedish Grand Prix — Anderstorp	Denny Hulme	McLaren-Ford DFV 061
French Grand Prix — Paul Ricard	Ronnie Peterson	Lotus-Ford DFV 101
British Grand Prix — Silverstone	Peter Revson	McLaren-Ford DFV 138
Dutch Grand Prix — Zandvoort	Jackie Stewart	Tyrrell-Ford DFV 091
German Grand Prix — Nurburgring	Jackie Stewart	Tyrrell-Ford DFV 066
Austrian Grand Prix — Zeltweg	Ronnie Peterson	Lotus-Ford DFV 097
Italian Grand Prix — Monza	Ronnie Peterson	Lotus-Ford DFV 118
Canadian Grand Prix — Mosport	Peter Revson	McLaren-Ford DFV 096
United States Grand Prix — Watkins Glen	Ronnie Peterson	Lotus-Ford DFV 147
1974		
Argentine Grand Prix — Buenos Aires	Denny Hulme	McLaren-Ford DFV 080
Brazilian Grand Prix — Interlagos	Emerson Fittipaldi	McLaren-Ford DFV 122
South African Grand Prix — Kyalami	Carlos Reutemann	Brabham-Ford DFV 150
Belgian Grand Prix — Nivelles	Emerson Fittipaldi	McLaren-Ford DFV 928
Monaco Grand Prix — Monte Carlo	Ronnie Peterson	Lotus-Ford DFV 130
Swedish Grand Prix — Anderstorp	Jody Scheckter	Tyrrell-Ford DFV 167
French Grand Prix — Dijon-Prenois	Ronnie Peterson	Lotus-Ford DFV 116
British Grand Prix — Brands Hatch	Jody Scheckter	Tyrrell-Ford DFV 162
Austrian Grand Prix — Zeltweg	Carlos Reutemann	Brabham-Ford DFV 174
Italian Grand Prix — Monza	Ronnie Peterson	Lotus-Ford DFV 118
Canadian Grand Prix — Mosport	Emerson Fittipaldi	McLaren-Ford DFV 919
United States Grand Prix — Watkins Glen	Carlos Reutemann	Brabham-Ford DFV 174
1975		
Argentine Grand Prix — Buenos Aires	Emerson Fittipaldi	McLaren-Ford DFV 919
Brazilian Grand Prix — Interlagos	Carlos Pace	Brabham-Ford DFV 154
South African Grand Prix — Kyalami	Jody Scheckter	Tyrrell-Ford DFV 162
Spanish Grand Prix — Montjuich	Jochen Mass	McLaren-Ford DFV 933
Dutch Grand Prix — Zandvoort	James Hunt	Hesketh-Ford DFV 197
British Grand Prix — Silverstone	Emerson Fittipaldi	McLaren-Ford DFV 072
German Grand Prix — Nurburgring	Carlos Reutemann	Brabham-Ford DFV 175
Austrian Grand Prix — Zeltweg	Vittorio Brambilla	March-Ford DFV 215
1976		
Spanish Grand Prix — Jarama	James Hunt	McLaren-Ford DFV 060
Swedish Grand Prix — Anderstorp	Jody Scheckter	Tyrrell-Ford DFV 214
French Grand Prix — Paul Ricard	James Hunt	McLaren-Ford DFV 120
German Grand Prix — Nurburgring	James Hunt	McLaren-Ford DFV 217
Austrian Grand Prix — Zeltweg	John Watson	Penske-Ford DFV 202
Dutch Grand Prix — Zandvoort	James Hunt	McLaren-Ford DFV 928
Italian Grand Prix — Monza	Ronnie Peterson	March-Ford DFV 174
Canadian Grand Prix — Mosport	James Hunt	McLaren-Ford DFV 928
United States Grand Prix — Watkins Glen	James Hunt	McLaren-Ford DFV 079
Japanese Grand Prix — Fuji	Mario Andretti	Lotus-Ford DFV 237
1977		
Argentine Grand Prix — Buenos Aires	Jody Scheckter	Wolf-Ford DFV 231
United States West Grand Prix — Long Beach	Mario Andretti	Lotus-Ford DFV

Spanish Grand Prix — Jarama	Mario Andretti	Lotus-Ford DFV
Monaco Grand Prix — Monte Carlo	Jody Scheckter	Wolf-Ford DFV 240
Belgian Grand Prix — Zolder	Gunnar Nilsson	Lotus-Ford DFV
French Grand Prix — Dijon-Prenois	Mario Andretti	Lotus-Ford DFV
British Grand Prix — Silverstone	James Hunt	McLaren-Ford DFV 261
Austrian Grand Prix — Zeltweg	Alan Jones	Shadow-Ford DFV 125
Italian Grand Prix — Monza	Mario Andretti	Lotus-Ford DFV 269
United States Grand Prix — Watkins Glen	James Hunt	McLaren-Ford DFV
Canadian Grand Prix — Mosport	Jody Scheckter	Wolf-Ford DFV 231
Japanese Grand Prix — Fuji	James Hunt	McLaren-Ford DFV
1978		
Argentine Grand Prix — Buenos Aires	Mario Andretti	Lotus-Ford DFV 262
South African Grand Prix — Kyalami	Ronnie Peterson	Lotus-Ford DFV 204
Monaco Grand Prix — Monte Carlo	Patrick Depailler	Tyrrell-Ford DFV 264
Belgian Grand Prix — Zolder	Mario Andretti	Lotus-Ford DFV 262
Spanish Grand Prix — Jarama	Mario Andretti	Lotus-Ford DFV 269
French Grand Prix — Paul Ricard	Mario Andretti	Lotus-Ford DFV 262
German Grand Prix — Hockenheim	Mario Andretti	Lotus-Ford DFV 267
Austrian Grand Prix — Zeltweg	Ronnie Peterson	Lotus-Ford DFV 204
Dutch Grand Prix — Zandvoort	Mario Andretti	Lotus-Ford DFV 262
1979		
Argentine Grand Prix — Buenos Aires	Jacques Laffite	Ligier-Ford DFV 299
Brazilian Grand Prix — Interlagos	Jacques Laffite	Ligier-Ford DFV 300
Spanish Grand Prix — Jarama	Patrick Depailler	Ligier-Ford DFV 298
British Grand Prix — Silverstone	Clay Regazzoni	Williams-Ford DFV 219
German Grand Prix — Hockenheim	Alan Jones	Williams-Ford DFV 310
Austrian Grand Prix — Zeltweg	Alan Jones	Williams-Ford DFV 320
Dutch Grand Prix — Zandvoort	Alan Jones	Williams-Ford DFV 320
Canadian Grand Prix — Montreal	Alan Jones	Williams-Ford DFV 313
1980		
Argentine Grand Prix — Buenos Aires	Alan Jones	Williams-Ford DFV 313
United States West Grand Prix — Long Beach	Nelson Piquet	Brabham-Ford DFV 325
Belgian Grand Prix — Zolder	Didier Pironi	Ligier-Ford DFV 298
Monaco Grand Prix — Monte Carlo	Carlos Reutemann	Williams-Ford DFV 337
French Grand Prix — Paul Ricard	Alan Jones	Williams-Ford DFV 295
British Grand Prix — Brands Hatch	Alan Jones	Williams-Ford DFV 313
German Grand Prix — Hockenheim	Jacques Laffite	Ligier-Ford DFV 338
Dutch Grand Prix — Zandvoort	Nelson Piquet	Brabham-Ford DFV 333
Italian Grand Prix — Imola	Nelson Piquet	Brabham-Ford DFV 330
Canadian Grand Prix — Montreal	Alan Jones	Williams-Ford DFV 313
United States Grand Prix — Watkins Glen	Alan Jones	Williams-Ford DFV 347
1981		
United States West Grand Prix — Long Beach	Alan Jones	Williams-Ford DFV 315
Brazilian Grand Prix — Jacarepagua	Carlos Reutemann	Williams-Ford DFV 310
Argentine Grand Prix — Buenos Aires	Nelson Piquet	Brabham-Ford DFV 330
San Marino Grand Prix — Imola	Nelson Piquet	Brabham-Ford DFV 332
Belgian Grand Prix — Zolder	Carlos Reutemann	Williams-Ford DFV 343
British Grand Prix — Silverstone	John Watson	McLaren-Ford DFV 354
German Grand Prix — Hockenheim	Nelson Piquet	Brabham-Ford DFV 424
Las Vegas Grand Prix — Las Vegas, USA	Alan Jones	Williams-Ford DFV 360
1982		
United States West Grand Prix — Long Beach	Niki Lauda	McLaren-Ford DFV 919
Belgian Grand Prix — Zolder	John Watson	McLaren-Ford DFV 353
Monaco Grand Prix — Monte Carlo	Riccardo Patrese	Brabham-Ford DFV 332
Detroit Grand Prix — Detroit, USA	John Watson	McLaren-Ford DFV 354
British Grand Prix — Brands Hatch	Niki Lauda	McLaren-Ford DFV 928
Austrian Grand Prix — Zeltweg	Elio De Angelis	Lotus-Ford DFV 269
Swiss Grand Prix — Dijon, France	Keke Rosberg	Williams-Ford DFV 310

Las Vegas Grand Prix — Las Vegas, USA	Michele Alboreto	Tyrrell-Ford DFV 264
1983		
United States West Grand Prix — Long Beach	John Watson	McLaren-Ford DFV 928
Monaco Grand Prix — Monte Carlo	Keke Rosberg	Williams-Ford DFV 312

FORD DFV-POWERED DRIVER SUCCESS RECORD
(World Championship races up to 1983 Monaco Grand Prix)

Driver	Wins
Stewart	25
Fittipaldi	14
Jones	12
Andretti	11
Hunt	10
Peterson	10
Reutemann	7
Scheckter	7
Hulme	6
Piquet	6
Rindt	6
Clark	5
Watson	5
Hill	4
Laffite	3
Depailler	2
Ickx	2
Lauda	2
Revson	2
Rosberg	2
Alboreto	1
Brabham	1
Brambilla	1
Cevert	1
De Angelis	1
Mass	1
McLaren	1
Nilsson	1
Pace	1
Patrese	1
Pironi	1
Regazzoni	1
Siffert	1
	154

The first victory for the short-stroke DFY engine came at the 1983 Detroit Grand Prix, won by Michele Alboreto in his Tyrrell-Ford. Although the winning engine carried the number DFY 001, it was equipped with the latest narrow-angle cylinder heads.

FORD DFV-POWERED CHASSIS SUCCESS RECORD
(World Championship races up to 1983 Monaco Grand Prix)

Chassis	Wins
Lotus	47
McLaren	30
Tyrrell	22
Williams	17
Brabham	15
Matra	9
Ligier	5
March	3
Wolf	3
Hesketh	1
Penske	1
Shadow	1
	154

Appendix B

Cosworth DFX CART/USAC race winners

1976

Pocono 500	Al Unser	Parnelli 6B
Milwaukee 200	Al Unser	Parnelli 6B
Phoenix 150	Al Unser	Parnelli 6B

1977

Phoenix 150	Johnny Rutherford	McLaren M24
Texas 200	Tom Sneva	McLaren M24
Milwaukee 150	Johnny Rutherford	McLaren M24
Pocono 500	Tom Sneva	McLaren M24
Michigan 200	Danny Ongais	Parnelli 6B
Texas 200	Johnny Rutherford	McLaren M24
Milwaukee 200	Johnny Rutherford	McLaren M24
California 500	Al Unser	Parnelli 6B

1978

Ontario 200	Danny Ongais	Parnelli 6C
Texas 200	Danny Ongais	Parnelli 6C
Indianapolis 500	Al Unser	Lola T500
Milwaukee 150	Rick Mears	Penske PC6
Pocono 500	Al Unser	Lola T500
Mosport 300Ks	Danny Ongais	Parnelli 6B
Michigan 200	Johnny Rutherford	McLaren M24B
Atlanta 150	Rick Mears	Penske PC6
Milwaukee 200	Danny Ongais	Parnelli 6B
California 500	Al Unser	Lola T500
Michigan 150	Danny Ongais	Parnelli 6C
Trenton 150	Mario Andretti	Penske PC6
Phoenix 150	Johnny Rutherford	McLaren M24B
Brands Hatch 120	Rick Mears	Penske PC6

1979 (Separate CART and USAC Championships)

CART

Phoenix 150	Gordon Johncock	Penske PC6
Atlanta 125	Johnny Rutherford	McLaren M24B
Atlanta 125	Johnny Rutherford	McLaren M24B
Trenton 100	Bobby Unser	Penske PC7
Trenton 100	Bobby Unser	Penske PC7
Michigan 126	Bobby Unser	Penske PC7
Michigan 126	Gordon Johncock	Penske PC6
Watkins Glen 150	Bobby Unser	Penske PC7
Trenton 150	Rick Mears	Penske PC7
California 500	Bobby Unser	Penske PC7
Michigan 150	Bobby Unser	Penske PC7
Atlanta 150	Rick Mears	Penske PC7
Phoenix 150	Al Unser	Chaparral 2K

USAC

Ontario 200	AJ Foyt	Parnelli 6C
Texas 200	AJ Foyt	Parnelli 6C
Indianapolis 500	Rick Mears	Penske PC6
Milwaukee 150	AJ Foyt	Parnelli 6C
Pocono 500	AJ Foyt	Parnelli 6C
Milwaukee 200	Roger McCluskey	Lola T500B

1980 (Combined CART-USAC Championship through to Mid-Ohio. Separate CART Championship based on entire season)

Ontario 200	Johnny Rutherford	Chaparral 2K
Indianapolis 500	Johnny Rutherford	Chaparral 2K
Milwaukee 150	Bobby Unser	Penske PC9
Pocono 500	Bobby Unser	Penske PC9
Mid-Ohio 156	Johnny Rutherford	Chaparral 2K
Michigan 200	Johnny Rutherford	Chaparral 2K
Watkins Glen 150	Bobby Unser	Penske PC9
Milwaukee 200	Johnny Rutherford	Chaparral 2K
California 500	Bobby Unser	Penske PC9
Michigan 150	Mario Andretti	Penske PC9
Mexico City 150	Rick Mears	Penske PC9
Phoenix 150	Tom Sneva	Phoenix

1981 (Separate CART and USAC Championships)

CART		
Phoenix 150	Johnny Rutherford	Chaparral 2K
Atlanta 126	Rick Mears	Penske PC9B
Atlanta 126	Rick Mears	Penske PC9B
Michigan 500	Pancho Carter	Penske PC7
Riverside 500Ks	Rick Mears	Penske PC9B
Milwaukee 200	Tom Sneva	March 81C
Michigan 150	Rick Mears	Penske PC9B
Watkins Glen 200	Rick Mears	Penske PC9B
Mexico City 150	Rick Mears	Penske PC9B
Phoenix 150	Tom Sneva	March 81C
USAC		
Indianapolis 500	Bobby Unser	Penske PC9B
Pocono 500	AJ Foyt	March 81C

1982 (Only USAC race was Indianapolis 500)

Phoenix 150	Rick Mears	Penske PC10
Atlanta 200	Rick Mears	Penske PC10
Indianapolis 500	Gordon Johncock	Wildcat Mk 8B
Milwaukee 150	Gordon Johncock	Wildcat Mk 8B
Cleveland 500Ks	Bobby Rahal	March 82C
Michigan 500	Gordon Johncock	Wildcat Mk 8B
Milwaukee 200	Tom Sneva	March 82C
Pocono 500	Rick Mears	Penske PC10
California 500Ks	Rick Mears	Penske PC10
Road America 200	Hector Rebaque	March 82C
Michigan 150	Bobby Rahal	March 82C
Phoenix 150	Tom Sneva	March 82C

COSWORTH DFX-POWERED CHASSIS SUCCESS RECORD
(CART/USAC races up to 1982 Phoenix 150)

Penske	33
Parnelli	14
McLaren	10
March	8
Chaparral	7
Lola	4
Wildcat	3
Phoenix	1
	80

COSWORTH DFX-POWERED DRIVER SUCCESS RECORD
(CART/USAC races up to 1982 Phoenix 150)

Rick Mears	17
Johnny Rutherford	14
Bobby Unser	11
Al Unser	8
Tom Sneva	7
Danny Ongais	6
A. J. Foyt	5
Gordon Johncock	5
Mario Andretti	2
Bobby Rahal	2
Pancho Carter	1
Roger McCluskey	1
Hector Rebaque	1
	80

Appendix C

Ford Cosworth V8 racing engine data

DFV

90-degree V8, water-cooled, normally aspirated Formula 1 engine. Aluminium alloy cylinder block and heads, aluminium alloy or magnesium alloy cam carriers, forged steel Cosworth pistons, connecting rods and crankshaft, cast iron, steel or aluminium cylinder liners. Lucas high-pressure fuel injection into inlet ports, initially Lucas transistorized ignition, later mainly Contactless or Lucas capacitive discharge ignition. Gear-driven twin overhead camshafts to each cylinder bank, two inlet and two exhaust valves per cylinder. Compression ratio 11:1 rising to 12:1. Valve angle: 16 degrees inlet, 16 degrees exhaust. Bore 85.67mm (3.373in), stroke 64.8mm (2.55in), displacement 2,993cc (182.64cu in). Maximum power initially 405bhp at 9,000rpm, rising progressively to approximately 510bhp at 11,200rpm. Maximum torque initially 245lb ft at 8,500rpm, rising progressively to approximately 270lb ft at 9,000rpm. Weight initially 356lb reducing to approximately 340lb. Number of engines produced to May 1983: 381, including 7 initial development engines.

DFW

Conversion of DFV with piston stroke reduced to 54mm to bring displacement within $2\frac{1}{2}$-litre limit for Tasman Championship racing. All engines converted to DFW specification were subsequently rebuilt as DFVs with standard stroke.

DFX

Turbocharged short-stroke version of DFV for use in CART/USAC racing in USA. Initially magneto ignition, later capacitive discharge ignition. Additional water cooling in cylinder heads. Variety of turbocharger units fitted. Bore 85.67mm (3.373in), stroke 57.30mm (2.256in), displacement 2,643cc (161.27cu in). Typical power output with turbo boost pressure restricted to 48in Hg: 720bhp at 11,000rpm, torque 350lb ft at 9,500rpm. Number of engines produced to May 1983: 176 plus 61 kits supplied to other engine builders.

DFL

Derivative of DFV for endurance racing. Initially produced as development engine with 90mm (3.543in) bore and standard 64.8mm (2.55in) stroke to give displacement of 3,298cc. Maximum power 490bhp at 9,500rpm, maximum torque 290lb ft at 7,000rpm. Subsequently developed into production engine with 90mm (3.543in) bore and 77.7mm (3.06in) stroke to give displacement of

3,955cc (241.35cu in). Maximum power 540bhp at 9,250rpm, maximum torque 340lb ft at 7,000rpm. Number of engines produced to May 1983: 5 in 3.3-litre and 25 in 3.95-litre form.

DFY
Short-stroke derivative of DFV engine for Formula 1 racing. Initially developed with cylinder heads based on DFV layout with inlet and exhaust valves each angled at 16 degrees. Subsequently fitted with new cylinder heads incorporating integral cam carriers and with inlet valves angled at 10 degrees and exhaust valves at 12½ degrees. Both heads designed to accept 1.42in diameter inlet valves and 1.25in diameter exhaust valves. Maximum power initially 520bhp at 11,000rpm, maximum torque approximately 280lb ft at 9,000rpm. Weight approximately 307lb initially, reducing to approximately 292lb with narrow-angle heads. Number of engines produced or in course of construction in May 1983: 25.

Appendix D

Engines manufactured by Cosworth Engineering

Year	Engine	CC	BHP	RPM	Description
1959	Mk I	997	—	—	Experimental modified Ford Anglia 105E engine, not made for sale.
1960	Mk II	997	75	7,500	Production racing engine developed from Mk I and used in Formula Junior with A2 camshaft.
1960	Mk III	997	85/90	7,500	Improved version of Mk II using A3 camshaft with strengthened bottom end and optional dry-sump lubrication.
1961	Mk IV	1,098	90/95	7,750	Bored-out version of Mk III with larger valves.
1962	Mk V	1,340	80	5,000	Inexpensive modified Ford Classic 109E engine for road use in Lotus 7.
1962	Mk VI	1,340	105	7,000	Racing version of Mk V. Very few made.
1962	Mk VII	1,475	120	7,000	Bored-out version of Mk VI. Very few made.
1963	Mk VIII	1,498	90	6,000	Inexpensive modified Ford Cortina 116E engine for road use in Lotus Super 7 with A2 camshaft, 5 main bearing crankshaft and twin Weber 40 DCOE carburettors. Very many made.
1963	Mk IX	1,498	125	7,000	Racing version of Mk VIII.
1963	Mk X	1,498	—	—	Experimental forerunner of production Lotus Twin-cam engine fitted to Elan with twin chain-driven overhead camshafts and cross-flow cylinder head. Production engine had capacity of 1,558cc.
1963	Mk XI	1,098	110	8,000	Updated version of Mk IV Formula Junior engine with much improved specification. Very successful and a major development in Cosworth's history.
1963	Mk XII	1,594	140	6,500	Bored-out racing version of Lotus Twin-cam engine with dry-sump lubrication and standard cast-iron connecting rods and crankshaft.
1963	Mk XIII	1,594	140	6,500	Development of Mk XII with improved dry-sump lubrication and latterly with steel rods and crankshaft.
1963	Mk XIV	1,498	100	6,000	Modified Ford 116E engine for Lotus Super 7 with more power than Mk VIII.
1963	Mk XV	1,594	140	6,500	Wet-sump Lotus Twin-cam engine fitted to Cortina Lotus for Group 2 racing.
1963	Mk XVI	1,498	140	6,500	81mm bore version of Mk XIII for racing in New Zealand and Australia.
1964	Mk XVII	1,098	120	8,500	Downdraught version of Mk XI with improved crank design. Few made, partly due to brazing problems involved in modifying cylinder head to downdraught configuration. A development rather than production project.

Year	Engine	CC	BHP	RPM	Description
1964	SCA	997	115	8,750	Single Camshaft type A. First extensively Cosworth-designed engine, based on Ford Cortina 116E cylinder block, for Formula 2 — won F2 Championship in 1964 and 1965. Gear-driven single overhead camshaft, 5 main bearing crankshaft and bowl-in-piston combustion chambers.
1964	SCB	1,498	175	8,000	$1\frac{1}{2}$-litre version of SCA made for experimental purposes only.
1965	SCC	1,098	135	9,500	Increased-bore version of SCA for North American sports car formula. Few made but many SCA engines sold for conversion.
1965	MAE	997	100	9,000	Modified Anglia series E (105E). Very successful Formula 3 engine made in large quantities. Modified cylinder head in 1966 and many kits and parts sold to other F3 engine specialists.
1967	FVA	1,598	218	9,000	Four Valve type A. Unbeaten Formula 2 engine, winning all F2 Championships from 1967 to 1971. Based on Ford 116E cylinder block with 4 valves per cylinder and gear-driven twin overhead camshafts.
1966	FVB	1,500	200	9,000	Experimental 1,500cc version of FVA made to examine power output possibilities for Formula 1 DFV.
1967	DFV	2,993	405	9,000	Double four Valve. Cosworth's first Formula 1 engine incorporating first Cosworth-designed cylinder block. Winner of first race and of 152 Grands Prix up to end of 1982. Rev limit raised to 10,250rpm in 1973 and 11,000rpm in 1980. Power output in excess of 500bhp in 1983.
1968	DFW	2,491	358	9,750	Successful short-stroke version of DFV for Tasman Series races.
1968	BDA	1,601	120	6,500	Belt Driven type A. Road-going engine for Ford for installation in Escort RS 1600. Based on FVA and cross-flow Ford block, but with toothed belt drive to twin overhead camshafts. 4 valves per cylinder.
1969	FVC	1,790	235	8,750	Long-stroke version of FVA for European 2-litre Sports Car Championship, which it won twice.
1970	BDB	1,700	200	8,250	Modified BDA development engine for Ford for rallying, with enlarged bore. Many sold in kit form.
1970	BDC	1,700	230	9,000	Fuel-injected racing version of BDB developed mainly for Group 2 saloon car racing. Many sold in kit form.
1971	BDD	1,600	200	8,750	Development version of BDA for Formula Atlantic racing. Many sold in kit form.
1972	BDE	1,790	245	9,000	Formula 2 version of BDA bored out to 85.6mm.
1972	BDF	1,927	270	9,250	Improved version of BDE with bore increased to 88.9mm by brazing liners into standard block. Won more 1972 Formula 2 races than any other engine.
1972	EAA	1,995	275	9,000	Cosworth's first stock-block engine based on other than Ford block. All-aluminium engine based on Chevrolet Vega block and similar to BDA in layout. Designed for sports car and Formula 2 racing, but never used in F2.
1973	BDG	1,975	275	9,250	Improved version of BDF for 1973 Formula 2 offering greater reliability.
1973	FVD	1,975	275	9,000	Modified version of FVA made for experimental purposes only.
1973	GAA	3,412	440	8,750	Ford V6 block-based engine under development for Group 2 saloon car racing.
1973	BDH	1,300	190	10,000	Small-capacity version of BDA based on Ford 1300 cross-flow block for sports car and Group 2 saloon car racing.
1974	JAA	750	65	7,000	Production motorcycle engine designed and built for Norton Villiers.
1974	BDJ	1,098	150	9,500	Small-capacity version of BDA designed for American SCCA Formula C.

Year	Engine	CC	BHP	RPM	Description
1975	JAB	750	95	9,750	Racing version of JAA motorcycle engine.
1975	BDM	1,599	225	9,250	Large-valve fuel-injected version of BDD.
1975	DFX	2,643	840	9,500	Turbocharged version of DFV with 57.30mm stroke designed for Indianapolis-type racing in the USA.
1978	KAA	2,400	240	7,000	Rally version of Opel Ascona 400 engine developed for 1980 season.
1979	OAA	1,600	170	7,800	Volkswagen-based engine for Formula Super Vee.
1981	BDP	1,975	230	8,250	Fuel-injected version of BDA for US Midget racing, running on methanol.
1981	BDU	1,975	235	8,250	Gasoline version of BDP for off-road racing.
1981	DFL	3,298	500	10,000	Interim larger-bore development of DFV engine for Group C endurance racing.
1982	DFL	3,955	540	9,250	Production version of DFL development engine incorporating increased stroke with enlarged bore.
1983	DFY	2,993	520	11,000	Short-stroke version of DFV for Formula 1.

Appendix E

Useful addresses

Cosworth Engineering Ltd., St James' Mill Road, Northampton NN5 5JJ
Tel: (0604) 51802 and 51214

Cosworth Research and Development Ltd., Hylton Road,
Worcester WR2 5JS
Tel: (0905) 427114

Cosworth Engineering Inc., 23205 Early Avenue, Torrance,
California 90505, USA
Tel: (213) 534 1390

The following have been appointed by Cosworth Engineering as officially approved rebuilders of the DFV engine:

Engine Developments Ltd., (John Judd), Engine Division, Somers Road,
Rugby, Warwickshire CV22 7DG
Tel: (0788) 71056 and 77958

Euroracing Engines Ltd., (Ken Horton), 149 Cardiff Road, Reading,
Berkshire RG1 8JE
Tel: (0734) 585355

Nicholson McLaren Engines Ltd., (John Nicholson), Green Lane, Hounslow,
Middlesex TW4 6HZ
Tel: (01) 572 3232

Alan W. Smith Racing (1977) Ltd., (Alan Smith), Manchester Street,
Derby DE3 3GA
Tel: (0332) 48974

Swindon Racing Engines Ltd., Crampton Road, Greenbridge Estate,
Swindon, Wiltshire SN3 3JJ
Tel: (0793) 31321

Heini Mader Racing Components, CH-1196 Gland, Ch Fossabot,
Switzerland